THE
BASQUE
BOOK

THE
BASQUE
BOOK

A LOVE LETTER IN RECIPES
from the
kitchen of Txikito

Alexandra Raij WITH Eder Montero
AND REBECCA FLINT MARX

PHOTOGRAPHY BY
PENNY DE LOS SANTOS

TEN SPEED PRESS
BERKELEY

CONTENTS

Heredad Ugarte 1'60
Bordon 1'50
Puerta Vieja 1'50
Cosechero
Heredad Ugarte 1.0
Albergada 0'8
Txakoli
Larrabe 1'4
Verdeio

FOR MAAYAN AND LUCIEN

"HERRI BERRIAH ADARRAK SUSTRAI."
—MIKEL URMENETA, 2010

INTRODUCTION

If, when I was a child, someone had told me, "One day, you're going to open a small Basque restaurant," I wouldn't have been too surprised. In fact, I would have probably shrugged my shoulders and said, "Yes, of course I am."

For as long as I can remember, I have wanted to open a restaurant. I grew up in Minnesota, but my parents emigrated from Argentina just before I was born, and my sisters and I were raised around a table with lively Spanish conversation and with food that was strange by midwestern standards (at the time, we may have been the only Argentine Jews in Minneapolis). Growing up, my favorite pastimes were playing restaurant, dreaming about food, and reading cookbooks, so opening a restaurant someday would not have seemed impossible.

As fate would have it, I grew up and opened a small restaurant in one of the biggest cities in the world. But the part that would have surprised me as a child—and, in a way, still surprises me today—is that my restaurant, Txikito, is Basque. I can imagine my ten-year-old self scratching her head and asking, "What does *Basque* mean?" I've been running Txikito since 2007, and I still don't have a definitive response to that question. But it's one that I strive to answer, for myself and for the people we feed, every day.

Cooking is a perfect vocation for people who like to find and make connections. To me, food is a way to tell a story, and even though I don't want to tell the same stories over and over again, I do want a common thread to connect the stories that I do tell. My husband, Eder, who is also my co-chef at Txikito, puts it a little differently: he says I'd open a new restaurant every week if I could. So it's not surprising that he is both frustrated by and supportive of this story, which is the story of how I met Basque food and found a home in a cuisine that has held my attention in ways that no other can.

Part of what made both Basque food and Eder, who is Basque, so attractive is that Basque cooking meant that I could return to living my life in Spanish. My affinity goes deeper than that, however: I love all of the cuisines of Spain, but Basque food has a very specific mystique. It doesn't hide behind strong

Mediterranean flavors. Instead, it celebrates single ingredients and tastes and constantly reminds the cook that "simple" doesn't necessarily mean "easy." Basque food makes you a better cook. It teaches you to respect ingredients, embracing and amplifying their natural flavors. I'd argue that many professional cooks would get better if they practiced Basque cooking, as it forces you to unlearn bad habits and pay attention to details. The Basque cook responds to *la materia prima*, or main ingredients, a tiny bit differently each time. Intuitively understanding how to make these minor adjustments is a sign of the cook's experience and skill.

My Basque journey started well before I met Eder. In Minnesota, my dad's best friend was nicknamed El Vasco, a terrific cook who made the most amazing homemade pizza and cherries jubilee, a dessert that turned my favorite fruit into a pyrotechnic miracle of flavors. El Vasco's real name was Nestor Riviere. He was my dad's tennis partner and a mathematician, and our families often cooked together. I had a girlish crush on Nestor: he drove a Fiat Spider and had salt-and-pepper hair, but in retrospect, what made him so seductive was how he cooked and what happened when he did. At home, cooking was always interesting, though a rather calm routine. El Vasco's cooking was flamboyant and extroverted and was meant to make people fall in love with him. It was a flirtation more similar to the kind you find in restaurant cooking, where customers are seduced by a combination of flavors and spectacle.

Every year our families held a huge pig roast at a place in Minneapolis called Hidden Beach, on Cedar Lake. Those roasts were epic, all-day parties that began early in the morning and went late into the night and seemed to bring out every Spanish- and Italian-speaking expat from the University of Minnesota. The men, who were mostly math professors, would build the roasting pits out of cinder blocks and old fences or mattress coils and then spend the entire day feeding the fire, drinking cans of Special Export, and talking tennis while the pigs slowly cooked. It was the 1970s, and everyone was tennis obsessed. Guillermo Vilas, Bjorn Borg, Ivan Lendl, and Jimmy Connors were popular topics of conversation, and some of the guys would go off to play a match while the rest of us waited for the pigs to be ready. Someone was always strumming a guitar and singing—again, this was the 1970s—while the women gossiped, cooked sausages and offal, and reheated empanadas on foil rafts, and we kids ran around, free to do whatever we wanted. My sisters and I would fall asleep on the car ride home, smelling like smoke, our faces dirty with soot, and the shirts over our full bellies stained with grease.

The sight of those men cooking together all day long and those magnificent pigs are some of my well-fed family's happiest memories, and it's no surprise that the aroma of meat cooked over charcoal still delivers me to those roasts. From an early age, I understood the rewards of patiently picking apart a pig's head or fighting over the threads of cheek meat and crisp skin. When I see my daughter doing this now, I beam with pride at her sticky, greasy fingers.

Everything we ate and the way we ate set us apart in our largely Scandinavian community, but at Hidden Beach, I felt at home: we all spoke either Spanish or Italian, looked the same, and enjoyed the same food. In my everyday life, I was conscious of the differences between my family and all of the blond, blue-eyed families in our area: we were dark, and the food I took to school didn't look or taste like anyone else's. At friends' houses, I was that kid who spent a lot of time talking to parents, always chose the dark meat and gristle, and left my bones embarrassingly clean, chewing the soft cartilage until it was gone. Experiencing alternating feelings of alienation and acceptance— of being part of one world but having occasionally to dip into another—is something that Eder and I share. I have always felt that I defined myself not by how I was like those around me but by how I was different. For historical and cultural reasons, this is also the Basque experience.

Even as a child, I knew I had to embrace my differences. Rejecting them would never give me a sense of belonging, but accepting them and holding them tight would bring me home. And eventually, it did. The myopic preoccupation with food and good cooking that has kept me company my entire life led me to a man from a culture where nearly everyone is obsessed with food. When I fell in love with my second Basque man, my childhood crush came of age. El Vasco, it turns out, wasn't that different from other Basque men I met later: a talented and passionate cook with a competitive edge that drove him to produce memorable meals where everyone participating became a better cook.

After graduating from culinary school, I moved to New York to look for work. A Brazilian friend told me that a Basque restaurant was opening in Tribeca, and a Basque teacher from the culinary school was helping to staff it. I'd heard that the chef there had worked for Martín Berasategui, one of the chefs who put Basque food on the map. I applied and got a job as *jefe de partida* in the kitchen's cold station. It turned out that the Galician owner of this would-be Basque restaurant actually opened a Basque-Galician place, which wasn't what I had signed up for but was something I innately understood. (My convoluted Argentine immigrant experience, after all, was rife with equal-opportunity appropriation and bastardization of Spanish recipes.)

When I arrived at the restaurant on the first day, there was Eder Montero. He was the sous chef, and he was sitting inside at nine in the morning wearing a suit, drinking a beer, and eating a sandwich. Did I mention it was nine o'clock?

He had his hair tied in a high ponytail that swung from side to side as he spoke. A full beard made him look at least my age, rather than six years younger.

There was something amazingly charismatic about him. He had this twinkle in his eye and possessed a kind of wise oldness. When I look at our kids now, I totally understand where they get their twinkle. I felt instantly drawn to Eder in a way that I can't explain.

Eder later told me that he thought I was the dumbest person he'd ever met because I was taking notes on that first day. But I don't think that's true. I knew he liked me from the beginning. He was playing hard to get, and not just with me but with the city. He had no intention of staying in New York, much less the United States. He had been recruited in Spain to go there to cook, and he had no intention of staying. He was a cocky kid—"a real pain in the ass," to use his own words—who wanted a brief adventure, get paid, and then go back to Europe or possibly to Japan. New York wasn't for him, and who could blame him? He was living in Ozone Park and had a thousand dollars in parking tickets. Eder was not only the consummate fish out of water in New York but also one who didn't quite make sense, even to worldly New Yorkers. He could not just be from Spain; there was something different, paradoxical about him. He was Basque. He was confident and sophisticated on one hand, yet he also had this primitive—though not provincial—side.

It's pretty awesome to have a crush at work: when you want to impress somebody, you go in every day and do the best job you can. Every night, we closed at 11:30 p.m. and then had to clean the kitchen from top to bottom. I still remember the night—Eder was standing on the *plancha*, scrubbing the kitchen range hood—that I realized that I had never worked so hard in my life. And that's also when I realized that Eder was the person for me. He was somebody who just made me better. I don't think there's anything more attractive than someone who does his or her job well, and for me, that was Eder.

Restaurant kitchens are gossip factories, and the last thing we wanted was for everyone to know our business, so when Eder and I started seeing each other, we were very discreet. The closer we became, the meaner he was to me at work, which both drove me crazy and encouraged me to just get faster, cleaner, better. But one day, everything changed: Valentine's Day, when the skunk balloon floated into our lives.

Eder was outside cleaning the restaurant's windows when a Pepé Le Pew balloon appeared from out of nowhere. It was so random and weird: not only was there no reason for Eder to be washing the windows in February but there was also no reason for a heart-shaped Mylar balloon that looked like a cartoon character to fall out of the sky and almost directly into his hands.

Eder grabbed it, carried it into the restaurant, and presented it to me like a rose, out in the open, right in front of everybody. That skunk balloon was a public declaration of what we were to each other. The entire kitchen crew reacted with mock disgust.

Later that night, I tied the balloon to my bag and began walking home from work. Somehow the balloon came loose and I didn't realize it was hovering behind me. Suddenly I heard a man's voice say, "Miss, miss! Your balloon!" I turned around and an incredibly handsome guy was standing there, holding Pepé Le Pew and smiling. It was almost as if I were being given the balloon all over again: the damn thing was trying to make a love connection. When I took it, I felt as if I were being presented with an opportunity to go in a different direction: I could strike up a conversation with this gorgeous man that could change my life entirely. Instead, I took the balloon, said thank you, and then turned and kept walking home. The balloon half-hovered in my apartment for months, acting as a silent, silly witness each time Eder would visit. Eventually, after all the air escaped, we put it on the refrigerator. When we moved to a new apartment, it disappeared. Well, it didn't disappear: Eder threw it away and I got really mad at him. Guess who cleans Txikito's fridges and pantries of unused experimental ingredients and trial dishes on exactly the day before I go looking for one of them?

The skunk balloon was this weird thing that came out of nowhere, and that's what Basque cuisine was for me, too. I couldn't have predicted that balloon, or Eder, or falling in love with him and his country's food. Sometimes in life, you find that you need exactly what needs you back. For me, those things were Eder and Basque cooking.

Just as I felt as if I were coming home when I began cooking Basque food, I want this book to be welcoming to home cooks. Although the most famous restaurants of the Basque Country—Michelin-starred high-end places like Mugaritz, Arzak, Akelarre, and Martín Berasategui—have introduced the world to a Basque *nueva cocina*, have helped put Spain on the culinary map, and have supplied professional cooks in every corner of the world with inspiration, Basque cooking is at its heart a cuisine of simplicity made exquisite. In an era where garnishes and condiments are often a substitute for substance, Basque cooking stands out as a cuisine of subtraction, where fancy embellishment is stripped away until you are left with the essence of an ingredient, be it a single, luscious piece of cod served with an oil emulsified with its own juices, or flash-fried *pimientos de Gernika* whose only adornment is a healthy sprinkling of sea salt. And in being a cuisine of subtraction, it is also one of paradox, where humble ingredients produce lavish flavors and rough materials yield dishes of exquisite refinement. Think, for example, of *txipirones en su tinta*, or squid in its own ink, a dish whose rather unglamorous appearance belies its sensuous, complex flavors. It's created by gently cooking the creature with little more than a few vegetables, olive oil, and a couple of packets of squid ink. It's earthy yet sublime, homely but astoundingly beautiful in its deceptive simplicity.

If you know how to pick out good raw ingredients, you can cook Basque food. It's a technique-based cuisine that isn't highly technical and doesn't require lots of specialized equipment. If you have a bottle of olive oil, a head of garlic, and a tin of tuna, you can make Basque food. Like a family, it is a cuisine that is much greater than the sum of its parts. And like a family, it is basic, instinctive, and comforting. Give it your time and care, and it will give you a home. If you are patient, the long-cooking Basque mother sauces will repay you with astounding depth of flavor. If you are in a hurry, you can make Basque food in the five minutes it takes to steam clams.

This book is the cooking of Txikito, New York City's only authentic Basque restaurant. It is a loving tribute to Eder's homeland and a legacy for our children, so that they may know our story. It is equal parts grandma's house, *cocina de autor* (high-end cooking), tapas bar, family restaurant, and roadside truck stop. It is, in short, a vibrant and layered answer to the question, "What does *Basque* mean?"

BEING BASQUE

Until I was in my twenties, most of what I knew about being Basque came from my fifth-grade Spanish book. The one-page description went something like, "There's this strange land in the north of Spain called 'Vascongadas' where there are these strange people called 'Los Vascos' and they speak this strange language called 'Vascuence.'" For all I knew, the Basques may as well have been leprechauns living under enchanted mushrooms.

It wasn't until I met Eder that he explained that Basques actually identify themselves as people who speak Euskera, the Basque language. (*Vascuence* is the Spanish word for their language.) During Franco's regime, speaking Euskera was forbidden, and as more and more immigrants from other areas of Spain moved in to take advantage of the region's resources, Euskera moved deeper into the foothills and remote towns. In the cities, the language survived mostly through culinary vocabulary and music—and behind the closed doors of *txokos* (see chapter 7), the private gastronomic clubs where Basques cook together.

I was lucky to begin my Basque education in 1999, almost twenty-five years after Franco's death and at a moment when several talented Basque chefs were sparking interest in Basque cooking around the world. Now I can see that the decades of isolation during the Franco era had the unintended benefit of preserving many aspects of Basque culinary culture, rather than being overtaken by the prevailing French vernacular. Cooking is very much its own language, and by maintaining their culinary traditions, the Basques kept alive a food-driven lexicon that ensured many Basque words lived on even for urban Basques.

ABOUT THE BOOK

This book is the product of two people falling in love. It is the distillation of fourteen years of shared kitchen space and two lives that have been woven into a unified personal history. It's a cookbook, of course, but it's also a story of love and homecoming told through 114 recipes.

Within these pages, you'll find dishes that reflect what Basque cuisine has given to Eder and me—classic recipes, in other words—and dishes that we have interpreted at our restaurant and given back to Basque cuisine. Some of them are so time-honored that a Basque grandmother could have made them. Others are drawn from tradition but assembled in a different—that is, modern—way.

Some very good cookbooks on classical Basque cuisine are already out there, and I had no interest in writing another one. Instead, I wanted to create a book that would demonstrate how Eder and I as chefs interpret a cuisine and keep it current. All of the recipes are prepared as they are at the restaurant, because Txikito is based on home cooking and the kitchen uses traditional methods to produce complex flavors.

Throughout this book, I want you to look differently at the ingredients that you think you know: here, for example, you'll see that a leek can be the center of a dish instead of a component of sauce. To that end, the recipes have been organized into chapters that might seem unconventional at first glance: instead of starters, mains, and desserts, you get vegetables, stews, fish, and eggs. What's important to understand is that in the Basque Country, cooks treat each of these categories with equal importance. That leek dish or a scrambled egg is prepared with the same care as a panfried trout or roasted pork loin.

At its most basic, Basque food can be divided into two main categories: food that you eat in private and food that you eat in public. Chapters 2 and 7 address the latter: the food of the *pintxos* bar (the Basque version of tapas) and the food eaten at festivals, in cider houses, in casual restaurants, and in Basque dining societies. Basque hospitality is rugged, informal, and refreshing; most of the *pintxos* are eaten standing up, hand to mouth, in one- or two-bite servings, and the vibe of the iconic Basque cider house is relaxed and communal.

One thing you'll notice is that many ingredients are repeated throughout the book. This repetition of dozens of high-quality foods is one of the cornerstones of Basque cooking. So at the end of the book you'll find an ingredient glossary that will help you stock your pantry with these essentials.

Building a Basque meal

Very few recipes in this book won't work well together, so the key when you're creating a menu is to seek out a variety of textures and temperatures. There's no need to confine yourself to convention: if you have meat, you don't need a starch and vegetable on the side. The Basques, after all, see nothing wrong or unusual about eating, say, three pepper dishes a day when peppers are in season, or multiple mushroom courses in a meal when the markets are filled with *boletus* (porcini). And although a Basque fine-dining restaurant will make textural variety a priority, more casual restaurants and home cooks don't worry that much about it. The idea is to take advantage of what's available and to celebrate it, rules be damned.

That said, the sample menus that follow will give you a sense of the traditional Basque meal. The key in preparing them is to remember that all of the dishes have equal value: meat need not be the star of the show. Sauce making is where you should really invest your time. Once you have the foundation of a good sauce, the rest of the meal is easy.

A SUMMERY SEASIDE-INSPIRED LUNCH OR DINNER

FIRST COURSE

- Chinatown-style periwinkles (page 163) or Grilled head-on shrimp (page 165)
- Summer tomatoes with sweet onion (page 106)
- Grilled sardines, Basque port style (page 152) or Anchovies, Bermeo style (page 157) with crusty bread
- Txakoli or manzanilla sherry

SECOND COURSE

- Butterflied bream (page 180)
- White wine, like Remelluri blanco or K5 Txakoli

DESSERT

- Gin and tonic

A CIDER HOUSE–INSPIRED DINNER

- Blistered shishito peppers with sea salt (page 105)
- Cider house cod omelet (page 225)
- Cider house–style prime dry-aged rib-eye steak (page 223)
- Idiazábal cheese with quince paste and nuts
- American craft cider, like Shacksbury, Aaron Burr, or Farnum Hill, and Basque cider, like Petritegi

A WINTER TXOKO-INSPIRED DINNER

FIRST COURSE

- Pureed leek and onion soup (page 195)
- Simple white wine, like Ostatu Rioja

SECOND COURSE

- Garden snails in bizkaína sauce (page 220)
- Still Txakoli wine, like Uriondo

THIRD COURSE

- Salt cod in pil pil sauce (page 175) or Poached monkfish with garlic soup (page 177)
- Grilled baby lamb chops (page 229)
- Rioja *reserva*, like Contino or Acodo (Tinto)

DESSERT

- Goat's milk junket with honey and walnuts (page 259)
- Black coffee or *carajillo* (coffee with brandy or other spirit)
- Digestif, like patxaran or Izarra

A NAVARRAN VEGETABLE-HAPPY MENU

- Gratin of artichoke hearts, Roncal, and jamón serrano (page 58)
- Little Gem lettuce hearts with anchovy and canned tuna (page 95)
- White asparagus from the tin with celery–black truffle vinaigrette and trout roe (page 85)
- Mussels with white beans (page 151)
- Piquillo peppers stuffed with cod (page 94)
- Wine: red, like El Chaparral Garnacha from Bodegas Nekeas, and white, like Castillo Monjardín Chardonnay, or rosado, like Marco Real or Príncipe de Viana

DESSERT

- Spice cookies (page 260)
- Pear and patxaran sorbet (page 248)
- Sweet Moscatel

1 | Basque Basics

FUNDAMENTAL TECHNIQUES AND INGREDIENTS

In this chapter, you'll learn about the techniques and ingredients that underlie much of Basque cooking. It includes recipes for the onion-based Basque mother sauces, such as *salsa bizkaína* and *salsa tinta*, as well as basic recipes for mayonnaise and stock.

Basque cooking is all about the details, which is why it's so important to understand the building blocks before you start cooking. Salt, onions, and oil may seem humble and unassuming, but they are at the very heart of everything the Basques prepare.

Salt

Salt has for centuries been a vital part of the Basque economy. In the Middle Ages, for example, the large, natural oceanic deposits found near Salinas de Añana made the Álava town one of the wealthiest in the Iberian Peninsula. And salt has also long been an enormously important part of Basque cooking. Far, far more than just a seasoning, Basques use salt to "tenderize" and break down textures, bring water-soluble proteins to the surface of meat for better browning, and concentrate and draw out delicately flavored liquids from foods that then sauce and season the dish. At the end of the day, if all you learn from this book is to be confident with salt, it will have done its job and I will be happy.

Brining

At Txikito, we brine everything from shellfish to onions. In Basque cooking, *salmuera* refers to a heavily salted cold-water brine, which is particularly useful for soaking oily fish like sardines and anchovies, as it both flavors their delicate flesh and tightens it so the bones can be more easily removed. When brined and then drizzled with vinegar and grapeseed oil, an anchovy becomes a *boquerón*. I've exported this treatment to many foods. In particular, it changed the way I prepare ingredients whose short cooking times make it difficult for them to absorb salt, which is why I brine my shrimp and shock blanched asparagus in salted ice water. I also like brining cucumber in salted ice water, which lends the vegetable flavor and an extremely crisp texture. That said, brining has taught me to exercise a judicious hand, as well: you don't want to smother an ingredient's natural flavor with the taste of salt.

Salt curing

The ancient method of directly applying salt to an ingredient to remove or drastically reduce its water content is used prolifically in Basque cooking. Both cod and hams are cured with salt and later air-dried until they've reached their ideal consistency and flavor. Anchovies and sardines are barrel cured, a process that involves first tossing the fish with salt and then alternating layers of fish and salt in a barrel. Although we don't make our own salt-cured anchovies or hams at Txikito (we leave that to the exceptional artisans in Spain), we do cure our cod and duck breasts to obtain more concentrated flavor and transformative textures.

Salt baking

Salt baking, which is especially well suited to crustaceans and fish, results in the most succulent and purely flavored seafood imaginable. The method, which involves entombing the seafood under a thick layer of salt, helps ensure even cooking, and when extended to such vegetables as beets and potatoes, it produces a remarkably concentrated flavor. You can use this technique on large cuts of meat with a tight pore structure with great success, too.

Seasoning

The Basques employ a pretty aggressive hand when using salt as a seasoning, but they're careful to apply it only at junctures when it will draw out the aromas and flavors of a dish in a layered and complex way. Paying attention to this kind of timing has radically changed the way I cook. Take, for example, the way I make onion-based sauces. Now, I add a generous amount of salt to the onions at the *beginning* of the cooking process, to draw out their moisture. This keeps the onions from browning prematurely or burning. It also helps control the evaporation of their sulfuric vapors by allowing those off flavors to percolate away instead of getting cooked into the final product. In the end you get the sweet, pure essence of onion without masking its natural flavors with overly caramelized notes. If you can learn how to harness a singular flavor like the Basques do, you can start to understand why, instead of working with many flavors, you just need to work with perfect flavors. This lesson will change your cooking, just as it did mine.

A final note on salt: The Basques say that if you're oversalting your food, it means you want to get married. When I met Eder, he made me use more salt in my cooking, and we ended up getting married. So you could say it's the salt's fault that I ended up with this crazy caveman.

Oil

The Basques are as generous with their use of oil as they are with salt, and oil is similarly used to cook, preserve, and flavor food. Extra-virgin olive oil is perhaps the most essential Basque ingredient, and it's one you shouldn't scrimp on. But by the same token (Eder's favorite expression), you do not have to spend a fortune on it. What you need to find is a pleasant-tasting oil that, when used in large quantities, doesn't become bitter or obscure your food with its own flavor. Know that whatever oil you choose is going to become a character in your cooking.

Fritos y refritos: deep-frying and "over-frying"

Fritos are fried dishes—everything from seafood to cutlets to croquettes—that are coated with starch or batter and fried until golden in hot oil (325°F to 375°F). These dishes do not keep or reheat well, so it's important to eat them right away.

Refrito can refer to both a technique and a sauce. It literally translates to "over-frying" (as opposed to its counterpart, *sofrito*, which is "underfrying"). The most common *refrito* in this book involves frying garlic—sliced or grated—until near golden. Vinegar is then added, which arrests the cooking and creates an aromatic, high-pitched cooked vinaigrette for fish, vegetables, lentils, or braised beans. You can also add herbs and spices or change up the acid in your garlic *refrito*. When making *refrito*, it's important to let the oil heat up gradually so that the garlic doesn't burn. The goal is a crispy, evenly golden garlic chip or crumb.

Sofrito and cebolla poachada

Slow-cooked vegetables—often *sofrito* (page 33) or *cebolla poachada* (its onion-based counterpart)—are the backbone of many Basque dishes, a sort of Basque equivalent to the French *mirepoix*. To make these marmalade-like bases, use slightly less oil then you would with a confit—in other words, the oil shouldn't completely submerge the main ingredient, and should get absorbed during the cooking process.

Confitar: poaching in oil

Poaching ingredients in oil, a technique frequently used with mushrooms, potatoes for tortillas, and cod for *pil pil*, allows the ingredient to cook at a very low and consistent temperature that promotes exquisite texture. In the process, water is drawn out of the ingredients so that they're semipreserved and have concentrated flavor. The juice left at the bottom of the pan is a distilled flavor of whatever you have poached, and when mixed with the oil at the top, it can be used as a broken or emulsified sauce. (Learning this pretty much changed my whole outlook on sauce making, so that I never again threw out a broken sauce.)

The by-products of poaching present numerous possibilities for the cook. For example, the oil and juices left over from preparing mushrooms will be on my pasta one night or in my risotto another night, or it might go into a batch of mayonnaise. It's a technique that ensures that nothing is wasted and that flavors that you could otherwise never obtain are harnessed and woven into unexpected places. Infused oils are a simple and effective way to add mystery to your cooking. Paying attention to this kind of opportunity is a very Basque way to cook.

The amount of oil used in poaching initially freaked me out. It seemed both vainglorious and wasteful and left me wondering whether oil-rich dishes could be made leaner and cleaner. In some cases, the answer was yes, but for the most part, the answer was to use the excess poaching oil to make greater things. So, like the Basques, I tell people to buy good or great oil and use it with abandon while keeping the other components of the dish humble and simple. I strongly recommend buying oil in the largest container that makes sense for your family. You won't be treating it as a precious thing to be used sparingly, and you'll end up paying less if you buy it in larger quantities. Use it and then reuse it.

Always buy and store your oil in a dark bottle in a cool place. If you are storing used oil—say, from poached mushrooms or potatoes for tortillas—remove and discard any garlic cloves and store it in the refrigerator (it will have traces of moisture that could spoil) and use it within a few days. Also, never reuse oils that you've used for sautéing or frying, as the high heat causes the oil to break down.

Mayonnaise

Americans might not believe it, but mayonnaise is an extremely sophisticated sauce. As an Argentine, I grew up in a family that prized mayonnaise, so when I discovered that Spaniards regard it the same way, I felt an immediate connection. Mayonnaise is a workhorse sauce that gives and accepts flavor equally. It's great for *pintxos* and shares DNA with *pil pil*, the famous Basque emulsion sauce. By looking at *pil pil*, I have learned to think of mayonnaise as a flexible sauce that can be imbued with numerous flavors and characteristics. And because my versions of mayonnaise contain a little water, you can replace the water with any flavored liquid, or use flavored oils, herbs, or spices to create new flavors. Just remember that because salt isn't fat-soluble and mayonnaise is very oily, it can be difficult to season properly. I recommend dissolving the salt in water or lemon juice. You can store any mayonnaise in an airtight container in the refrigerator for up to 3 days. Always bring it to room temperature before serving.

Mayonnaise | MAYONESA

MAKES 4 CUPS

2 egg yolks

1 tablespoon Dijon mustard

1 teaspoons salt dissolved in ½ cup room-temperature water

2 cups extra-virgin olive oil

2 cups canola oil

1 to 2 tablespoons fresh lemon juice

This thick version of mayonnaise makes an excellent binder. If you are mixing by hand or have access to a mini-processor, feel free to halve the recipe. Add a chopped clove of garlic to make aioli.

In the bowl of a food processor, combine the egg yolks, mustard, and a small splash (about 2 tablespoons) of the salted water and process for about 20 seconds, just until combined; scrape down the sides. Combine the olive and canola oils in a container with a spout. With the processor running, slowly add the oil in a thin, steady stream. When an emulsion forms and begins to thicken, lighten it with another teaspoon or so of salted water. Then slowly add more oil, followed by another splash of salted water, and then the remainder of the oil. Add the lemon juice to taste, salting it first if the mayonnaise needs more salt, and pulse briefly to mix.

NOTES: If your mayonnaise is about to break, you will see a ring of oil start to form around the perimeter of the processor bowl. Turn off the processor, add a splash of lemon juice or water, and restart the processor before adding more oil.

Thin mayonnaise | MAYONESA LIGERA

MAKES ABOUT 2 CUPS

1 egg yolk

2 teaspoons Dijon mustard

½ cup extra-virgin olive oil or flavored oil of choice

1 cup canola oil

½ teaspoon salt dissolved in ⅓ cup water

2 teaspoons fresh lemon juice

This version of mayonnaise contains less oil than regular mayonnaise, which makes it more of a sauce than a binder. It should be a little thicker than heavy cream. To test the consistency, slip a metal spoon into the mayonnaise and lift the spoon: the mayonnaise should leave a thin coating on it. If your emulsion is too thick, loosen it with warm water.

In the bowl of a food processor, combine the egg yolk, mustard, and a small splash (about 2 tablespoons) of the salted water and process for about 20 seconds, just until combined. Scrape down the sides with a spatula. Combine the olive and canola oils in a container with a spout. With the processor running, slowly add the oil in a thin, steady stream. When an emulsion forms and begins to thicken, lighten it with another teaspoon of salted water. Then slowly add more oil, followed by another teaspoon of the salted water, and then the remainder of the oil. Add the lemon juice, salting it first if the mayonnaise needs more salt, and pulse briefly to mix.

Green peppercorn mayonnaise | MAYONESA DE PIMIENTA VERDE

MAKES ABOUT 2 CUPS

3 tablespoons Spanish green peppercorns in brine, rinsed

¼ teaspoon fresh rosemary needles (optional)

⅓ cup water

1 egg yolk

1 teaspoon Dijon mustard

½ cup extra-virgin olive oil

1 cup canola oil

2 teaspoons fresh lemon juice

½ teaspoon sugar

Green peppercorns in brine have a salty flavor and citrusy burn that is delicious with crab and with fowl like duck, squab, and quail.

In a blender, combine the peppercorns, rosemary, and water and process until the pepper and rosemary are pulverized. Strain the mixture through a fine-mesh strainer into a small container, discard the solids, and reserve the water.

In the bowl of a food processor, combine the egg yolk, mustard, and a splash of the peppercorn water (about 1 tablespoon) and process for about 20 seconds. Combine the olive and canola oils in a container with a spout. With the processor running, slowly add the oil in a thin, steady stream. When an emulsion begins to thicken, lighten it with another teaspoon of the peppercorn water. Then slowly add more oil, followed by another ½ teaspoon of the peppercorn water, and then the remainder of the oil. Add the lemon juice, sugar, and more peppercorn water if the mayonnaise needs more salt, and pulse to mix.

Taking stock

In Spain, stocks are called *fondos*, or bases. They are an important building block for a variety of dishes and a great way to reuse leftover proteins and vegetables, whether it's bones from a meaty braise or trimmings from cleaning produce. It's always a good idea to ask whether you can make stock from something you're about to compost. At the restaurant, we even use the liquid left over from hydrating peppers or mushrooms to flavor our stocks. The only things I don't like to use are very oily fish such as mackerel. I've tried making *fondos* from their bones but the color is foggy and the flavor isn't clean. If you are looking for a fishy *fondo* (and by the way, *fishy* is not a bad word in Basque), opt for dashi, the Japanese kelp and bonito stock.

Keep your stock relatively salt-free until you know how you're going to use it. The following recipes appear throughout this book. Although they are simple to make, they add a great deal of complexity to dishes and even stand on their own as soups with simple floating garnishes. Most stocks can keep for 3 to 5 days in the refrigerator or 3 months in the freezer.

Shrimp stock | CALDO DE GAMBA

MAKES 2 QUARTS

4 cups shrimp shells, from raw shrimp

2 quarts water

This simple shrimp stock has a clean, delicate flavor and makes a great base for soups and rice dishes. If you want a stronger, more iodine-infused flavor, roast the shells in a preheated 350°F oven for 6 to 8 minutes, or sweat them in the stockpot with olive oil before adding the water.

In a stockpot, combine the shrimp shells and water and bring to a simmer over medium-high heat. As soon as the shells begin to change from gray to pink and foam begins to collect on the surface of the stock (after about 5 minutes), remove from the heat and cover the pot with plastic wrap, aluminum foil, or a towel and let steep for 1 hour.

Strain the stock through a fine-mesh strainer into a container and discard the shells. Use immediately, or cool and transfer to airtight containers and refrigerate for up to 3 days or freeze for up to 3 months.

Jamón stock | CALDO RANCIO

MAKES 3 QUARTS

Caldo rancio is stock made from scraps of *jamón ibérico*, *jamón serrano*, or chorizo. It's a bit like the bean pot likker or ham hock stock found in the American South and is great for cooking rice, as a base for fish and garlic soups, to add to braised beans or greens, or for cutting with milk to make croquettes. A true flavor-saver stock, it's common throughout the Basque Country—and also nowhere near as rancid as its name suggests. *Rancio*, literally "spoiled," describes the funky umami flavors that *jamón* acquires as it ages. Although you want *some* funk, be sure to cut off any suspicious or very dark parts from the *jamón* before using it.

1 Spanish onion, ends removed and peel left on, cut in half crosswise

2 cups jamón serrano or ibérico scraps, plus any hocks or bones on hand and/or optional dry-cured chorizo ends

3 quarts water or chicken stock, homemade (page 26) or store-bought

1 bay leaf

Splash of manzanilla sherry (optional)

Heat a dry cast-iron frying pan over high heat. Add the onion halves, cut side down, and cook, pressing down with a spatula, until they stick and are flush with the pan. Cook until the onions release themselves from the pan and are charred and blackened, about 3 to 5 minutes. Remove from the heat.

In a stockpot, combine the onion halves, jamón scraps, water, and bay leaf and bring to a boil over high heat. Turn down the heat to a simmer and cook for 1 hour, until the broth is hammy and has taken on a bit of color. (Alternatively, combine in a pressure cooker and cook for 8 minutes.)

Remove from the heat and strain through a fine-mesh strainer into a container, then stir in the sherry. Let cool, then skim off any fat from the surface. Use immediately, or transfer to airtight containers and store in the refrigerator for up to 3 days or in the freezer for up to 3 months. Season with salt only when you know how the stock will be used.

Double chicken stock | CALDO DE POLLO

MAKES 4 TO 5 QUARTS

2 whole chickens, about
4 pounds each, or
8 pounds chicken wings
and/or feet

If you have a big pressure cooker, you can use it to make this stock in little more than a half hour. The pressure cooker will also clarify the stock for you, which makes it easy to snag the fat off the top for other delicious things, like matzo balls or croquettes (pages 70 and 71). Both the stock and its fat freeze well. You can also pick the cooked meat from the carcass and save it for sandwiches and salads.

Place the chickens in a large stockpot with as much water as the pot can accommodate (ideally 4 to 6 quarts). Bring to a boil over medium-high heat, turn down the heat to a simmer, and cook for 2 hours. Every 30 minutes, skim off any impurities that rise to the surface. (Alternatively, place in a pressure cooker and cook for 35 minutes.)

Remove from the heat, lift out and set aside the solids, and pass the stock through a fine-mesh strainer into a container. Let cool to room temperature, then skim off the fat from the surface and save for another use. It can be stored in an airtight container in the freezer for up to 1 month. The cooled stock will be thick and gelatinous. Use immediately or transfer to airtight containers and refrigerate for up to 3 days or freeze for up to 3 months. Pick the meat off the bones and reserve for another use. Store tightly covered in the refrigerator for no more than 3 days or in the freezer for 3 months.

Beef tongue stock | CALDO DE LENGUA

MAKES 4 TO 5 QUARTS

1 Spanish onion, unpeeled, coarsely chopped

2 carrots, peeled and cut into 2-inch chunks

2 leeks, cut into 1-inch pieces

4 flat-leaf parsley sprigs

1 cup canned tomatoes, crushed by hand, or 4 plum tomatoes, halved lengthwise, grated on the medium-coarse holes of a box grater, and skins discarded

1½ cups white cooking wine

2 large beef tongues, at room temperature

4 to 6 quarts water, or as needed to cover

½ teaspoon kosher salt

You can make this stock and store it so you have it on hand for soups and braises, or you can produce it as a by-product of the braised tongue recipe on page 210. If you decide to make the stock, you can slice the tongue and use it for making deli-style sandwiches or you can bread and fry the slices (a Basque favorite), or you can chop the tongue for tacos.

Preheat the oven to 475°F. Scatter the onion, carrots, leeks, and parsley in a single layer in a roasting pan and sprinkle with the salt. Place in the oven and roast, stirring once about halfway through the cooking, for about 25 minutes, until charred and tender. Transfer the roasted vegetables to a heavy pot just large enough to fit the tongues side by side. Add the crushed tomatoes, place over medium-high heat, and cook, stirring, for 5 minutes, until dry. Add the wine, bring to a simmer, and cook for about 8 minutes, until the wine has almost evaporated. The timing will depend on how wide your pot is.

Place the tongues in the pot and add the water to cover the tongues three-quarters of the way up. Bring to a simmer over high heat, then reduce the heat to a simmer and cover. Braise the tongues for about 3 hours, until a wooden skewer can be easily inserted into the thickest part of the tongue but meets a bit of resistance when removed. (Alternatively, to cook the stock in a pressure cooker, roast the vegetables and reduce the wine as directed, then add the tongues and water to just cover and cook for 60 to 70 minutes.)

Remove the tongues from the water, sprinkle generously with salt, and let cool. Wrap tightly with plastic to store and reserve for another use. Strain the stock through a fine-mesh strainer into a container and discard the vegetable solids. Let the stock cool, then skim off any fat or impurities from the surface. Use immediately or refrigerate for up to 3 days or freeze for up to 3 months.

BEEF STOCK | CALDO DE TERNERA

When we don't have tongue, we use beef neck, which has all the assets of oxtails and shanks (high in gelatin, high meat-to-bone ratio) but at a much lower cost. Proceed as directed when making tongue broth, but use 4 pounds of beef neck (or shank) for every 3 quarts of water. If you want a really deeply flavored stock, brown the meat in the stockpot (or pressure cooker).

Fish stock | CALDO DE PESCADO

MAKES 4 TO 5 QUARTS

This stock could be the textbook definition of the old proverb "waste not, want not." You can toss in shellfish shells, fish bones, and fish heads (be sure to cut away the gills, as they can turn the stock bitter); whitefish bones, for the record, yield a particularly flavorful and clean-tasting result. I do not recommend using the bones of oily fish like mackerel. We do not add vegetables or wine here to keep the stock more neutral and flexible. You can add shrimp shells, but keep in mind that they are stronger flavored and not as versatile as fish-bone stocks.

When you make this stock, be careful never to let it boil hard. Think of the cooking process as steeping tea. The finished product has many uses, from a base for fish soups to the cooking liquid for the white rice served with Squid in Its Ink (page 171).

2 to 5 pounds fish bones and heads and/or shellfish shells

10 flat-leaf parsley sprigs

4 to 6 quarts water

In a large stockpot, combine the fish and shellfish remnants with cold salted water to cover and let soak for 5 minutes to remove any excess blood. (If using only shellfish shells, you can skip this step.) Drain the contents of the pot through a strainer and return the solids to the pot. Add the parsley sprigs and water to cover and bring to a bare simmer over medium-low heat. Cook for 10 minutes, skimming off any impurities that rise to the surface. Turn off the heat and let the stock steep for 20 minutes.

Scoop out the large solids with a slotted spoon and discard. Strain the stock through a fine-mesh strainer into a container, being careful not to allow any of the solids that have settled at the bottom of the pot to pass through the strainer. Let cool, then use immediately or transfer to airtight containers and refrigerate for up to 3 days or freeze for up to 3 months.

Onions: the Basque mothership

Sweet onions are the foundation of all of the Basque mother sauces. Part of the secret to the complexity of these sauces is *cebolla pochada*, or the technique of slow poaching the onions with a little oil in their own juices, creating a kind of single-subject *sofrito*. The onions are then traditionally passed through a food mill (at Txikito, we use a blender) to produce the body of the sauce, which negates the need for starches or other thickeners and results in the rich flavor and ethereal texture that defines so many Basque sauces.

More often than not, the appearance of these sauces doesn't prepare you for the flavors they impart. *Tomate frito* looks like a plain tomato sauce, but its large proportion of slow-cooked onion makes it unexpectedly sweet. Likewise, *salsa bizkaína* is a rust-hued sweet pepper sauce that is unlike any other I have had. Its palate and texture aren't what you're expecting: the color suggests tomatoes, but the flavor screams onions, which makes its effect disorienting. And although the bottomless black of *salsa tinta*, or squid ink sauce, suggests the depths of the sea, its foundation of onions tells a different story.

I've thought a lot about this custom of onion-based sauces, and I've come to two conclusions. The first is that because Basques are ingenious and resourceful, they use things that can be stored all year-round with no refrigeration, such as dry peppers, onions, garlic, ham, chorizo, and canned goods. The second is that Basque onions are the best I have ever had. Not since my young adult years living in Seattle, where Walla Walla onions were the prize of the season, have I tried onions of such sweetness, even when raw. Keep your eyes open at farmers' markets for sweet red onions, which approximate the *cebollas de zalla*, puck-shaped onions native to Bizkaia Province whose quality and rarity has earned them protected designation of origin status. Of course, Walla Wallas and Vidalias are great too, as are Spanish onions.

Squid ink sauce | SALSA TINTA

MAKES 4 CUPS

5 Spanish onions, halved and thinly sliced

1 green bell pepper, seeded and cut into small dice

1½ tablespoons extra-virgin olive oil

Kosher salt

2 cups water

½ cup canned whole plum tomatoes, crushed by hand

1½ tablespoons squid ink

Pinch of sugar, if needed

Black as night and sweet as honey, this briny sauce is considered by many Basques the national sauce. It certainly contains all the mystery and beauty of the Basques themselves. You can use this sauce for everything from risotto to vinaigrettes; see page 171 for the iconic Squid in Its Ink.

In a heavy saucepan, combine the onions, bell pepper, oil, and a little salt, cover, place over medium-low heat, and sweat the onions, stirring occasionally, for about 15 minutes, until the onions are soft and melty but not caramelized beyond a light blond. Uncover, raise the heat to medium, add the tomatoes, then bring to a boil and cook for about 4 to 6 minutes, until the tomato has lost some of its acidity and the onions have melted further. Turn down the heat to a simmer and add the squid ink, cooking for 2 minutes. Then add the water and continue to cook for 25 to 30 minutes, stirring occasionally, until the onions and pepper have almost entirely melted out and the sauce is sweet and complex.

Taste the sauce and adjust the salt. The sauce should have a very light hint of sweetness, so add the sugar if needed. Blend in a blender until completely smooth. Use immediately, or store in an airtight container in the refrigerator for up to 3 days or freeze for 3 months.

Sweet pepper sauce | SALSA BIZKAÍNA

MAKES ABOUT 6 CUPS

10 dried choricero or guajillo peppers, or 2 cups choricero pepper paste (page 39)

3 tablespoons extra-virgin olive oil

8 cups thinly sliced Spanish onion

1 bay leaf

4 cloves garlic, thinly sliced

1 tablespoon kosher salt

4 ounces mixed chorizo and/or jamón ends, diced small

1 teaspoon sweet Spanish paprika

1 cup canned whole plum tomatoes

Ground Cheyenne chile, if using choricero peppers

This is one of those sublime sauces that changes in each cook's hands. There's a lot of discussion about whether *salsa bizkaína* should have tomatoes; I use tomato but judiciously, as too much cheapens the sauce. You can use this sauce on potatoes, oil-poached salt cod, or tripe, but my favorite way to enjoy it is with snails, because the snails are just an excuse to eat the sauce, which is doped up with bacon and chorizo (see page 220).

Heat a dry frying pan over medium heat, add the peppers, and toast, turning once, for about 30 seconds total, just until pliable. Remove from the heat, trim away the stems, tear the peppers open, and shake out their seeds. Place the peppers in a heatproof bowl, add boiling water to cover, and top with a weight to keep them submerged in the water. Let the peppers soak for about 20 minutes, until they are plump and you can scrape their pulp from their skin with a spoon. Scrape the pulp into a bowl, discard the skin, and reserve the pepper pulp and soaking water separately.

In a 3-quart saucepan, gently heat the oil over low heat. Add the onion, bay leaf, and garlic, coating them with the oil, and cook for 5 minutes, stirring. Add the salt, cover, and cook over low heat for 10 minutes. Uncover, stir well, add the chorizo and jamón, and cook, stirring occasionally, for 5 minutes. Re-cover and continue to cook for another 20 minutes, until the onions are sweet and wilted.

Uncover the pan and continue to cook over low heat, stirring, for about 5 minutes, until the onion is very sweet and uniformly golden but not brown. The goal here is to melt the onion. Add the reserved pepper pulp and paprika and cook, stirring, for 5 minutes. Raise the heat to medium-high and add the tomatoes, crushing them with your hands as you drop them in. Cook, stirring, for about 8 minutes. Remove from the heat and let cool and rest for 20 minutes.

If you have used choricero peppers, you can add some Cheyenne chile for punch; if you have used guajillos, the sauce should have plenty of punch. Working in batches, transfer the sauce to a blender or food processor and puree while it is still warm but not hot. If the sauce is too thick, thin it with the reserved pepper soaking water. Use immediately, or transfer to airtight containers and refrigerate for up to 3 days or freeze for up to 3 months.

Sweet vegetable "marmalade" | SOFRITO

MAKES 4 TO 6 CUPS

A sauce of sweet poached onions and peppers, *sofrito* builds the flavor in many Basque dishes, but at Txikito and in my home kitchen, it has become a condiment unto itself. By looking at how many Basque dishes rely on this vegetable marmalade, I began to appreciate its versatility, and now I use it to build flavor in rice dishes and soups and smear it on bread to keep *pintxos* from getting soggy from their toppings and to bump up flavor a thousand percent.

This recipe produces a large batch, but it's worth making a big amount because *sofrito* is a time-intensive project, it can be added to any number of dishes to lend depth of flavor and complexity, and it freezes well. Freeze it in small containers so you can thaw just as much as you need. At home, I freeze it in ice-cube trays.

You need to exercise patience and attentiveness when making *sofrito*. If it burns, its flavor will be bitter.

5 Spanish onions, cut into chunks

1 green bell pepper, seeded and cut into chunks

Extra-virgin olive oil

Kosher salt

1 small pinch saffron threads (about 10 threads, optional)

1 tablespoon choricero pepper paste (page 39)

¼ cup canned plum tomatoes, crushed by hand

Working in small batches, combine the onions and green pepper in a food processor and pulse until finely minced but not watery. Be sure to keep the batches small so you have control over the texture. As you go, pour each minced batch into a large strainer set over a large bowl. When all of the vegetables are minced, allow them to drain for 30 to 60 minutes. The more liquid you drain, the quicker the cooking will go.

Coat the bottom of a large heavy saucepan with a lid with a film of oil to a depth of ⅛ inch. Warm the oil over low heat, then add the drained onions and peppers and about 2 tablespoons salt. Cover and cook over medium-high heat for 10 minutes. Uncover and continue to cook, stirring occasionally, for about 10 minutes, until the onions are translucent and have reduced significantly.

Turn down the heat to low and continue to cook, stirring occasionally, for 2 to 3 hours, until the bitterness of the mixture is cooked out. Raise the heat to medium, add the saffron, and stir to cook in its flavor. Add the pepper paste and tomatoes and cook, stirring, for 6 minutes, until the mixture is dark and sweet. Taste and adjust the salt if needed.

Let cool completely, then transfer to airtight containers (see headnote) and refrigerate for up to 1 week or freeze for up to 3 months.

Tomato sauce | TOMATE FRITO

MAKES 8 CUPS

8 plum tomatoes, halved lengthwise

1 cup plus 1 tablespoon extra-virgin olive oil

Kosher salt

2 large Spanish onions, cut into small dice

5 cloves garlic, minced

Leaves from 14 marjoram sprigs

1 dried guindilla or árbol chile

10 cups canned plum tomatoes (approximately 3½ [28-ounce] cans), crushed by hand

½ bunch flat-leaf parsley, chopped

Tomate frito is both a finished sauce and a component of myriad Basque dishes like Braised Tongue in Tomato Española (page 210) and Smothered Okra with Sweet Basque Tomato Sauce and Minted Yogurt (page 108). In the Basque Country, the sauce is sold in jars and cans, but I find it is often too sugary, so even though I can now buy it here, I prefer to make my own. At Txikito, the sauce is a little more complex than the typical *tomate frito,* but in true Basque form, it's the best we can do. I promise it will become your pasta sauce by default; your Italian dishes will thank us, too.

Preheat the oven to 500°F. Line a baking sheet with parchment paper. In a bowl, toss the tomatoes with 1 tablespoon of the oil and a pinch of salt. Spread the tomatoes, cut side down, on the prepared baking sheet and roast for 15 to 20 minutes, until the skins are charred. Remove from the oven and let cool to room temperature. Transfer to a food processor and pulse until a chunky sauce forms. Set aside.

In a large saucepan, combine the onions, garlic, marjoram, chile, and the remaining 1 cup oil and season generously with salt. Place over low heat and cook, uncovered, stirring occasionally, for about 25 minutes, until the onions are very soft, sweet, and translucent. You do not want to brown the onions, so cover the pan or add a few tablespoons of water if they cook too fast. Add the canned tomatoes and the reserved tomato puree and raise the heat slightly so that the sauce simmers gently but does not boil. Season with salt and then cook uncovered, stirring occasionally, for about 1 hour, until the acidity of the tomatoes cooks out and the sauce is sweet and thick.

Stir in the parsley and remove from the heat. Use immediately, or let cool, transfer to airtight containers, and refrigerate for up to 1 week or freeze for up to 3 months.

Peppers

Peppers are an essential ingredient in the Basque pantry, and specific towns take great pride in their seasonal crops: piquillo peppers from Lodosa or green peppers from Guernica, for example. At Txikito we're lucky enough to know farmers who will grow specific pepper varieties for us, but at home you can often substitute North American varieties (see Chile Peppers, page 277, for more information).

Habanero vinegar | VINAGRE PICANTE

MAKES 4 CUPS

2 cups seasoned rice vinegar

2 cups champagne vinegar

½ cup sugar

Kosher salt

1 fresh habanero chile, stemmed and seeded

We make this versatile and very spicy vinegar at Txikito and use it in *escabeche* and pickled fish dishes. The vibrancy of the habanero chile makes it stand out just enough to provide some fruity notes without becoming overwhelming. It is incredibly easy to make at home. Splash some in your stews or on top of a shucked raw oyster.

In a small saucepan, combine the vinegars, sugar, and salt over low heat and heat gently, stirring often, for about 5 minutes, until the sugar and salt have dissolved. Remove from the heat, add the chile, and let cool to room temperature. Transfer to a tightly capped jar and let stand at room temperature for 24 hours before using. You can discard the chile after that point, though we leave it in longer because we prefer more spice. Store indefinitely in an airtight container.

Roasted peppers | PIMIENTOS ASADOS

MAKES 2 PEPPERS

2 bell peppers

3 tablespoons extra-virgin olive oil

½ teaspoon kosher salt

Sweet red peppers—jarred, stuffed, or topped—are a hallmark of Basque cooking. The flavor of wood-fired peppers in their own liquor is sweet and assertive, not unlike the Basques themselves.

Preheat the oven to 500°F. Line a baking sheet with parchment paper. Cut the bottom and the stem end off of each bell pepper, then seed the peppers. In a large bowl, toss the peppers with the oil and salt to coat evenly. Stand the peppers on the prepared baking sheet and roast, rotating the pan back to front at the halfway point, for 20 to 25 minutes, until the skins char and the flesh is tender.

Remove the peppers from the oven, place in a metal bowl, and cover with plastic wrap. When the peppers are cool enough to handle, peel them, discarding the skin and saving any juices that have collected at the bottom of the bowl for another use. Store refrigerated for up to 1 week.

Choricero pepper paste | PURE DE PIMIENTO CHORICERO

MAKES 8 CUPS

Any Basque sauce that is red and appears to contain lots of tomato but doesn't taste like it is probably choricero sauce. The bittersweet choricero pepper is one of the hallmarks of Basque cooking: its pulp adds body and flavor to many typical Basque sauces, and its sun-scorched red hue is immediately recognizable—and was the inspiration for the primary color of the Basque flag. Choricero peppers are dried in the sun but aren't smoked like some paprika peppers favored in other parts of Spain.

Many Basques buy the pulp of the choricero, but Eder's grandmother taught me how to use the tip of a spoon to scrape the flesh from the hydrated peppers and pass it through a food mill. It's an arduous task but yields sauces and soups with a more traditional finish. At the restaurant, we put the pulp in a blender, which creates a smooth paste. Still, when I want to produce a "grandma" dish, I take the trouble of pulling out a spoon to make the paste the old-fashioned way, just as sometimes you want to use a mortar and pestle to make a more traditional aioli or pesto.

If you can't find choriceros, I recommend substituting Mexican guajillos. Their heat level can vary from batch to batch, so be careful not to inhale as you're pureeing them. You can also adjust the amount of peppers you use based on their heat level. I like a little heat.

2 pounds dried
choricero peppers

Salt

Preheat the oven to 350°F. Arrange the peppers on a baking sheet, place in the oven, and toast for 2 to 5 minutes, until fragrant and pliable. While the peppers are still warm, remove their seeds and stems.

Fill a large saucepan about two-thirds full with lightly salted water and bring to a boil. Add the toasted peppers, then turn off the heat and cover with a lid. Leave the peppers to steep for about 20 minutes, until very soft.

Drain the peppers, reserving the soaking water. Working in batches, process the peppers in a blender using only enough of the soaking water as needed to form a puree. Pass the puree through a fine-mesh strainer and then store in airtight containers in the refrigerator for up to a week or in the freezer for up to 3 months. Freeze any remaining soaking water to use as a flavorful vegetarian stock.

2 | Txikiteo

THE ART OF PINTXOS

The simplest way to define *pintxos* is to say that they are the Basque equivalent of tapas. But the word *pintxos* (pronounced PEEN-chos) actually embraces many meanings and variations. It describes a world of vibrant, festive food that's eaten all day and all night—bar food that stretches the boundaries of what bar food can be.

Pintxos encompass everything from a piece of ham draped over a slice of garlic-rubbed bread or a simple *croqueta* to small, colorful multilayered sandwiches almost too tall to cram into your mouth. Some involve twenty ingredients, including sauces and vinaigrettes, others are little stews, and still others are simply poached or scrambled eggs with caviar. All of them, however, are designed to be eaten standing up, held in one hand; the other hand, of course, should be holding a drink. They're also intended to tempt the eye: at bars throughout the Basque Country, they're displayed on platters, positioned more or less as the first thing you see when you step up to order a drink. Tiers of these canapé-style snacks cascade over the bar, which, unlike the American bar, is not a place to sit with a plate or drink but rather a place to stand at the same level as the bartender.

Ordering a *pintxo* is a personal experience: the bartender will often pass you a small plate and encourage you to pick your own. Alternatively, you point and the bartender uses small tongs to transfer a couple onto your plate. But eating these one- or two-bite delicacies is also social. You enjoy them with friends, hopping from bar to bar as the evening blooms into night, and you return to them the morning after to help ward off a hangover, as I did the day after my wedding, when I found myself, still wearing my dress, propped up at a bar and devouring a *tortilla* at 7:00 a.m.

That said, when Basque people are out on the town, they don't eat *pintxos* at every bar they visit. As an American, the food can be hard to resist because it is so lovingly prepared everywhere you go. But Basques, being party-loving people, often prioritize alcohol over food, and *pintxos* can get expensive.

The best *pintxos* bars offer a parade of irresistible delicacies: small, buttery tart shells filled with *bakalao al pil pil*, ethereal poached eggs balanced atop pureed porcini, pristine open-faced tuna sandwiches. But what makes their food even more remarkable is that the bars themselves tend to be so unremarkable—plain rooms that aren't done any favors by the daylight or the harsh glare of fluorescents.

In this book, *pintxos* fall into five categories: *banderillas*, or savories skewered with a pick; *montaditos*, or little sandwiches; *hojaldres*, pastries with savory fillings; *cocina en minatura*—literally, "miniature cuisine"—fancy food designed to showcase the ability of the cook or bar owner; and *raciónes*, foods meant for sharing, like *croquetas* or charcuterie. Of these categories, only *raciónes* are meant to be shared. All of the others are intended to be eaten individually.

Pintxos are of such great importance to Basque life that an entire vocabulary has been built around them. When people go out for a *pintxos* crawl, they meet with their *kuadrilla* (group of friends). Going from place to place is known as going out for *potes* (drinks). Usually the crawl starts in a central place where one person is given the task of holding the money for the evening. Everyone contributes to the *bote*—a typical contribution is fifteen euros—and the person in charge of the *bote* pays the bill at every bar.

Once you get to the bar, you can have a *zurrito*, or little glass of beer, or a *txikito*, or small glass of wine. If you're thirstier, there is a *caña*, or bigger glass of beer, or even a *katxis*, or liter of beer. There is also a *kalimotxo*, a mix of wine and cola similar to a wine cooler, but it is consumed primarily by younger people and is a drink you're meant to outgrow. Then there is *vermut* in the form of Marianito blanco y rojo.

Part of the beauty of *pintxos* is how creative they can be: although this chapter contains recipes, it's also a compendium of suggestions for building *pintxos* to your own specifications. Regardless of what you make, keep in mind that it's best to stick with multipurpose ingredients that, when combined, bring out the best in each other. Remember, too, that many ingredients used to make *pinxtos* taste best when eaten at room temperature—think cheeses, meats, anchovies, and pickles—and they won't turn the bread soggy if they sit out for a while. *Pintxos* are Basque party food, and like any great party food, they're built to endure as much as delight.

Banderillas

Served pierced with a toothpick, *banderillas* are one-bite salty, savory snacks that are easily popped into your mouth, leaving your hands free. Their components are usually cured or pickled and are firm enough to skewer. This chapter includes recipes for *banderillas* we serve at Txikito, but we encourage you to experiment. No rules exist for building *banderillas*, and the picks can be short or long. It can be fun to treat them as deconstructions of classic dishes. For example, you can riff on a (definitely non-Basque) muffaletta sandwich (skewer grilled cubes of thick-cut mortadella and halloumi cheese dressed with chopped olive and pimiento vinaigrette, then drizzled with pistachio oil) or on a zucchini tart by rolling up feta and mint in a thin slice of zucchini and then broiling it. Shrimp, octopus, mussels, and other seafoods work well for *banderillas*, as do olives, firm cheeses, cured meats, fresh herbs, hard-boiled quail eggs, grilled vegetables, and any *conservas* (tuna, anchovies, or roasted or pickled peppers). *Banderillas* are best served on a platter under a veil of olive oil, which provides both flavor and sheen. If you're looking for inspiration, a delicatessen's display case is a great place to start.

Montaditos y bocadillos

The most common type of *pintxo*, these little sandwiches are served open-faced or pressed shut on bread whose main purpose is to transport delicious ingredients to your mouth. Baguette-style loaves are ubiquitous, either sliced or in miniature sub-style form, but *pain de mie* (white Pullman loaf) and Parker House–style rolls are also used. Some *montadito*s have a few ingredients; others are piled high with what seems like the entire contents of the pantry.

If you like steak with onion rings, make a *montadito* with fried shallots, a sliver of steak, and a dab of horseradish sauce. If you're an eggplant fan, layer thin slices of lightly grilled eggplant with piquillo peppers and *boquerones*. If a cheesy gratin is your thing, spoon some onto a baguette slice and broil it. Want to replicate the classic pairing of chicken liver and prunes? Buy some pâté and top it with a smear of prune marmalade. Or if you prefer simplicity to the point of austerity, make a *serranito* by slipping scraps of *jamón* fat between two slices of bread and pressing the stack in a sandwich press until the fat is hot and translucent. If you're feeling generous, cut the sandwich into fingers and you'll have plenty to share with your friends.

A *montadito* is a good vehicle for showcasing ingredients beloved by Basques but challenging for many Americans. In other words, use it to convert your friends who don't think they like anchovies or blood sausage. The key is to layer such ingredients with complementary, more accessible flavors: pair an anchovy with a juicy slice of tomato to cut the saltiness of the fish, or marry blood sausage with a thin green apple slice for a sweet-tart contrast to the rich, earthy meat. Let flavor and color be your guide and you won't go wrong.

Hojaldres

Hojaldre literally translates to "puff pastry," a laminated dough with lots of layers, but in the *pintxos* section of this book, it is more broadly used to refer to any savory pastry. Crisp, rich pastries with savory fillings are some of the most spectacular-looking members of the *pintxos* family. All of them are appealing jewel-box-like presentations that wouldn't be out of place on a plate of wedding hors d'oeuvres. They typically appear in the following guises.

Buttery, flaky, delicate vols-au-vent, or puff pastry cases with savory fillings, evoke a classic formality that is both old-fashioned and luxurious. The fillings are varied, ranging from salads or gratins to stewed meats, braised vegetables, or high-quality canned tuna, and are limited only by your imagination and your pantry. A garnish of microgreens, such as a tangle of microcilantro, is an effective and easy way to bump up their elegance.

Although you can make puff pastry, I recommend buying it, as it is time-consuming to make. Look for puff pastry made with 100 percent butter; I recommend Dufour brand.

Pasta brick or *feuilles de brick* (or often simply *brik*) are North African wheat pastry sheets that boast a shattering crispiness when fried, making them a great

VOL-AU-VENT PASTRY CASES

Making vol-au-vent pastry cases may seem challenging, but it is actually fairly simple. All you need is a thawed sheet of puff pastry, a 3-inch pastry ring cutter, and a 2-inch pastry ring cutter. To make each case, stamp out 3 circles of pastry with the 3-inch cutter. With the 2-inch cutter, cut out a circle from the center of 2 of the 3-inch circles, creating 2 doughnut-like rings. Use a little egg white to glue the doughnut rings onto the remaining solid 3-inch circle. Repeat with the remaining pastry and then freeze the cases. When the pastry is completely frozen, preheat the oven to 425°F, arrange the cases on a baking sheet, and bake for 15 to 20 minutes, until golden brown. It's important that you start with very cold or frozen dough to get a proper rise.

substitute for phyllo sheets. Their thinness and crunch deliver a compelling textural contrast to their soft interior. The pastry's provenance makes a global-style *pintxo* that beautifully illustrates how Basque cooks incorporate foreign ideas while maintaining their own tastes.

Look for *feuilles de brick* at Middle Eastern markets. If you cannot find them, purchase Vietnamese spring roll wrappers (made from wheat, not rice), which are available at Asian grocers, or Indian samosa wrappers. The key to success when making spring roll–style *pintxos* is to limit the moisture. The filling should be compact and moist but not too wet. You can fill the pastries with a variety of different foods, from blood sausage and leeks (page 63) to tuna, chopped hard-boiled egg, and *sofrito*, for an empanada-like *pintxo*. I also like to use raw shrimp: it cooks perfectly in the time that it takes to fry the wrapper crisp and golden.

Tarteletas, or miniature tarts (tartlets), typically use *pasta quebrada*, or shortcrust pastry, for the pastry shell. You can sometimes find these shells in the frozen-foods section of grocery stores, but I like making the shells from *pan de molde*, which is nothing more than buttered thin white bread slices pushed into small, fluted molds. This technique is easy, festive, and leaner than a buttery pastry dough, and, unlike many store-bought shells, usually tastes great. At the restaurant, we use crustless *pan de mie* and Pepperidge Farm Very Thinly Sliced White Bread, also with the crust removed. If you prefer to use store-bought shells, look for Dufour's all-butter frozen tartlet shells. I love filling these with caper-studded steak tartare and topping them with a raw quail egg yolk. Also great is the Russian potato salad on page 101 topped with salmon roe, or blue cheese and caramelized onion with fig.

Cocina en miniatura

The dishes that make up this category could be served as a course at a restaurant, except that they're consumed standing up. The *cocina en miniatura* tradition is where refined, elegant main courses—a glazed quail, braised pork belly, single pork cheek, or even surf and turf—are made into tiny versions of themselves, often with the same elaborate garnishes—purees, microgreens, edible flowers, seaweeds, and even gold leaf—seen in restaurants. This tension between high and low cuisine is in part the essence of the *pintxo* experience, but it is important to strike a balance between the exotic and familiar. *Cocina en miniatura* is most commonly enjoyed by well-heeled patrons who frequent the high-end *pintxos* bars in the best parts of town, and the dishes often reflect whatever ingredients du jour are being used at Michelin-starred restaurants—of which the Basque Country has an abundance.

Raciónes

Ración describes a shareable portion of food. Ordering *raciónes* or *media raciónes* (half portions) works well if you're eating with a group of people and is often done in lieu of having a formal meal. Typically, plates of *jamón* and charcuterie are served as *raciónes*, but the term encompasses a variety of dishes, including *cazuelas* of fried chorizo and *txistorra* (a kind of fresh chorizo); steamed octopus Galician style, with paprika and potatoes; and scrambled egg dishes. *Croquetas* are a favorite *ración*: a sauce or stew encased in a crisp breaded exterior, they're adored by adults and children alike throughout Spain. At Txikito, we serve them two at a time, but in Spain you usually get six.

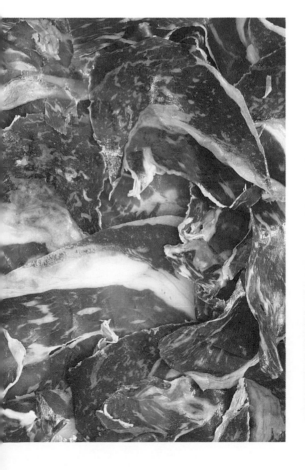

Manzanilla olives, pickled guindilla peppers, and anchovy

GILDA

The most iconic *pintxo* of them all, the *banderilla* known as *gilda* is a layered skewer of Manzanilla olives, pickled guindilla peppers, and an anchovy. It is traditionally layered to suggest a woman's figure, specifically that of Rita Hayworth in the 1946 movie *Gilda*: an olive for the head, the peppers for the arms, the anchovy and another olive on the bottom for more curves. But what's even more compelling than the shape are the flavors, which are best friends and support one another perfectly. Stacked just right, the ingredients also look like a Basque dancer, arms out and embracing the sky. | SERVES 6

12 Manzanilla olives, pitted

6 olive oil–packed anchovy fillets

12 pickled green guindilla peppers, stems trimmed

1 cup extra-virgin olive oil

Have ready six 4-inch bamboo skewers or toothpicks. Thread 1 olive about halfway down a skewer, followed by 1 anchovy folded accordion-style. Next, skewer 2 peppers, one after the other, to make the "arms," piercing the trimmed end so that the narrow tips stick out. Finish with a second olive. The whole assembly should occupy the upper third of the skewer, with the olive on the tip. If it doesn't, just slide everything up. Repeat with the remaining ingredients and skewers, and then arrange the finished skewers in a shallow dish. Cover with the oil and serve at room temperature.

Marinated mushrooms with vermouth and garlic

BANDERILLA DE SETAS AL AJILLO

Drop one of these into a martini! *Txampis al ajillo*, or slow-cooked garlicky mushroom caps, are the specialty of one of Eder's favorite bars in Bilbao. The bar makes a ritual of grilling each mushroom for ten minutes, repeatedly basting it with a secret garlicky mixture in an unmarked squeeze bottle. I could have eaten ten of them, but that afternoon, when I declared I wanted another, Eder said no dice, and we were off to the next place. Part of what made that mushroom so good is that you kept longing for another, a reminder that a *pintxo* is just the right amount of food to be memorable.

Buy the smallest, uniform-size button mushrooms you can find. You must cook them so that they release their juices, which means high heat and moving them around in the pan. You can opt to skip the skewers and instead serve the mushrooms in a *cazuela* with plenty of bread and toothpicks on the side. And if you want to use them in martinis, which I highly recommend, reduce the oil to 1½ tablespoons, which is just enough to conduct heat and be absorbed but not enough to leave behind an oily film. | SERVES 6

1 teaspoon minced garlic

½ cup extra-virgin olive oil

1½ pounds small white button mushrooms

Kosher salt

1 teaspoon red pepper flakes

1 bunch flat-leaf parsley, coarsely chopped

3 tablespoons dry vermouth (preferably Atxa or Perucchi brand) or fino sherry

Juice of 1 lemon

In a large saucepan, warm the garlic and oil over medium heat for about 30 seconds, until opaque. Raise the heat to high, add the mushrooms and 1 teaspoon salt, and cook, stirring often, for about 5 minutes, until the mushrooms begin to release their juices and shrink. Add the pepper flakes and parsley and cook, stirring, for 2 minutes longer. Add the vermouth and deglaze the pan, stirring to dislodge any browned bits. Reduce the heat to medium, then cook for about 6 more minutes, until the liquid reduces to a syrupy consistency. Add a pinch of salt, remove from the heat, and stir in the lemon juice. Transfer the mushrooms and their liquid to a dish, let cool, cover, and refrigerate for at least 1 hour.

Have ready six 4-inch bamboo skewers. Thread the chilled mushrooms onto the skewers, dividing them evenly, and arrange on a platter. Pour the liquid from the storage dish over the mushrooms and serve.

Cold poached shrimp with white asparagus

BANDERILLA DE GAMBA ROJA

Banderillas of shrimp are served both cold and hot *a la plantxa*, or griddled. Brining and poaching the shrimp, as is done here, makes them particularly flavorful and succulent. I recommend seeking out wild-caught Florida royal red or North Carolina brown shrimp in order to approximate the sweet and supple texture of Spanish *gambas de Palamós*. Ask your fishmonger for 20/30 count, which are bite-size. Traditionally, shrimp threaded on skewers are served topped with mayonnaise and grated hard-boiled egg, but you will also find them in *pintxos* bars dressed with a variety of vinaigrettes. At the restaurant, we like to pair them with white asparagus, which is traditional. You might try mixing minced green bell peppers and onion with vinegar and oil for a colorful vinaigrette. Feel free to improvise. | SERVES 6

1 pound shell-on shrimp (20/30 count)

1½ cups water

¼ cup kosher salt

3 tablespoons sugar

1½ cups ice cubes

6 medium tinned white asparagus, drained

2 tablespoons mayonnaise, homemade (page 22) or store-bought (optional)

2 hard-boiled eggs (page 115), peeled and chopped or grated (optional)

Using kitchen scissors, and starting at the head end, cut an incision down the back of each shrimp to the tip of the shell, exposing the dark intestinal tract. Peel the shrimp and lift out and discard the tract. Save the shells for stock (page 24). Rinse the shrimp and set aside.

To make a brine, in a large bowl, combine the water, salt, and sugar and stir to dissolve the salt and sugar. Add the ice cubes. Place the peeled shrimp in the brine for 7 minutes, depending on their size.

Meanwhile, bring a saucepan of salted water to a boil over high heat. Prepare an ice bath and place a metal bowl in the bath to chill. When the shrimp are ready, remove them from the brine and blanch them in the boiling water for about four 1 minute, stirring, just until they turn pink. Using a slotted spoon or spider, and working quickly, transfer them to the chilled metal bowl. Let cool.

Have ready six 4-inch bamboo skewers. Drain the asparagus and pat dry, then slice crosswise into four 1-inch pieces. Skewer a piece of the asparagus, followed by a shrimp. Repeat so that each skewer has 4 shrimp and 4 pieces of asparagus. Arrange on a platter and serve topped with the mayonnaise and grated egg.

Open-faced fried quail egg and chorizo sandwich

ARRAULTZA

This charming *pintxo* is a real crowd-pleaser: who doesn't love fried eggs and chorizo? In the version we make at Txikito, we cut the chorizo into very thin matchsticks, which makes it easier to eat and ensures that all of the flavors come through in each bite. Make sure that the chorizo is at room temperature, as cold chorizo is waxy and not as tasty and will make your eggs cold. | SERVES 6

5 ounces dry-cured spicy chorizo, at room temperature

6 tablespoons sweet vegetable "marmalade" (page 33), at room temperature, or 1 Spanish onion, ¼ cup extra-virgin olive oil, and pinch of kosher salt

6 (½-inch-thick) slices baguette, cut on the bias

¼ cup extra-virgin olive oil

6 quail eggs, at room temperature

Maldon salt, for finishing

Using a sharp knife, cut off the tips of the chorizo, then cut it in half at its U bend to create 2 logs. Carefully make a shallow incision along the length of each log and peel off the thin casing. Slice the chorizo crosswise into 1-inch-thick pieces. Cut each piece lengthwise into thin slices and then cut the slices into matchsticks. Alternatively, cut the chorizo logs crosswise into thin coins. Set aside.

If using the vegetable marmalade, spread 1 tablespoon of it onto each baguette slice. If using the onion, dice it very small, then cook it very slow and low in a frying pan with the oil and salt for about 25 minutes, until very soft and sweet. Let cool to room temperature, then spread about 1 tablespoon onto each bread slice. Top the marmalade or slow-cooked onion with a generous amount of the chorizo, then make a small well in the middle of each mound of chorizo.

In a very small frying pan, heat the oil over high heat. Add the quail eggs one at a time, then reduce the heat and fry (see page 116 for tips on frying eggs). Nestle a fried egg in each chorizo well. Sprinkle a little Maldon salt over each yolk and serve at room temperature.

Tutera, page 58 (left),
and *arraultza* (right)

Open-faced sandwich of jamón, anchovy, and roasted pepper

MARIJULI

Every *pintxos* bar has a *marijuli* or a *matrimonio*. *Marijuli* means, among other things, "whatchamacallit" or "what's her name?"; *matrimonio* means "marriage" and usually includes one vinegar-brined anchovy and one oil-cured one. This *marijuli* is a cured "surf and turf" *montadito*—its ingredients complement one another and the mixture of flavors is so Spain. | SERVES 6

2 roasted green bell peppers (page 38)

2 tablespoons extra-virgin olive oil

Kosher salt

2 plum tomatoes

6 (½-inch-thick) slices baguette, cut on the bias

6 slices paleta de jamón ibérico or jamón ibérico

6 olive oil–packed anchovy fillets

Using your fingers, rip the peppers into pieces and place in a bowl. Add the oil and a pinch of salt and toss to coat evenly. The peppers can be prepared a day ahead, but bring them to room temperature before using.

Meanwhile, cut the tomatoes in half lengthwise, scoop out and discard the seed sacs, and grate each half on the medium-coarse holes of a box grater, collecting the pulp on a plate. Keep grating until you have about ¼ cup of tomato pulp. Discard the skins and season the pulp with a pinch of salt.

To assemble each montadito, spread a spoonful of tomato pulp on a baguette slice. Place 2 pieces of roasted pepper on the pulp, followed by a slice of paleta or jamón. Top with an anchovy. Serve at room temperature.

Pressed sandwich of mushrooms, Roncal, and sage

TXAMPI

This is a duxelles-style mushroom spread pressed between soft white bread and heated until warm, gooey, and irresistible. Although a combination of king oyster, white button, and porcini mushrooms is suggested here, any hearty mushroom will do. Bread slices from a white Pullman loaf are ideal because they press down nicely and crisp up beautifully. You can use this same mushroom mixture for filling vols-au-vent (see page 47). | SERVES 8

2 tablespoons unsalted butter

2 shallots, minced

2 cloves garlic, minced

1 pound mushrooms (such as a combination of king oyster, white button, and porcini), trimmed and minced

Kosher salt

2 tablespoons Madeira or brandy

1 tablespoon heavy cream

¼ cup grated Roncal, Manchego, or Grana Padano cheese

4 thin slices white Pullman bread, crusts removed

½ cup mayonnaise, homemade (page 22) or store-bought

16 small fresh sage leaves

In a large saucepan, melt the butter over medium heat. Add the shallots and garlic and cook, stirring occasionally, for 5 minutes, until translucent. Raise the heat to high, add the mushrooms and 1 teaspoon salt, and cook, stirring occasionally, for about 15 minutes, until the mushrooms release their juices and the liquid evaporates. Add the Madeira and cream and cook for another 2 minutes. Remove from the heat and let cool for a minute or two, then fold in the cheese. Let cool for about 30 minutes, until room temperature.

Divide the mushroom mixture between 2 of the bread slices, spreading it evenly, and then top with the remaining 2 slices. Heat a large cast-iron or nonstick frying pan over low heat until very hot. Spread about 2 tablespoons of the mayonnaise on the top of each sandwich. Press 4 sage leaves into the mayonnaise on each sandwich, placing 1 leaf in each quarter of the bread.

When the pan is hot, add the sandwiches, mayonnaise side down. Using a large spatula, press down on the top of both sandwiches and sear them without moving them for 1 minute, until they begin to brown. Before flipping them, spread the remaining mayonnaise on the tops of the sandwiches, using 2 tablespoons for each sandwich, and then press the remaining 8 sage leaves into the mayonnaise. Now flip and sear for 2 minutes on the second side, again pressing down on the sandwiches with a spatula. Cut each sandwich into quarters, and arrange on a platter. Serve immediately.

Gratin of artichoke hearts, Roncal, and jamón serrano

TUTERA

This is a *montadito gratinado*, which means it receives a golden finish in your broiler or oven. Think of it as a hot dip smeared on bread and then toasted. It is a great party item because you can build it ahead and fire off a few at a time. I like a warm *pinxto*, and this one takes equal inspiration from the Basque love of artichokes with *jamón* and my lingering affection for the artichoke dip served at Minneapolis's Loring Cafe in the 1980s. *See photo on page 54.* | SERVES 6

10 freshly trimmed artichoke hearts, or 2 cups frozen artichoke hearts, thawed and patted dry

2 tablespoons extra-virgin olive oil

Kosher salt

½ cup thinly sliced jamón serrano

2 tablespoons mayonnaise, homemade (page 22) or store-bought

1 cup grated Roncal, Parmesan, or Manchego cheese

Juice of 1 lemon

½ teaspoon freshly ground pepper

6 (½-inch-thick) slices baguette, cut on the bias

Preheat the oven to 425°F. Line a baking sheet with parchment paper.

In a bowl, toss the artichoke hearts with the oil and a pinch of salt. Spread on the prepared baking sheet and roast for 10 minutes, until lightly browned. Remove the artichokes and let cool. Meanwhile, stack the jamón slices, roll them up, and cross-cut the rolls into thin ribbons.

Pulse the roasted artichokes in a food processor until they are finely chopped but not pureed. Transfer to a bowl and fold in the mayonnaise, cheese, jamón ribbons, lemon juice, pepper, and 2 teaspoons salt.

Spread about 2 to 3 tablespoons of the artichoke mixture on each baguette slice and arrange the slices on the prepared baking sheet. Bake at 425°F for 4 to 6 minutes, until browned and bubbly. Serve immediately.

Gratin of deviled crab

TXANGURRO

Like the artichoke gratin on page 58, this is a *montadito gratinado*. Txikito's version of *txangurro* approximates the flavor of stuffed crab that is so beloved in the Basque Country. As with other broiled or baked *pintxos*, this little open-faced sandwich is bubbly and brown and great to make for a group. The cream cheese here is a funny nod to the Basque love of *queso Philadelphia* and is proof that one man's delicacy is another's comfort food. | SERVES 6

1 pound blue crabmeat, picked over for shell fragments

2 ounces cream cheese, at room temperature

1 tablespoon heavy cream

2 tablespoons sweet vegetable "marmalade" (page 33)

1 teaspoon kosher salt

1 teaspoon Sriracha sauce

Juice of ½ lemon

6 (½-inch-thick) slices baguette, cut on the bias

Preheat the oven to 425°F. Line a baking sheet with parchment paper.

In a bowl, combine the crabmeat, cream cheese, cream, vegetable marmalade, salt, Sriracha sauce, and lemon juice and mix well. Spread about 3 tablespoons of the mixture on each baguette slice and arrange on the prepared baking sheet.

Bake for about 6 minutes, until brown and bubbly. Serve immediately.

Pressed sandwich of jamón ibérico fat

EL SERRANITO DE IRUÑA

4 tablespoons extra-virgin olive oil

8 (2-inch-wide) slices jamón ibérico or serrano fat, shaved from stored jamón fat

4 (⅓-inch-thick) slices country or crustless Pullman bread

Saving *jamón* fat and bones is something that the Basques and Spaniards do. We do it at Txikito as well, for the simple reason that it's saving flavor. You can do all sorts of wizardry with *grasa* or *lagrima ibérica*—more polite names for fat—but one of the most delicious things you can make with it is pressed sandwiches. The first time I had this delicacy I had to pry open the sandwich to see what was going on in there. The funky fat was translucent and had mostly melted into the bread, while the rest was a clear, flabby layer, soft and luxurious. The second time I had a *serranito* was at my wedding, where the sandwiches were a tremendous hit. | SERVES 8

In a nonstick frying pan, heat 2 tablespoons of the oil over medium-low heat. While the oil heats, place 4 slices of the jamón fat on each of 2 slices of the bread and top with the remaining bread slices. When the pan is hot, add the sandwiches and, using a large spatula, press down on the top of both sandwiches and sear them without moving them for 3 to 4 minutes, until golden brown. Remove the sandwiches from the pan and add the remaining 2 tablespoons oil to the pan. When the oil is hot, return the sandwiches, browned side up, to the pan and sear the second side for 2 minutes, again pressing down on the sandwiches with a spatula.

Transfer the sandwiches to a cutting board, cut each sandwich into quarters, and wrap each quarter in waxed paper. Serve immediately.

Cigarillos de morcilla, page 63 (above), *el serranito de iruña* (below)

Chorizo hash in puff pastry

TXITXIKI EN HOJALDRE

Txistorra en hojaldre, the Basque version of pigs in a blanket, has two things that any Basque loves: pork and puff pastry. *Txistorras* are the fresh ropes of chorizo that we make in-house at the restaurant, and *txitxiki* is our quick cheat: it is the cooked ground meat mixture that we eat as a test run before we stuff the casings with chorizo mixture. When shopping for this recipe, look for high-quality pork shoulder, preferably from Berkshire or another heritage breed, with some fat content. Ask your butcher to grind the pork for you at the store; a blend of half medium and half fine grind makes for an ideal texture. If you decide to grind your own pork, as we do, cut it into 1-inch cubes, toss the cubes with all of the other ingredients, let the mixture marinate for 30 minutes, and then freeze it for 15 minutes before grinding. You will end up with more hash than you need for the vol-au-vent cases (about 8 cups), but the extra can be used for other dishes, such as lasagna or mini shepherd pies. | SERVES 6, WITH LEFTOVER HASH

¼ cup extra-virgin olive oil

1 pound medium-grind pork shoulder

1 pound fine-grind pork shoulder

2 cloves garlic, minced

Kosher salt

3 tablespoons hot Spanish paprika

2 tablespoons Calabrian chile paste or Sriracha sauce

6 to 12 vol-au-vent pastry cases, baked and cooled to room temperature (see page 47)

Coat the bottom of a large saucepan with the oil and place over high heat. When the oil begins to smoke, add all of the pork, the garlic, and 1 tablespoon salt and cook, stirring and breaking up the pork with a wooden spoon, for about 6 minutes, until the pork just begins to brown. Turn down the heat to medium-low, add the paprika and chile paste, and cook for another 3 minutes to allow the fat and spices to mingle. Taste and adjust the seasoning with salt. Remove from the heat. You should have about 8 cups hash, more than you need for this recipe. Reserve the leftovers for another use. You can use the hash immediately, or let cool, cover, and refrigerate for up to 3 days, then reheat in a microwave or frying pan over medium heat before continuing.

To serve, spoon 2 to 3 tablespoons of the hash into each pastry case so that it fills the pastry and comes up over the top, arrange on a platter, and serve immediately dusted with more paprika if you like.

Crispy bundles of morcilla

CIGARILLOS DE MORCILLA

At Txikito, we make our own *morcilla*, or blood sausage, from blood, pork fat, onions, and sometimes rice. But you can buy blood sausage from your favorite purveyor and doctor it to get a similar result. Here, leeks are cooked down until soft and sweet and then added to the crumbled sausage. That filling gets rolled up spring-roll style into *feuilles de brick*, North African pastry sheets, and then fried. *See photo on page 60.* | SERVES 6

3 leeks, white and light green parts only, thinly sliced

¼ cup extra-virgin olive oil

Kosher salt

1 pound blood sausages

6 (12-inch) feuille de brick rounds or wheat-based Vietnamese spring roll wrappers

1 egg, lightly beaten

Canola oil, for frying

In a saucepan, combine the leeks, olive oil, and a pinch of salt and sweat over low for 25 minutes, until very soft and melty.

While the leeks are cooking, remove the sausages from their casings. When the leeks are ready, crumble the sausages into the pan, fold the leeks and sausages together, and cook, stirring occasionally, for about 5 minutes, until the flavors have melded and the sausage fat binds the mixture. Let cool for about 30 minutes, until room temperature.

Cut a pastry round into quarters. With the pointed end of a quarter facing you, place a small oblong lump of filling (about 1½ tablespoons) near the tip and then roll the dough away from you, folding in the sides as you would an egg roll and creating a snug cylinder. Seal the seam with a drop of beaten egg. Repeat with the remaining pastry and filling. You can freeze any leftover filling for up to 3 months, or fry it to serve with eggs.

Pour the canola oil to a depth of about 1 inch into a deep saucepan and heat over high heat to about 365°F. Lower the heat to medium. Line a large plate with paper towels. Working in batches, fry the pastry bundles, turning them once, for about 2 minutes on each side, until golden brown. Using tongs or a spider, transfer the bundles to the towel-lined plate to drain. Serve immediately.

Scallop in its shell (or spoon) with jamón ibérico fat and soy-sherry-ginger vinaigrette

VIERIA CON SOJA, VINAGRE DE JEREZ, VELO DE GRASA IBÉRICA, GENJIBRE

Cucharillas are *pintxos* served in spoons, often of the Chinese soupspoon variety. If you're lucky enough to have access to the incredible Taylor Bay scallops farmed on Cape Cod, I recommend using them and portioning three scallops per shell or spoon. Served nearly raw, the sweet scallops make a great match for salty *jamón ibérico* fat, and the sherry vinegar and the soy lend some acidity to cut through both. Although the use of soy may seem incongruous, Asian ingredients are popular among chefs in the Basque Country, who consider them *"muy moderno."* | SERVES 6

2 cups kosher salt

3 green onions, white and light green parts only, minced

2-inch piece fresh ginger, peeled and minced

¼ cup sherry vinegar

2 teaspoons light soy sauce

½ teaspoon toasted sesame oil

¼ teaspoon red pepper flakes

½ teaspoon sugar

12 scallop shells (ask your fishmonger) or ovenproof Chinese soupspoons

12 medium scallops, small outer muscle removed

24 very thin (1-inch square) slices jamón ibérico fat or Italian or Spanish lardo

½ cup microcilantro, or ½ bunch cilantro, coarsely chopped

Preheat the broiler or oven to 500°F. In a bowl, combine the salt with enough water (about ¾ cup) to create the texture of wet compacted sand.

To make the vinaigrette, in a bowl, stir together the green onions, ginger, vinegar, soy sauce, oil, red pepper flakes, and sugar. Depending on the acidity of your vinegar, you may want to add an additional pinch of sugar. If your soy sauce has made the vinaigrette too salty, stir in a little water, too.

Place 12 small mounds of wet salt (about 1½ teaspoons each) on a baking sheet and balance a scallop shell on top of each mound. (You may have to do this in batches.) Place a scallop in each shell and top with a slice of the jamón fat. Broil or bake until the scallops are warmed through and the fat is transparent, about 1 minute. Repeat as needed with the remaining scallops.

Remove from the broiler and top each scallop with about 1½ teaspoons of the vinaigrette and some microcilantro. If serving the scallops in shells, apply more wet salt to a platter and balance the shells on top. If serving in spoons, forgo the salt and set the spoons directly on the platter. Serve immediately.

Sardine "lasagna" with blue cheese

LASAÑA DE SARDINAS CON QUESO AZUL

I made this *pintxo* one night when a sardine-loving chef came to Txikito for dinner, improvising it on the fly with ingredients on my station. It was incredibly tasty and reflected everything that Basques like, and showed off their creativity and their naïve, fish-out-of-water approach to anything Italian. Just as lasagna is comfort food to Americans and exotic to the Basques, sardines are comfort food to the Basques and exotic or polarizing to Americans. | SERVES 6

12 fresh sardines, filleted, or 3 (4- to 5-ounce) tins high-quality Spanish sardine fillets in olive oil, such as Ramón Peña brand

2½ ounces provolone cheese, grated

½ cup crumbled blue cheese

1½ cups tomato sauce (page 36)

1 teaspoon red pepper flakes

Leaves from 5 marjoram sprigs

Preheat the oven to 375°F. Line a small (5 by 7-inch) loaf pan with enough parchment paper to leave a 3-inch overhang on one side. The overhang will help you to unmold the lasagna.

Layer the ingredients: Start with a layer of sardines, placing them head to tail, shiny skin side up, and with no gaps. Sprinkle the fish evenly with one-fourth of the provolone and a little of the blue cheese. Dot the cheese with the some of the tomato sauce, then sprinkle with the some of the pepper flakes and marjoram. Repeat the layers up to three times; how many layers you get will depend on the size of your sardines. Finish the lasagna with an extra layer of provolone, pepper flakes, and marjoram. With oiled hands, lightly and evenly press down the lasagna.

Bake the lasagna for approximately 12 minutes if you're using canned sardines and up to 15 minutes for fresh, until the sardines are cooked and the cheese has melted. Let cool completely, cover, and refrigerate for at least 2 hours or overnight.

To unmold the lasagna, run a knife along the inside edge of the pan to loosen the sides of the lasagna, then pull up the parchment overhang enough to sneak an offset spatula under the lasagna and carefully tip it out onto a cutting board. Using a very sharp knife, portion the lasagna into small rectangles.

To serve, carefully transfer the portions to a baking sheet and reheat quickly in a hot oven. You want the lasagna to be warm but not so hot that it slides apart. Serve immediately.

Seared foie gras with maple syrup

FOIE A LA PLANTXA CON JARABE DE ARCE

Foie gras is a luxury in the Basque Country, but like caviar, it is also ubiquitous. Seared foie is a common *pintxo* at places like San Sebastián's jewel, La Cuchara de San Telmo. This is the kind of *cocina en miniatura* that really matters (at least to me): every day, La Cuchara serves hundreds of tiny masterpieces that could pass as appetizers at fine dining restaurants if its trappings weren't so relaxed and pared down.

Foie gras isn't difficult to find—it's just expensive. But it's so easy to prepare that it's worth treating yourself on a special occasion. If you don't live near the Hudson Valley, where Hudson Valley Foie Gras makes and sells an excellent product, ask your butcher or go online. Rougié and D'Artagnan are good brands. Foie gras is sold sliced and as whole lobes; slicing it yourself is best, as you can control the cooking more easily by cutting thicker slices. | SERVES 6

6 (¾-inch-thick) slices foie gras

½ cup grade B dark maple syrup

1 tablespoon sherry vinegar

Maldon salt and freshly cracked pepper

2 pears, peaches, plums, or another tender seasonal fruit, pitted and thinly sliced

Preheat the oven to 225°F. Place the foie slices on a plate or baking sheet and freeze for 25 minutes.

In a small bowl, stir together the maple syrup and vinegar and season with a pinch of salt and a twist of black pepper.

Heat a large nonstick frying pan over medium heat until it is just hot. Add the foie gras slices and sear for about 30 seconds, until golden on the first side. Flip the slices and sear on the second side for 30 additional seconds or until a mahogany color, then transfer the foie gras to a nonstick baking sheet and place in the oven for about 2 minutes, until the foie is warm in the center. To test for doneness, slide a needle or cake tester into the thickest part of a slice and then hold the needle to your lip.

Meanwhile, season the sliced fruit with salt and pepper, then caramelize in the nonstick frying pan with the rendered foie gras fat until golden around the edges and warm through, about 30 seconds per side.

Arrange the slices of foie gras on a platter and top each slice with some of the warmed fruit. Drizzle each slice with the vinegar syrup, garnish with a few crystals of salt, and serve immediately.

Croquettes

CROQUETAS

The classic Basque *croqueta* involves shaping a rich, flavorful béchamel sauce into balls, double coating it with egg and bread crumbs, and then frying it. There are many opinions about the ideal texture of a *croqueta*. Some very modern versions are liquid, but I fall into the classic camp, which is creamy and silky but not too runny. I was born to *"croquetiar,"* as only someone who has rolled thousands of *croquetas* might call it. If my husband and I are phoning each another, one of us might say, "I can't talk now," or *"Estoy croquetiando."* Translation: "I'm rolling croquettes." My entire childhood could be called "white sauce days": my mom made béchamel sauce about three times a week, so I learned at her hip how to rid white sauce of lumps and to use nutmeg sparingly. The trick is to make a solid sauce with a delicate flavor of the primary ingredient. A chicken *croqueta* that doesn't taste like chicken is poorly made, no matter how great the béchamel.

I've included recipes for chicken *croquetas* and ham *croquetas*, plus two variations. You can shape the croquettes, coat them with bread crumbs and then freeze them for up to 1 month. Make sure they are fully thawed before you fry them or they will be cold in the center. For the best results, make and bread the croquettes at least one day before frying so the breading is set and they don't crack while frying.

CONTINUED

Chicken croquettes | CROQUETAS DE POLLO

SERVES 6 TO 8

4 cups double chicken stock (page 26)

Kosher salt

¼ cup unsalted butter

¾ cup rendered chicken fat, left over from making chicken stock or sourced from your butcher, or unsalted butter

1 small Spanish onion, cut into small dice

1 cup all-purpose flour

2 cups whole milk

1 cup shredded cooked chicken

2 hard-boiled eggs (page 115), peeled and coarsely chopped

Pinch of freshly grated nutmeg

8 cups panko bread crumbs

3 eggs

Canola oil, for frying

In a saucepan, bring the stock to a boil over high heat, then turn down the heat to maintain a steady simmer and cook until the liquid has reduced by half, about 6 to 8 minutes. Season with about 1 tablespoon salt, then remove from the heat and cover to keep warm.

Meanwhile, melt the butter in a large saucepan over low heat. Add the chicken fat, onion, and ¼ teaspoon salt and sweat the onions for about 25 minutes, until very soft and sweet.

When the onion is ready, raise the heat to medium-low, add the flour, and cook, whisking constantly, until the flour is very pale blond and bubbly, about 8 minutes. Raise the heat to high and begin to add the milk, whisking constantly to ensure a smooth paste forms. Whisk in the stock as quickly as possible, then turn down the heat so the mixture is barely gurgling. Continue stirring, taste, and add another pinch of salt if needed. Continue cooking for about another 8 minutes or so. Fold in the chicken and hard-boiled eggs, then turn down the heat to low and cook, stirring, for 1 minute longer. Remove from the heat; add the nutmeg.

Coat a baking sheet with a thin film of canola oil and spread the béchamel mixture over it. Cover with plastic wrap, pressing it directly onto the surface (to prevent a skin from forming), let cool, and then refrigerate for at least 1 to 2 hours. It is ready when it has a firm, slightly plastic consistency. Lightly oil your hands, roll the béchamel mixture into 1-inch balls, and place on a clean baking sheet. Cover and chill while you prepare the bread crumbs, approximately 20 minutes.

In batches, pulverize the bread crumbs in a food processor and transfer to a shallow, wide baking dish. In a separate bowl, beat the raw eggs until blended. One at a time, coat the chilled balls with the bread crumbs, tapping off the excess; dip them in the eggs, allowing the excess to drip off; and then coat once again with the bread crumbs. Set aside on a clean baking sheet.

Pour the oil to a depth of 1 inch into a deep saucepan and heat to 365°F. Working in batches, fry the croquettes, turning them once, for about 2½ minutes total, until deep golden brown; drain on a paper towel–lined plate then serve.

Ham croquettes | CROQUETAS DE JAMÓN

SERVES 6 TO 8

½ cup unsalted butter

½ cup minced jamón serrano or ibérico

4 cups whole milk, or mixture of whole milk and jamón stock (page 25)

Kosher salt

1 cup all-purpose flour

8 cups panko bread crumbs

3 eggs

Canola oil, for frying

In a large saucepan, melt the butter over low heat. Add the jamón and cook, stirring occasionally, for about 10 minutes, until the butter is infused with its flavor. Meanwhile, in a small saucepan, warm 2 cups of the milk and about 2 teaspoons salt over low heat. Remove from the heat and cover to keep warm.

When the jamón is ready, raise the heat to medium-low, add the flour, and cook, whisking constantly, for 6 to 8 minutes, until very pale blond. Raise the heat to high and begin to add the remaining 2 cups cold milk, whisking constantly to break up any lumps. As the mixture comes to a boil and begins to thicken, quickly whisk in the warm milk. Turn down the heat so the béchamel is barely gurgling, then continue stirring, making sure the bottom doesn't brown, until the sauce has finished thickening. Taste and add another pinch of salt if needed. Reduce the heat to low and continue to cook for 6 to 8 more minutes.

Coat a baking sheet with a thin film of canola oil and spread the béchamel mixture over it. Cover with plastic wrap, pressing it directly onto the surface (to prevent a skin from forming), let cool, and then refrigerate for at least 1 to 2 hours until firm. Shape the croquettes, ready the bread crumbs and beaten eggs, and then coat, fry, and serve the croquettes as directed for Chicken Croquettes (page 70).

CORN CROQUETTES | CROQUETAS DE MAÍZ

Follow the recipe for Ham Croquettes (using all milk), then fold 1 cup of chopped corn kernels into the béchamel mixture after cooking out the flour. Stir in a pinch of freshly grated nutmeg before spreading to cool, then proceed as directed.

TUNA CROQUETTES | CROQUETAS DE BONITO

Follow the recipe for Chicken Croquettes (using all butter and no rendered chicken fat), but omit the chicken, hard-boiled eggs, and nutmeg. Sweat ½ cup minced green bell pepper with the onion. Fold 1 cup well-drained olive oil–cured canned bonito into the béchamel mixture before spreading it on the baking sheet for chilling. Proceed as directed.

Sunday afternoon battered and fried squid

RABAS

Rabas, like so many Basque foods, are not just a recipe but also a tradition, even a behavior. Every Sunday afternoon, bars have a competition to see who makes the best fried squid rings. I like to try them all and make a lunch and dinner out of it. Some cooks coat the squid with flour and egg—*a la romana*—for frying; others use only flour. I like to take the time to make an Orly batter, which is an egg-enriched tempura batter with baking powder. The key to great *rabas*, however, is high-quality squid that will stay soft and sweet when fried. If you can't find good squid, you can substitute cuttlefish to make *chocos fritos.* | SERVES 6

1¾ pounds medium-size squid, or 1 pound cleaned squid

2 cups all-purpose flour

1 tablespoon baking powder

½ teaspoon kosher salt

1 egg, lightly beaten

1 (12-ounce) bottle club soda, ice-cold

Extra-virgin olive oil, for frying

½ cup rice flour or cornstarch

If using whole squid, clean the squid as directed on page 172. Cut the bodies crosswise into ½-inch-wide rings, or snip the bodies open lengthwise, score them lightly, and then cut into 1- to 2-inch squares. Leave the tentacles whole. Cover and refrigerate the squid until needed. If you have purchased cleaned squid, cut as directed for the cleaned whole squid.

In a bowl, whisk together the all-purpose flour, baking powder, and salt. Make a well in the center and pour the egg into the well. Whisk in the club soda, a little at a time, until the mixture is the consistency of loose pancake batter. Do not overmix or the batter will toughen. Let the batter relax for 15 to 20 minutes. Do not make it more than 30 to 40 minutes before frying.

When ready to fry, pour the oil to a depth of 2 inches into a deep saucepan and heat to 365°F. Put the rice flour in a bowl, add the squid, toss to coat evenly, and then lift out, shaking off the excess flour. Line a plate with paper towels.

Working in batches, dip each piece of squid into the batter and then gently slip it into the oil. Without crowding your oil, fry the pieces in batches, turning and submerging them in the oil—long chopsticks are a great tool for this—for about 2 minutes, until golden brown. Using a slotted spoon, transfer the squid to the towel-lined plate to drain. Repeat with any remaining squid. Serve immediately.

Spiced lamb meatballs with warm pea salad

ALBÓNDIGAS DE CORDERO

3 tablespoons extra-virgin olive oil

2 Spanish onions, chopped, plus ½ onion, minced

1 carrot, peeled and chopped

2 leeks, white and light green parts only, chopped

1½ cups red cooking wine

12 cups double chicken stock (page 26), or beef tongue stock (page 27)

1 bunch fresh mint

2½ pounds ground lamb

1 cup panko bread crumbs

1 egg, lightly beaten

1 teaspoon sweet Spanish paprika

¼ teaspoon cayenne pepper

½ teaspoon allspice

Canola oil, for frying

PEA SALAD

1 small Spanish onion, minced

1 bay leaf

Diced jamón ends (optional)

3 tablespoons extra-virgin olive oil

3 cups (about 1 pound) fresh or frozen shelled English peas, blanched for 1½ minutes

In the Basque Country, meatballs are typically served as a light stew with fried potatoes and peas added to the mix. Here, fresh mint and parsley wake up the dish, while the warm pea salad is my fresher take on the Basque tradition of braising everything together. | SERVES 6 TO 8

In a large saucepan, warm the olive oil over high heat. Add the chopped onions, carrot, and leeks and cook, stirring often, for about 7 minutes, until they begin to brown. Add the wine and simmer for a few minutes until most of the alcohol cooks off. Add the stock and mint, bring to a boil, and then immediately lower the heat to a gentle simmer. Simmer the stock gently for 1 hour. Remove from the heat, strain through a fine-mesh strainer, and return to the saucepan. Set aside.

While the stock is simmering, make the meatballs. In a large bowl, combine the lamb, bread crumbs, minced onion, egg, paprika, cayenne, and allspice and fold together, making sure to incorporate the spices evenly without overworking the meat. Line a couple of dinner plates with paper towels and set aside.

Shape the lamb mixture into balls about 1 inch in diameter. Pour the canola oil to a depth of ¾ inch into a deep sauté pan and place over high heat. Working in batches, add the meatballs to the hot oil and fry, turning as needed, for 2 to 3 minutes, until evenly browned on all the sides. Using a slotted spoon, transfer to the paper towel–lined plates and reserve.

To make the pea salad, in a small saucepan, combine the onion, bay leaf, jamón, and oil over medium-low heat and sweat for about 7 minutes, until the onion is translucent. Add the peas and cook until heated through.

Meanwhile, bring the stock to a boil over high heat and turn down the heat to a simmer. Add the meatballs and simmer for a few minutes, until cooked through. Using a slotted spoon, transfer the meatballs to a serving dish, add the pea salad, and fold together. Serve immediately.

3 | Huerta

THE BASQUE KITCHEN GARDEN

As you drive around the Basque Country, you'll see small garden plots of acid lime and dark green speckling the landscape. They're striated with perfect little rows of lettuces, greens, and squashes that sometimes give way to a few fruit trees, pea and tomato vines, and some flowers for the bees.

These small family gardens, or *huertas*, are as common today as they were in the past and are emblematic of the Basques' deep connection to their food and landscape. But they also reflect the poverty and challenges of the Basque terrain: alternately rugged, hilly, forested, and blighted by poor soil and drainage. Because most of the Basque Country isn't suited to industrial farming, small-scale subsistence cultivation has prevailed. This intimacy with homegrown products is the defining characteristic of Basque cuisine: people know what to do with what they have and are flexible during hard times and celebratory at all times. They use availability as inspiration, which is why they give primacy to such vegetables as beans and onions and even borage and cardoons that are secondary or rejected in many other cultures.

Vegetables were often all a family had to eat, which is why the Basques became adept at treating them like meat—frying, boiling, braising, and roasting them to yield a rich variety reflective of the wealth of originality born of poverty. Where else in the world do they make *chuletas*, or "lamb chops," by breading and frying Swiss chard stems? Mock meatballs are similarly fashioned from the chard leaves as part of the classic *menestra de verduras* (vegetable medley).

Some families sell their vegetables at local markets. At the Mercado de la Ribera in Bilbao, the tables set up by these villagers, or *aldeaños*, stand in stark contrast to the sleek stalls burgeoning with shiny nonlocal produce. The town of Ordizia is home to one of the most famous markets in the Basque Country, and the majority of vegetables sold there are grown by area families. During the late summer and early fall, the market entrance is perfumed with the smoky, sweet aroma of peppers being blistered in the *tamboril*, a large drum-shaped cage hand-cranked over an open fire. The glowing cinders floating in the air are a siren call to all cooks, and the smell of charred sweet peppers is intoxicating. Inside the market, like a staged renaissance fair, a grid of square tables displays a bounty of fall mushrooms, beans, eggs, nuts, and large squashes in orderly baskets or stacks. Next to a cheese stand, a man with weathered hands plucks feathers from small game birds. In another square, *bakalados* (sides of salt cod) are stacked high. It is a culinary portrait that depicts meat as a supporting player.

This relationship to vegetable gardens and markets is at the heart of the Basque affinity not just for seasonality but also for microvarieties of produce. The Basques will drive from one market to the next to find that one special seasonal ingredient, so that they might buy it in bulk and then put it up to enjoy during the rest of the year. Excursions to Lodosa in Navarra, a town known for its piquillo peppers, *pochas* (white beans), and asparagus, compete with trips to the Guipuzkua towns of Tolosa and Guernica for prized dark red and black beans and green peppers, respectively.

The Basque palate favors tender texture, which is why vegetables there are eaten either raw or thoroughly cooked, but never served al dente. This helps explain the Basques' love of canning and pressure cooking. Tinned white asparagus, which practically dissolves on contact with the tongue, is as prized as fresh. The Basques also embrace bitterness in a way that most Americans do not. That means they go for sharp-flavored greens like endive and frisée rather than young, multicolored lettuces in a "spring mix." And although in recent years we've been taught to fetishize rainbow-striped heirloom tomatoes, the Basques prefer plain-looking red or reddish green tomatoes, which is why at Txikito we favor Jersey beefsteaks or Oxhearts over the multicolored varieties. Generally, we choose produce that looks like what people eat in the Basque Country, and we're fortunate to have built relationships with farmers who will grow certain Basque ingredients, like piparra (guindilla) peppers and *pochas* for us. That said, we don't limit ourselves: sometimes we'll take something that isn't particularly Basque and use it in a Basque way. Txikito's *pastel de maíz*, or corn pâté, for example, is a summertime riff on the Basque *pastel de verduras*, which typically uses green asparagus or leeks.

At Txikito, we feel we have a responsibility to tell an honest story through our cooking, and we do that in part by improvising in a way that befits a cuisine built on deprivation and innovation. The manner in which the Basques use their landscape has influenced how we use ours, collaborating with farmers and rejecting fashion in favor of traditionally good ingredients. You won't find rainbow tomatoes at Txikito, but you will discover cooking that gives vegetables equal footing with meat and luxury ingredients and makes them the star of their own dish.

Poached leeks in their own juices with chopped egg

PUERROS SENCILLOS CON ACEITE Y HUEVO PICADO

12 small or 6 medium leeks

3 tablespoons extra-virgin olive oil, plus more for drizzling

Kosher salt

1 bay leaf

Juice of 1 lemon

4 hard-boiled eggs (page 115), peeled and coarsely chopped

1 tablespoon black truffle paste (optional)

Sencillo means "simple," but not in a disparaging way. Just as the word *typical* is a compliment in the Basque Country, so too is simple. Its meaning falls close to "plain," which in American culture is also an insult. As such, these simple, typical, plain leeks illustrate the difference between American core values and those of the Basques. That said, I think a new generation of American cooks is placing greater emphasis on seeking the purity of a single flavor and creating single-subject dishes whose quality requires no camouflage.

Choose the tightest leeks you can. Eat them at room temperature, as if they came from a jar that you brought back from Rioja and forgot about until you were hungry one night. That is the inspiration for this dish. | SERVES 4 TO 6

Trim the leeks down to the white and lighter green parts and save the dark green parts for another use. If the leeks are very long, cut them in half crosswise. Using a sharp knife, butterfly the leeks: make one cut down the center to get approximately 4-inch sections, and then rotate the leek 90 degrees and cut down the center lengthwise without cutting all the way through. You want to be able to fan out the upper parts to make the leek easier to clean. Rinse the leeks in three changes of water, making sure to shake them under the water to remove their grit. Peel away the two outermost layers to reveal the tender inner layers. Set aside the outer layers.

Using kitchen twine, tie the leeks together in bundles of 3 leeks. You should have 4 bundles total, depending on the length of the leeks and whether you halved them.

Cut the reserved outer layers into narrow strips. Place in a large saucepan, add the oil, 1 teaspoon salt, and the bay leaf, and sweat over low heat for about 10 minutes, until the strips are sweet and melt in your mouth.

CONTINUED

Poached leeks in their own juices with chopped egg

CONTINUED

Meanwhile, cut a circle of parchment paper slightly smaller than the diameter of the saucepan. When the leeks strips are ready, nestle the leek bundles atop the strips and add water just to cover and about 2 teaspoons salt. Raise the heat to medium and bring the water to a bare simmer. Turn down the heat to low and cover the leeks with the parchment to keep them submerged. Braise for about 10 minutes, until a wooden skewer is easily inserted into the leeks but still meets with a little resistance on the way out. Avoid moving the bundles around as they braise, as they are fragile.

Carefully remove the leeks from the braising liquid. Snip off the twine on each bundle and peel away the outermost layer of each leek to reveal the smooth layer beneath. Chop the removed layers and set aside in a bowl.

Strain the braising liquid through a fine-mesh strainer and save for another use; it is essentially a sweet vegetable stock. Remove and discard the bay leaf and then add the contents of the strainer to the bowl holding the chopped outer layers. Add the lemon juice, eggs, truffle paste, and a pinch of salt and mix well.

To serve, place the braised leeks on plates or a platter and mound the egg salad decoratively on top. Drizzle with oil and serve immediately.

White asparagus from the tin with celery–black truffle vinaigrette and trout roe

ESPÁRRAGOS COJONUDOS CON APIO Y HUEVAS

Cojonudo is a high compliment in the Basque country; it means a dish has balls! Perhaps because so many Basque men cook, it doesn't surprise me that the highest compliment—*esto esta cojonudo*—is a pretty good measure of quality, even for me. Tinned white asparagus fall into the *cojonudo* category, literally: when they're packed less than eight to a tin and of the highest quality, you will see "Cojonudos" proudly displayed on the tin. The stalks must be very soft and tender, or, as the Basques like to say, *como mantequilla*—"like butter." And when it comes to Navarran white asparagus, bigger is always better. Because the asparagus has a mild flavor, the vinaigrette here respects and flatters its character rather than trampling it. White asparagus are rather expensive, but the payback is that this recipe requires little work and typically yields high fives from friends. Feel free to buy smaller, less expensive white asparagus of exceptional quality, but treat yourself to a proper *cojonudo* at least once. A little homemade thin mayonnaise (page 23) is great here, too. | SERVES 4

⅔ cup extra-virgin olive oil

1 celery heart, trimmed and minced

1 teaspoon black truffle paste

1½ teaspoons fresh lemon juice

2 teaspoons kosher salt

1 (250-gram-drained-weight) can white asparagus

1½ ounces smoked trout roe

Thin mayonnaise (page 23), for serving

In a small bowl, whisk together the oil, celery heart, truffle paste, lemon juice, and salt. Arrange the white asparagus on a plate. Top with the vinaigrette, scatter with trout roe, and serve with the mayonnaise on the side.

Artichokes with lima beans and Spanish ham

HABITAS CON ALCACHOFAS Y JAMÓN

A *conserva* is a preserved or semipreserved product, usually fish or vegetables, though foie and pâté are also in the *conserva* family. I think of this stew of spring vegetables as an "unconserved *conserva*." The vegetables, which are gently braised in olive oil and seasoned with a little *jamón* for umami, show how the Basques use meat as a condiment. The dish is good on its own or makes a great bed for poached salmon or poached eggs. | SERVES 4 TO 6

8 cups fresh or frozen shelled lima beans

8 artichokes

½ cup plus 3 tablespoons fresh lemon juice

6 green onions, white and light green parts only, sliced (not too thinly)

1 cup thin ribbons of jamón serrano or cubed meat from ham hock

Extra-virgin olive oil, to cover

Kosher salt

1 bunch flat-leaf parsley, coarsely chopped

Fill a large saucepan with water and bring to a boil over high heat. Prepare a large ice-water bath. Add the lima beans to the boiling water and blanch for 45 seconds. Using a slotted spoon, immediately transfer the beans to the ice bath. Once they are cool, drain them and remove their tough outer white skins. Pat dry and reserve.

To trim the artichokes, fill a large bowl with water and add the ½ cup lemon juice. Working with 1 artichoke at a time, cut off the bottom of the stem, leaving about 1 inch intact; the stem makes a good grip as you work. Cut off the top 1 to 1½ inches of the artichoke so that the leaves open and expose the core. Trim off the tough leaves around the base, and then cut away the outer leaves until only the pale light yellow and tender inner leaves remain. Using a vegetable peeler or a paring knife, shave off the woody green outer layer from the base and stem. The entire artichoke should now be pale and tender. Trim down the stem to ½ inch. Cut the artichoke heart in half lengthwise, scoop out the hairy and purple parts with a spoon, and slip the halves into the lemon water.

When all of the artichokes are trimmed, drain them, pat them dry, and place them in a saucepan. Cut a circle of parchment paper slightly smaller than the diameter of the saucepan. Add the lima beans, green onions, and jamón to the artichokes, pour in oil just to cover, and season with salt. Gently cook the vegetables in the oil over low heat, covered with parchment to keep them submerged. Maintain the temperature around 140°F to avoid browning or frying the artichokes, for about 15 minutes, until tender and silken. Check the mixture often, as both the artichokes and the beans can quickly turn to mush if left in the oil too long.

Using a slotted spoon or spider, carefully transfer the vegetables to a bowl. Strain the oil through a fine-mesh strainer and drizzle some of it over the stew. Save the remainder for another use, such as poaching salmon. Fold the remaining 3 tablespoons lemon juice into the vegetables, then taste and adjust with salt if needed. Garnish with the parsley and serve immediately.

Charred eggplant with bonito tuna

BERENJENA CON CEBOLLA ROJA Y BONITO CASERO

Here, the smokiness of charred eggplant evokes the Basque tradition of cooking vegetables over grapevines. At Txikito, we've been lucky to find a good equivalent of the Basque Country's sweet, violet Zalla onion at our local greenmarket. It's important to char the flesh of the eggplants well, as it is the only cooking they receive. If some charred flecks remain after you have peeled off the skin, that's fine. Serve this *ensaladilla* cold or at room temperature as a light lunch, with a fork or scooped up with bread. | SERVES 4 TO 6

3 medium or 2 large eggplants

Kosher salt

Juice of 1 lemon

¼ cup extra-virgin olive oil, plus more for drizzling

3 small sweet red onions, or 2 medium Vidalia or Walla Walla onions

1 cup champagne vinegar

½ cup sugar

4 plum tomatoes

2 cups large flaked home-cured tuna (page 141) or canned tuna in olive oil

4 plum tomatoes, halved lengthwise and seeded (optional)

3 tablespoons chopped fresh flat-leaf parsley

Over a flame on your gas stove top or on your grill, char the eggplants on all sides and on the top and bottom until the flesh collapses, about 3 minutes per side for medium eggplants or 5 minutes for large eggplants. Use tongs to turn them, but be sure to allow them to char thoroughly before you move them. It is okay if they smoke or flare up occasionally.

Place the charred eggplants side by side in a bowl and let them cool slightly. When they are cool enough to handle, peel off and discard the skin, then transfer the flesh to a cutting board and chop into a rough mash. Don't overdo it, as you don't want a smooth puree. Return the flesh to the bowl, season it with salt and the lemon juice, and toss with the olive oil.

Halve and peel the onions, then slice them crosswise paper-thin. In a saucepan, combine the vinegar, sugar, and 1½ tablespoons salt and heat over medium-low heat to a bare simmer. Add the onions, remove from the heat, and let steep for 6 minutes. Cover and refrigerate until needed. (This step can be done up to 3 days in advance.)

To serve, grate each tomato half on the medium holes of a box grater, collecting the pulp and discarding the skins. Spread the tomato pulp on a platter, top with the eggplant, and then scatter the tuna over the eggplant. Drain the onions and strew over the top. Drizzle with oil and sprinkle with parsley. Serve at room temperature or slightly chilled.

Mushroom confit

SETAS CONFITADAS

Poaching wild mushrooms in olive oil allows Basques to enjoy a short season for a little longer. Use the leftover poaching oil in rice dishes and vinaigrettes and to poach egg yolks. Kept under oil, this confit can be stored for up to 4 days in the refrigerator. | SERVES 4 TO 6

4 pounds wild mushrooms (such as porcini, hedgehog, chanterelle, milk cap, or Saint George's), trimmed

Extra-virgin olive oil, to cover

Kosher salt

6 cloves garlic

4 to 6 thick slices country bread

Juice of 1 lemon

Chopped fresh flat-leaf parsley, for garnish

Place the mushrooms in a saucepan, add oil to cover, and season with salt. Smash 1 garlic clove with the back of a knife and toss it into the oil. Gently heat the oil over medium-low heat until the liquid appears to be simmering. What you are seeing is the water the mushrooms release as they become saturated with oil. Turn down the heat to low (you want the mushrooms to gently percolate in the oil, not fry) and cook the mushrooms for about 20 minutes, until they are creamy, silken, flavorful, and have absorbed the salt. Remove from the heat and let cool. As they cool, their juices will naturally separate from the oil; pour off the oil, reserving it and the juices separately. Remove and discard the garlic, then add the mushrooms back into their oil until ready to use them. Save the mushroom juices for another use.

Preheat the oven to 350°F. Rub both sides of each bread slice with one garlic clove, place the slices on a baking sheet, drizzle with oil, and toast in the oven for about 6 minutes, until crispy and golden brown.

While the bread toasts, line a plate with paper towels. Thinly slice the remaining 4 garlic cloves. In a small saucepan, combine the garlic slices and ½ cup of the mushroom oil over medium heat and cook for about 35 seconds, stirring, until golden brown. Using a slotted spoon, transfer the garlic slices to the towel-lined plate to drain.

To serve, gently reheat the mushrooms in their oil. Reheat the mushroom juices. Drain the warm mushrooms, transfer them to a bowl, and toss with the lemon juice. Place each slice of toast in an individual bowl and divide the mushrooms among the bowls, spooning them over the bread. Pour in some of the warm mushroom juices and garnish each serving with a drizzle of the garlic-infused oil, a few of the garlic chips, and a sprinkle of parsley.

Roasted red peppers with oil-cured anchovies

PIMIENTOS RIOJANOS

The sweetest, pepperiest, purest pepper you will ever have: that's what Rioja Alavesa, the Basque region of Rioja where *pimientos riojanos* are grown, wants you to remember when you leave. That's exactly what you will take away from this dish, which I hope will forever change the way you roast peppers and think of singular flavors. I have been chasing this flavor all the way from Rioja to this dish; for me, it's every bit an amazing reflection of *terroir* as the Tempranillo grape with a little Garnacha and Graciano in it. And the best part is that I can make it at home. When you're buying the red bell peppers called for here, choose bells that are large and meaty looking and feel heavy for their size. Once you have roasted and peeled the peppers, don't worry if a few black bits of skin are still clinging to them. | SERVES 4 TO 6

12 roasted red bell peppers (page 38)

Extra-virgin olive oil, for coating and to cover

2 cloves garlic, smashed

Kosher salt

8 to 12 olive oil-packed anchovy fillets

Using your fingers, pull the roasted peppers apart into thirds. Place the pepper pieces in a small saucepan, add oil to cover and the garlic, and season with salt. Gently heat the oil to a bare simmer and poach the peppers slow and low for 10 minutes, until silky and flavorful. Remove from the heat, remove the garlic, and let cool in the oil.

Carefully drain the peppers, reserving the oil. At this point, the peppers can be stored in an airtight container in the refrigerator for up to 3 days or frozen for up to 1 month. Store the oil in a separate container in the refrigerator. Bring the peppers and oil to room temperature or warmer before serving.

To serve, place the peppers on a plate, drizzle with some of their oil, and drape the anchovies on top.

Pimientos rellenos con bacalao, page 94 (above), and *pimientos riojanos* (below)

Piquillo peppers stuffed with cod

PIMIENTOS RELLENOS CON BACALAO

The Basque stuff peppers with just about anything: braised meat, deviled crab, and tuna are just three possibilities. Sweet, arrow-shaped piquillos pack a lot of flavor in their thin, pliant flesh. *See photo on page 93.* | SERVES 4 TO 6

1½ cups extra-virgin olive oil

2 whole cloves garlic, plus 6 cloves, thinly sliced on a mandoline

2 (15-ounce) cans imported piquillo peppers

Kosher salt

6 to 7 ounces quick salt-cured cod (page 142)

1 cup thin mayonnaise (page 23)

In a small saucepan, combine 1 cup of the oil and the whole garlic cloves. Drain the piquillos, reserving the liquid for later use. Add the peppers to the oil and garlic and place over medium-low heat. Bring the oil to a bare simmer and heat the peppers for 10 minutes, until they are tender and flavorful. Remove from the heat and let the peppers cool in the poaching oil for at least 30 minutes so they will be easier to work with.

Preheat the oven to 350°F. Line a small plate with paper towels. In a small saucepan, combine the remaining ½ cup oil and the sliced garlic over medium-low heat and heat, stirring constantly, for about 40 seconds, until the garlic is barely golden. Using a slotted spoon, transfer the garlic to the towel-lined plate to drain. Let the oil stand until cool enough to dip your fingertip into it without burning it.

Add the cod to the garlic oil, place over low heat, and poach the cod for about 4 to 5 minutes, until the flesh is just opaque and flakes when prodded. Remove from the heat and drain the cod, reserving the oil, then transfer the cod to a bowl. Put aside 3 tablespoons of the oil for later use and save the remaining oil for another use. Let the cod cool to room temperature, then use your fingers to flake it apart into the bowl. Drizzle the flakes with 1 tablespoon of the reserved garlic oil.

When the piquillos have cooled, remove them from their oil and pat dry. Stuff each pepper with about 2 tablespoons of the poached cod. Line the stuffed peppers in a baking dish and drizzle with the remaining 2 tablespoons garlic oil. Bake for about 15 minutes, until the peppers are bubbly and dark.

Serve the stuffed piquillos in the baking dish drizzled with the mayonnaise, reserved piquillo juices, and garlic chips.

Little Gem lettuce hearts with anchovy and canned tuna

COGOLLOS

In Spanish, *cogollo* means tender lettuce heart, but it is also a metaphor for the heart of all things, such as the heart of a city. For this dish, baby lettuce hearts, bright green and a little bitter on the outside and sweet and lighter yellow-green inside, are halved, topped with anchovies of exceptional quality, and finished with a little vinaigrette. It's difficult to top such a combination, unless you add some tuna, which makes it even better.

Use Boston lettuce with the outer layers removed if you can't find Little Gem or Sucrine heads. Be sure to have bread on hand for cleaning plates properly in the Basque style. | SERVES 4 TO 6

1 cup extra-virgin olive oil

¼ cup sherry vinegar

2 teaspoons kosher salt

4 to 6 heads Little Gem or Sucrine lettuce (1 to 2 heads per person)

8 to 12 olive oil–packed anchovy fillets

2 (8-ounce) cans tuna in olive-oil, drained, or flaked home-cured tuna (page 141)

In a small bowl, whisk together the oil, vinegar, and salt.

Depending on the size of the lettuce heads, cut into halves or thirds lengthwise and divide evenly among individual salad plates. Drape the anchovies over the lettuce, portioning 2 fillets per serving. Divide the tuna among the plates, crumbling it over each serving. Drizzle with the vinaigrette and serve immediately.

Frisée salad with golden garlic and parsley

ESCAROLA

Anointed with only toasted garlic and good olive oil, *escarola*, or pale yellow frisée, is an absolute delicacy. No, I have not forgotten the vinegar: this salad has no acid at all, relying instead on a veil of warm oil to balance the bitterness of the frisée. It made me dispense with the notion that sweet, salty, sour, and bitter or funky flavors have to coexist at all times. Sometimes, two tastes are enough. Consider serving this alongside the Plaza Nueva Salt Cod Salad (page 149): both use garlic crumbs, and they complement each other's flavors beautifully. | SERVES 4 TO 6

5 cloves garlic, minced

½ cup extra-virgin olive oil

Kosher salt

8 cups white frisée leaves, trimmed of dark green parts and torn into 1- to 2-inch sections

1 bunch flat-leaf parsley, coarsely chopped

Line a plate with paper towels. In a frying pan, stir and toast the garlic in the oil over medium-low heat for about 40 seconds, stirring, until it turns light golden brown. Remove from the heat before it turns dark. Working quickly and using a small fine-mesh metal strainer, lift out the garlic from the oil and transfer to the towel-lined plate to drain, then season with a pinch of salt. Leave the oil in the pan.

In a bowl, toss together the frisée, parsley, and a large pinch of salt. Drizzle the warm oil over the frisée mixture and toss to coat evenly. Sprinkle with the garlic and serve immediately.

Eder's avocado salad

AGUACATE DE EDER

3 ripe Hass avocados, halved and pitted

1½ to 2 tablespoons Txakoli wine vinegar, white balsamic vinegar, or seasoned rice vinegar

3 tablespoons smoked Spanish paprika, preferably from Rioja, or 2 tablespoons sweet La Vera smoked paprika mixed with 1 tablespoon sweet Spanish paprika

Maldon salt

About ¼ cup extra-virgin olive oil

Every summer when we visit the Basque Country, Eder's great aunt Mila gives us baby-food jars filled with the most extraordinary paprika from Rioja. Made by her friend, it is fruitier than *pimentón de la Vera* and the smoke is more delicate, which is why the long bus ride to pick it up is more than worth the trip. When those jars start to run out, we get nervous. They are what make good food great at our house.

One evening, Eder halved an avocado, seasoned it with salt, and dusted it generously with the Riojan paprika. Embellished with a little sweet vinegar made from the Basque white wine Txakoli and enough olive oil to dissolve the paprika, it was a genius salad with pitch-perfect flavor. Calculate half an avocado per person, although I guarantee you'll end up eating both halves if you make it for yourself. | SERVES 6

Thinly slice an avocado half and array the slices on an individual salad plate. Do not fan the slices; they should be close together. (You can also just peel the half and lie it cut side down on a plate.) Repeat with the remaining avocado halves. Drizzle each half with about ½ teaspoon of the vinegar. Using a small fine-mesh strainer or a shaker, dust each serving with a thin layer of paprika. Season with salt, drizzle generously with the oil—you want enough oil to dissolve the paprika and give each half the appearance of a rusty car door—then serve.

Lourdes's Russian potato salad

RUSA

4 Carola potatoes, peeled

Kosher salt

½ cup peeled and finely diced carrot

½ cup frozen shelled English peas, thawed

2 tablespoons extra-virgin olive oil, plus more for drizzling

About 3 tablespoons seasoned rice vinegar

2 cups mayonnaise, homemade (page 22) or store-bought

1 (8-ounce) can tuna in olive oil, flaked

Chopped fresh flat-leaf parsley, for garnish

2 hard-boiled eggs (page 115), peeled, halved, and sliced

Green olives, for garnish (optional)

Peeled and diced roasted beets, for garnish (optional)

Pulled cold cooked chicken meat, for garnish (optional)

Poached shrimp, for garnish (optional)

1 piquillo pepper, cut into thin ribbons, for garnish (optional)

Crumbled cooked bacon, for garnish (optional)

Ensaladilla rusa, or Russian salad, has been in my life longer than Eder has. Argentines like potatoes and mayonnaise as much as the Spanish do, and I've been making *rusa* since I was a child, when my Argentine Russian grandmother, Victoria, taught me how to make mayonnaise with two forks.

At Txikito, we layer the salad so you can see its gorgeous colors, but feel free to fold it into a delicious mess like Eder's Aunt Lourdes does. No matter how you serve it, the palate understands it as comfort food. We like to use sunny yellow–fleshed Carola potatoes when they're in season, but any good creamy or starchy fleshed potato, including russets, will do. Just avoid waxy new potatoes. | SERVES 4 TO 6

Cut the potatoes into ½-inch cubes and place in a saucepan full of generously salted water. Bring to a boil over high heat. Cook for approximately 2 minutes after the water comes to a boil, until the potatoes are barely tender. Using a slotted spoon, transfer the potatoes to a bowl. Return the water to a boil, add the carrots, and cook for about 3 minutes, until barely tender. Add the peas and immediately drain both and combine with potato.

Add the oil and vinegar to the warm vegetables, adding the vinegar about 1 teaspoon at a time to taste. Season the mixture with salt and let cool to room temperature.

Stir the mayonnaise into the cooled mixture. Gently fold in the tuna and adjust salt as needed.

Serve immediately, topped with a drizzle of oil, the chopped parsley, the sliced egg, and any combination of the optional garnishes (choose two or three at most). Alternatively, chill the salad before topping with the oil and garnishes.

Gratin of Belgian endive and Basque blue cheese

ACHICORIA CON QUESO AZUL

Although I had never eaten cooked endive until I "went Basque," I quickly came to appreciate how well the vegetable lends itself to roasting: it keeps its character and becomes sweeter as it cooks. In this recipe, its lingering bitter notes play off nicely against the creamy, salty blue cheese—bitter loves nothing more than salt and fat—creating a dish that is rich yet light and full of compelling textures.

Bleu des Basques is less salty than other French or other Spanish blues, which makes it ideal here, but feel free to substitute your favorite blue and use a little less. It may seem like a lot of mayo is used, but it breaks and separates during the cooking: its oil braises the endives, making them tender and flavorful, and its yolk turns crispy and golden brown. I like to make the gratin in a pretty baking dish that can go straight from the oven to the table. | SERVES 4 TO 6

3 or 4 large heads Belgian endive

Kosher salt

1½ cups mayonnaise, homemade (page 22) or store-bought

1 cup crumbled bleu des Basques cheese

1 tablespoon red pepper flakes

Leaves from 14 marjoram sprigs

Juice of 1 lemon

3 tablespoons chopped parsley

Extra-virgin olive oil

Preheat the oven to 450°F. Peel off the outer layer of each endive and discard, then trim off the base of the stem. Cut each endive lengthwise into thirds. Place in a baking dish and sprinkle with salt. Spread the mayonnaise on the endive portions, dividing it evenly. Scatter the cheese over the top and sprinkle with the pepper flakes and marjoram.

Bake for approximately 15 minutes, until the endives are tender and the cheese is bubbly and golden brown. Remove from the oven, sprinkle with the lemon juice and parsley, and drizzle with olive oil. Serve immediately.

Blistered shishito peppers with sea salt

PIMIENTOS GERNIKA

As addictive and easy to eat as a bag of potato chips, small blistered peppers are wildly popular at the moment, but they are so much more than a bar snack du jour. The first time I ate a pimiento de Gernika—the variety used for this dish in the Basque Country—was with a rib eye eaten at a picnic table on a Basque hillside. I quickly became obsessed with the tender, wrinkled skin and mild but deep flavor of the heat-seared peppers and was excited to discover the similar shishito pepper at Nobu, the Japanese restaurant where Eder used to work.

That same year, I took a job at a small wine bar, and as luck would have it, I befriended a Korean vegetable farmer who, like a proper Basque *aldeana*, was growing shishitos for herself. She was picking about six pounds a week, and I was buying them all. By the next summer, when I opened my first tapas bar, she was growing forty pounds a week just for us. Since then, we have expanded her Basque vegetable repertoire, and every year I bring her more seeds as I discover varieties I've never seen. Finally (and thankfully), these little peppers have helped bring green peppers back into favor after years of being rejected for their red cousins.

A word about Maldon salt: it is truly like no other. None of the local versions I've tried—not even Basque salt from Álava—is as good. Maldon and shishito peppers have come into their own together thanks to this dish, so do yourself a favor and buy both. | SERVES 4 TO 6

Extra-virgin olive oil, for frying

1½ to 2 pounds shishito or Padrón peppers or mild thin-skinned Italian frying peppers

Maldon salt

Line a plate with paper towels. Pour the oil to a depth of ⅓ inch into a wide, deep frying pan and place over medium heat. When the oil is hot, in batches, scatter the peppers in the pan without crowding them and cook, turning once or twice with tongs, for 1 to 2 minutes until barely golden brown. (Be careful of splattering oil.) Using a slotted spoon, transfer them to the towel-lined plate to drain and sprinkle generously with salt. Serve immediately.

Summer tomatoes with sweet onion

TOMATES CON CEBOLLETA

1 cup extra-virgin olive oil

¼ cup sherry vinegar

Kosher salt

1 sweet onion (such as Vidalia or Walla Walla) or a few spring onions, thinly sliced

3 or 4 perfectly ripe but firm large summer tomatoes

Country bread, for serving

The Basques don't need to be told never to chill a tomato. It's something they know, even if they've never heard it. Their respect for tomatoes, which they'll often leave on the vine right up to the minute they're ready to use them, is captured in the salads of tomato and sweet spring onion that are a constant fixture in the Basque Country. | SERVES 4 TO 6

Bring a saucepan of salted water to a boil. While the water is heating, in a small bowl, whisk together the oil, vinegar, and 2 teaspoons salt to make a vinaigrette. (Vinegars have different acid values, so you may want to add more vinegar to taste.)

When the water boils, add the onion, then immediately remove the saucepan from the heat, let the onion soften in the water for 15 seconds, and drain.

About 5 minutes before you serve the salad, slice the tomatoes, arrange on a plate, and then sprinkle them with salt to make them weep a bit. Scatter the onions over the tomatoes. Briefly whisk the vinaigrette and spoon it over the tomatoes and onions, reserving any extra for another use. Serve immediately with bread.

Smothered okra with sweet Basque tomato sauce and minted yogurt

OKRA CON YOGUR DE MENTA Y TOMATE FRITO

This dish uses *tomate frito*, a Basque mixture of oniony *sofrito* and tomatoes. The sweet, rich tomato sauce can transform any summer vegetable into a Basque dish capable of charming the pants off a southern-food lover. If okra isn't your thing, you can substitute any charred summer vegetable; baby eggplants, zucchini, and green onions all work well here. Depending on the vegetable you use, this can be a main course or a side. At Txikito, we like to run lamb chops *a la plantxa* and this okra on the same day. They're great in the same meal. | SERVES 4 TO 6

3 pounds okra

2 to 3 tablespoons extra-virgin olive oil, plus more for drizzling

Kosher salt

2 cloves garlic, grated on a fine-rasp grater

2 cups plain full-fat Greek yogurt

½ cup lightly packed fresh mint leaves, cut into narrow ribbons

3 tablespoons chopped fresh marjoram

2 cups tomato sauce (page 36)

Chopped fresh flat-leaf parsley, for garnish

Preheat the oven to 425°F. Cut the okra crosswise into ¼-inch-thick slices, transfer to a bowl, drizzle with oil, season with salt, and toss to coat. Spread the slices on a baking sheet and roast for 13 to 16 minutes, until they start to char around the edges.

Meanwhile, make the yogurt sauce. In a small saucepan, combine the garlic and 2 tablespoons of the oil and heat over medium-low heat, stirring constantly, for about 30 seconds, until the garlic is cooked and turns a very light golden brown. Scrape the garlic and oil into a bowl, add the yogurt, mint, and marjoram, season with salt, and mix well. Add a little more oil, up to about 1 tablespoon, to loosen the consistency. (The yogurt sauce will keep in an airtight container in the refrigerator for up to 2 days.)

Remove the okra from the oven. It can be served hot or at room temperature, so let it cool, if you like. In a bowl, fold together the okra and tomato sauce. To serve family style, garnish the okra with parsley, drizzle with oil, and serve the yogurt sauce on the side. Or, to serve on individual plates, swirl the yogurt sauce on the plates, top with the okra, garnish with parsley, and finish with oil.

Cauliflower with refrito of paprika and white balsamic vinegar

COLIFLOR CON REFRITO DE PIMENTÓN

1 head cauliflower, outer leaves removed and stem trimmed

Kosher salt

Extra-virgin olive oil, for frying, plus ¼ cup

2 tablespoons white balsamic vinegar

3 cloves garlic, thinly sliced

1 tablespoon sweet Spanish paprika

1 bunch cilantro, coarsely chopped

Cauliflower loves a *refrito*, the Basque condiment of choice for many vegetables and fish. The addition of paprika (*pimentón*) and a sweet vinegar like white balsamic (or rice vinegar) to the *refrito* yields a rich dressing for a lean wintery vegetable; it works nicely with cabbage, too. | SERVES 4 TO 6

Bring a saucepan of generously salted water to a boil over high heat. Prepare a large salted ice-water bath. Add the cauliflower to the boiling water and cook for about 10 minutes, until tender throughout but not mushy. Immediately transfer the cauliflower to the ice bath to halt the cooking. When the cauliflower has cooled completely, remove it from the ice bath and pat it dry. Cut the cauliflower vertically into ½-inch-thick slices; you want the florets to stay together. Set aside any pieces that crumble off to use later for garnish.

Heat 3 tablespoons oil in a cast-iron frying pan over medium-high heat. Working in batches, sear the cauliflower slices, turning once and adding more oil as needed, for about 3 minutes on each side, until golden brown. As the slices are ready, transfer them to a large platter or a couple of large plates and keep warm.

Combine the vinegar and ¼ teaspoon salt in a medium-size heatproof bowl. To make the refrito, in a small saucepan, combine the garlic and the remaining ¼ cup oil and heat over medium-low heat, for about 40 seconds, until golden brown. Remove from the heat, quickly add the paprika, and pour the mixture into the vinegar, being careful the oil doesn't sputter and burn you. Stir in any stray cauliflower crumbs.

Divide the refrito evenly among the cauliflower slices, spooning it over the top, and sprinkle with the cilantro. Serve immediately.

4 | Huevos

EGGS ALL WAYS

The Basques love eggs cooked every way and at every meal, and none of the dishes in the Basque repertoire better conveys the tension between humble modesty and luxury than those made with eggs. It might be an egg fried in olive oil, its white transformed into exquisite lace, and then topped with a scattering of chorizo, *jamón*, or sautéed squid. Or maybe a slowly poached egg set in a glistening nest of wild mushroom confit. Both are three-star dishes made in five minutes for five dollars.

Choosing good eggs is essential to a good result. A great fresh egg has a very hard shell, an oval shape, a yolk that stands tall when cracked into a pan or bowl, and a white that has viscosity and does not spread. I strongly recommend buying eggs at a farmers' market, as they will be fresher and of better quality than most commercial eggs, which can have thin shells, loose whites, and wan yolks. If you will be hard boiling the eggs, buy them a few days in advance of cooking, as fresher eggs are harder to peel.

Because there are so many textural differences in cooked egg dishes, and such a fine line between a perfect egg and an overcooked one, learning to cook with them will teach you how to control heat. And while nonstick pans get a bad rap because of fears about some coatings, they are essential for cooking eggs. Just be sure to heat the pan with the oil in it. I prefer pans with an enamel coating.

Poached eggs | ESCALFADOS

Kosher salt

2 tablespoons champagne
or cider vinegar

Eggs

When you're poaching eggs, you always want the white to be gently set around the yolk and the yolk to be liquid. That way, the yolk essentially functions as a sauce for whatever you're serving it with.

Fill a large, wide saucepan with water, salt the water, add the vinegar, bring to a boil over high heat, and then turn down the heat so the water is just below simmering. You don't want bubbles breaking on the surface, but you do want tiny bubbles streaming up from the bottom of the pan.

Prepare an ice-water bath. Set out as many ramekins or other small containers as eggs you are cooking, and break 1 egg into each ramekin (using a ramekin for each egg will give you more control when you add the eggs to the hot water). Set a kitchen timer to 2 minutes. Working as quickly as possible, slide the eggs into the hot water and then immediately start the timer. When the timer beeps, using a slotted spoon or a spider, gently lift each egg from the water. It should feel soft but not break when touched. If it feels too loose and jelly-like, allow it to cook for an additional 30 seconds. As the eggs are removed, place them in the ice bath to stop the cooking, being careful not to crowd them.

Just before serving the eggs, place them briefly in a bowl of very hot tap water to warm them through.

Soft-boiled "three-minute" eggs | MOLLETS

The *huevo mollet* is big in the Basque Country because it's fundamentally a peelable soft-boiled or three-minute egg. If you start them in cold water, "three-minute" eggs are really five- or six-minute eggs; if you start them when the water is boiling, the timing is closer to three minutes. The white of the egg should be tender, the yolk wobbly, and the shell easy to peel. As with poached eggs, a soft-boiled egg functions as a sauce.

Using a pushpin, poke a hole into the wide bottom of each egg. Fill a saucepan with water and bring the water to a boil over high heat. Prepare an ice-water bath. Set the timer for 6 minutes. Using a slotted spoon or a spider, gently lower the eggs into the boiling water, turn down the heat so the water simmers, and start the timer. When the timer beeps, lift out the eggs and immediately place them into the ice bath to stop the cooking. After 5 minutes, transfer the eggs to a warm-water bath until you are ready to peel and serve them. Or, peel them and keep them in barely warm water until ready to serve.

Hard-boiled eggs | COCIDOS

My mother taught me the trick to peeling hard-boiled eggs: before you boil the egg, insert a pushpin all the way into its wide bottom. This helps create an air gap between the shell and the membrane. Eggs are easiest to peel when they are still a little warm. Gently cracking the shell all over and then peeling the egg under running water also helps. Because the whites of hard-boiled eggs are often stuffed, they should be strong but not rubbery.

Prepare an ice-water bath. Using a pushpin, poke a small hole into the wide bottom of each egg. Fill a saucepan with water. Using a slotted spoon or a spider, gently lower the eggs into the water. Set the timer for 7 minutes. Bring the water to a boil over high heat. Turn down the heat until the water is at a bare simmer and start the timer. When the timer beeps, lift out the eggs and immediately place them into the ice bath to stop the cooking. Allow them to sit until they are cool enough to touch, then peel them. The eggs can be stored peeled in the refrigerator for up to 2 days in an airtight container, but they taste best eaten at room temperature.

Fried eggs | FRITO

3 to 4 tablespoons
extra-virgin olive oil

1 egg, at room
temperature

Kosher salt

Maldon salt,
for finishing

This recipe works best in a small nonstick frying pan, preferably one that can accommodate only one or, at most, two eggs. Generally, you should never fry more than two eggs at a time, as they can easily stick together. A good guiding principle is to cook the white until set while keeping the yolk loose. You want to treat the yolk as a sauce that you're warming through rather than frying. A generous amount of olive oil is used here, so use caution that it doesn't splatter and burn you. The end result—a lacy white, known as *puntilla*, and a creamy yolk—is worth the extra care. | SERVES 1

Generously coat the bottom of a small nonstick frying pan with the oil; you want enough oil so that it will pool when the pan is tilted. Heat the oil over medium-low heat. When the oil is hot, crack the egg into the pan and season it with a pinch of kosher salt. If the oil was heated properly, the egg will spread out and form lacy edges and small bubbles will begin forming in the white. Tilt the pan so that the oil pools on one side. Dip a spatula in the hot oil before making contact with the egg to prevent it from sticking, then use the spatula to break up the bubbles and chip small holes in the white and its viscous parts. This allows the white to cook evenly and quickly while keeping the yolk loose. Continue to cook the egg until its edges are lacy and the viscous white is cooked through. Once the white is set, tilt the pan to pool the excess oil and, using a spoon, baste the white near the yolk five or six times with the oil. Using the spatula, remove the egg from the pan and serve it immediately, sprinkling the yolk with Maldon salt.

Scrambled eggs | REVUELTOS

This recipe works best in a nonstick pan small enough to accommodate just the eggs. To achieve a soft, creamy texture, Basques often crack their eggs directly into the pan, and they don't try to make the egg mixture all one color, preferring instead streaks and spots of yellow and white. Scrambled eggs are often a plate shared among a table of diners, unlike here where they are typically treated as a quick dish for someone eating alone, and garnishes range from seafood to vegetables to mushrooms. These eggs take very little time and yet they receive the same appreciation as more labor-intensive dishes. It's all about the quality of the *prima materia*. | SERVES 1

Extra-virgin olive oil, for frying

2 eggs, at room temperature

Kosher salt

Coat a nonstick frying pan with a thin layer of oil (about 1 tablespoon). In a bowl, lightly mix the eggs with a pinch of salt. Be careful not to overmix; there should be striations of white and yellow. Heat the oil over medium-low heat. When the oil is hot, add the beaten egg to the pan. Dip a spatula in a bit of the hot oil to prevent the egg from sticking to it, then tilt the pan toward you. Use the spatula to push the egg halfway up the pan, letting its raw parts pool and fill the bottom of the pan. Repeat this process three or four more times. When the egg is nearly cooked through but still appears wet, remove the pan from the heat and transfer the egg to a plate. It will continue to cook in the residual heat. Serve immediately.

Classic Spanish tortilla

TORTILLA ESPAÑOLA CLASSICA

Tortillas can be juicy or dry, and either way is correct. It's just a question of how you like them. Spaniards prefer their *tortillas* soupy, but you can cook them through if you're concerned about raw eggs. No one can teach you how to perfect a tortilla; you have to learn as you go. But here are a few tips: Use the smallest pan you can, one that will just accommodate the size of the tortilla—I like a 9- to 10-inch pan— and, if you can, work over a gas burner. You want the flame to lick up the sides of the pan, which is essential for forming the sides of the *tortilla* and preventing broken edges. Commit to flipping the *tortilla*: use deliberate, purposeful movements and don't hesitate once you've begun. You can patch up any cracks or holes with a bit of beaten egg, should the need arise. The side of the *tortilla* that you sear first should be facing up at the end. That's important because it made contact with the pan when the surface was at its hottest, so it is the sturdiest.

| MAKES 1 (9- TO 10-INCH) TORTILLA; SERVES 8 AS A SMALL MEAL OR 12 AS A TAPA

4 or 5 medium russet potatoes (about 2 pounds)

1 Spanish onion, thinly sliced

½ cup canola oil, or as needed

½ cup plus 3 tablespoons extra-virgin olive oil, or as needed

Kosher salt

10 eggs, at room temperature

1 cup sweet pepper sauce (page 32), warmed (optional)

Peel 4 of the potatoes, then rinse under cool running water and cut lengthwise into quarters. Cut the quarters crosswise into ⅛-inch-thick slices. You should have 4 cups potato slices. If you're short, cut up another potato.

In a large saucepan, combine the potatoes and onion and add the canola oil and ½ cup of the olive oil to cover, adding more of each if needed to cover. Add enough salt to season the vegetables, not the oil. Place over low heat and cook for 30 to 40 minutes, until the vegetables are tender. Remove from the heat; drain the vegetables, reserving the oil. Set the vegetables aside. Carefully strain the oil through a fine-mesh strainer and store in the fridge for future use.

Heat 2 tablespoons olive oil in a 9- to 10-inch nonstick frying pan over high heat. While the oil is heating, in a bowl, beat the eggs with ½ teaspoon salt just until blended. If you're not squeamish about raw eggs, taste them and adjust the seasoning. Add the potatoes and onion to the eggs, folding them in with a heat-resistant spatula to combine.

CONTINUED

Classic Spanish tortilla

CONTINUED

When the oil is smoking, make sure to swirl it up on the sides of the pan to prevent the tortilla from sticking. Pour the egg mixture into the pan and toss the mixture aggressively, as if sautéing it or flipping pancakes, about three times, then stop to give it time to form a skin. You want to heat what will be the inside of the tortilla, but you want to make sure that it doesn't coagulate so much that it doesn't form a foundation. Prod the mixture with the spatula around the edges to give it shape and to prevent it from sticking to the bottom of the pan. Begin to shape the sides of the tortilla by using the spatula to pull the mixture gently from the sides of the pan, shaking the pan to make sure the mixture isn't stuck.

When the egg just begins to set, after about 1 minute, turn down the heat to medium-low and cook 1 more minute. Invert a large plate on top of the pan. Firmly grasp the pan handle, choking up on it with the help of a kitchen towel, place your free hand palm down over the plate, and flip the pan and plate over together, dropping the tortilla onto the plate. Place the pan back on the burner, wipe it clean of any stuck-on bits, and recoat it with the remaining 1 tablespoon oil. Heat the oil over high heat until it begins to smoke and then quickly and deliberately slide the tortilla off the plate into the pan, using a pushing-and-pulling motion. Pat down the tortilla and begin shaping its sides again. Cook for 1 minute. Repeat the flip and return process and cook for another 2 minutes over very low heat; you shouldn't need more oil at this point. Repeat the flip one more time, cooking for 3 more minutes over low heat. Now repeat the flip one final time to get the presentation side facing the bottom of the pan. Using a clean plate, flip the tortilla out so the pretty side is up.

It tastes best if you let it rest for an hour before serving, but do not refrigerate it. Cut into wedges to serve. If you do have to chill it, warm it slightly before serving. If using the sauce, warm it and spoon it over the tortilla just before serving.

Poached egg with chorizo-jamón broth and chanterelles

HUEVO ESCALFADO CON CALDO RANCIO Y PERRETXIKOS

The Basques aren't precious about their mushrooms, using them liberally and often. In the spring, Saint George's mushrooms, called *perretxikos*, or "little dogs," are the must-have Basque ingredient. (The term has become a generic term used for any small mushrooms, even there.) Because they are not readily available in the United States, at Txikito we use chanterelles, which are known as *zizas* or *rebozuelos* in the Basque Country. For this recipe, you can use any small wild mushrooms; just be sure to choose tight, firm ones. I especially like matsutake mushrooms in this dish because of their light, piney flavor. | SERVES 4

2 cups dry-cured chorizo or jamón serrano trim, or a combination

Extra-virgin olive oil, for sautéing

2 cups chanterelle mushrooms (about 6 ounces)

Kosher salt

4 poached eggs (page 114)

Maldon salt and Espelette or Aleppo pepper, for finishing

In a small saucepan, combine the chorizo with water to cover barely and bring to a boil over high heat. Turn down the heat to a simmer and cook for 15 to 20 minutes, until the meat has released its flavor into the broth. Little globules of fat should be floating on the surface of the broth. Strain the broth and discard the meat scraps. Return the broth to the sauccpan and keep it warm over low heat. Resist the temptation to skim off the fat, which contributes flavor.

Generously coat a frying pan with oil and place over medium heat. When the oil is hot, add the mushrooms and a pinch of salt and sauté for about 4 minutes, until the mushrooms begin to soften. Transfer the mushrooms to a plate. (The mushrooms can be cooked a few hours ahead and gently rewarmed.)

To serve, divide the chanterelles and any of their oil and juices evenly among 4 small bowls and make a well in the center of each pile. Reheat the poached eggs in the broth for about 2 minutes, until just heated through. Using a slotted spoon, lift out the eggs, one at a time, and slide each egg into a mushroom well. Pour a little broth—no more than 3 tablespoons—over the eggs, season them with Maldon salt and pepper, and serve immediately.

Warm three-minute egg with loose mayonnaise, green beans, and new potatoes

HUEVO MOLLET CON PATATAS, VAINAS Y MAYONESA LIGERA

8 ounces flat green beans or romano beans, trimmed and cut on the bias into 1-inch lengths

8 ounces new potatoes (the smallest you can find)

4 soft-boiled "three-minute" eggs (page 115)

1 cup thin mayonnaise (page 23), made just before serving

Kosher salt

Extra-virgin olive oil, for drizzling

This dish is a favorite of mine: all four of its components are beloved Basque staples and are foods that I grew up with when my family spent summer and winter breaks in Argentina. The key to this salad is to make sure the beans, potatoes, and eggs are a little warm. The mayonnaise must be just made, never refrigerated. The tenderness and temperature of the ingredients mimic a sunny day. Sometimes a few soft textures together don't want any crunch. | SERVES 4

Bring a saucepan of salted water to a boil over high heat. Prepare an ice-water bath. Add the beans to the boiling water and cook for 4 to 12 minutes, until tender; the timing will depend on the natural tenderness of the bean. It is more important that the beans become tender than vibrant green. I recommend doing a test run with 1 or 2 beans to see how long they take, and then cooking the remainder. Drain the beans and immediately immerse them in the ice bath to stop the cooking. When cool, drain well and dry on a kitchen towel to remove excess moisture.

Refill the saucepan with salted water and bring to a boil. Add the potatoes and cook for 6 to 8 minutes, until fork-tender. Drain well and dry on a kitchen towel. While the potatoes are cooking, prepare the eggs. When they are finished cooking, peel them and hold them in a tepid water bath until ready to serve.

While the potatoes are still hot, flatten them with your palm or the back of a metal spatula, using even, medium pressure so that they squish but don't break apart or crumble. Scatter an equal amount of the beans over each plate and top with the warm smashed potatoes. Cover the potatoes completely with a few tablespoons of the mayonnaise. Finally, if necessary, gently rewarm the eggs and dry them before adding 1 whole egg to each plate. Season with salt and drizzle with oil and serve immediately.

Blood sausage omelet

TORTILLA DE MORCILLA

Making *morcilla* is so popular in the Basque Country that there are *concursos*, or "competitions," to see who can make the best version. Often the same family or butcher will take the prize year after year, though occasionally a dramatic upset occurs. My favorite thing about Basque food competitions is that whoever wins is usually declared "best in the world." It's taken for granted that all of the best food is Basque, so if you win a Basque competition, it must follow that you are the best in the world, period. | SERVES 2 TO 4

2 leeks, white and light green parts only, halved and thinly sliced

2 cups thinly sliced cabbage

Kosher salt

Extra-virgin olive oil, for cooking

3 small blood sausages (about 4 to 6 ounces total weight), removed from their casing and crumbled

4 eggs, at room temperature

In a nonstick frying pan, combine the leek, cabbage, a pinch of salt, and 2 teaspoons of oil and sweat over low heat for 15 to 20 minutes, until the vegetables are soft and sweet. Raise the heat to medium-high, add the sausage and another pinch of salt, and cook, stirring occasionally, for about 8 minutes, until the sausage has caramelized a little and is aromatic. Transfer to a bowl and reserve.

Wipe out the pan, lightly coat it with oil (about 1 tablespoon), and heat over medium-high heat. While the oil is heating, in a bowl, lightly beat the eggs with a pinch of salt. Be careful not to overbeat the eggs; you want striations of yolk and white. When the oil is hot, add the cabbage-sausage mixture to the pan, then pour in the eggs and let them set for 1 minute. Dip a heat-resistant rubber spatula into a bit of the hot oil to prevent the egg from sticking to it and then tilt the pan toward you. Use the spatula to push the egg halfway up the side of the pan, letting the raw egg pool at the bottom. Repeat this process one more time, then let the egg set for 20 seconds, until it is very lightly colored. Invert a large plate on top of the pan. Firmly grasp the pan handle, choking up on it with the help of a kitchen towel, and place your free hand palm-down on the plate. Confidently flip the pan and plate over together, dropping the tortilla onto the plate. Reheat the pan, adding a thin slick of oil, and slide the tortilla back into the pan and finish cooking over low heat for 1 minute.

Slide or flip the tortilla onto a serving plate, cut it into wedges, and serve immediately.

Lourdes's deviled eggs with tuna and foie

HUEVOS RELLENOS DE BONITO Y FOIE

Every Christmas, Eder's Aunt Lourdes makes these eggs *para picar*, or "to nibble," before main courses. I appreciate that she buys a foie gras terrine and then uses it to make these doped-up surf-and-turf deviled eggs. They're pretty old-school and would be very much at home at a fancy San Sebastián *pintxos* bar. | SERVES 6

12 hard-boiled eggs (page 115)

½ cup mayonnaise, homemade (page 22) or store-bought, plus more for garnish

1 tablespoon Dijon mustard

Kosher salt

2 teaspoons black truffle paste (optional)

1 (4-ounce) can tuna in olive oil, drained and crumbled

3 tablespoons minced fresh chives, plus more for garnish

1 (5-ounce) can foie gras terrine, at room temperature

A pinch of piment d'espelette (optional)

Peel the eggs and cut them in half lengthwise. Alternatively, for a more modern presentation, peel them, then trim the ends and cut them crosswise through the center. Remove and save the yolks and then rinse off the whites. Fill a bowl with water and hold the whites in it until ready to serve.

Place the yolks in a food processor and add the mayonnaise, mustard, and a pinch of salt. Process until smooth. Pulse in the black truffle paste until evenly combined. Transfer the mixture to a bowl.

Fold the tuna and chives into the yolk mixture. Use a fork to smash the foie terrine, and then fold that in as well, making sure there are no lumps. Taste and adjust with salt if needed. Spoon the yolk-foie mixture into a piping bag with a wide star tip or into a large plastic zip-top bag (snip off the corner after chilling). Chill for 1 hour.

Remove the egg whites from the water and pat them dry. Pipe the filling into the egg whites and decorate them with chives, a bit of mayonnaise, and the piment d'espelette. (I like to decorate them with truffle shavings, too.) You can make the filling up to a day ahead and chill it until needed, and the whites can be stored immersed in water in the refrigerator for the same amount of time. Make sure the whites are at room temperature before serving or they will be tough. The filling should be slightly chilled, so it may need a little tempering, too, if it's been chilled too long.

"Messy eggs" with rough-cut potatoes

HUEVOS ROTOS VASCOS

This is a typical way of serving fried eggs, the Basque equivalent of what in diner parlance would be "two eggs sunny side up over fries, wreck 'em!" Much fuss is often made over the best way to cook French fries, but Basque fries are their own thing. They are golden and crispy on the outside, extremely tender on the inside, and more shards than sticks. The best are boiled first and then fried in olive oil. My grandmother Victoria made them this way, too, so eating fries in the Basque Country carries a remarkable nostalgia for me. As I eat them, I always remember how the two of us would fry potatoes and then eggs from her hens and eat them together as a late-night snack. | SERVES 2 TO 4

Kosher salt

2 russet potatoes

Extra-virgin olive oil, for frying

3 ounces dry-cured chorizo, casing removed and thinly sliced

4 eggs, at room temperature

Bring a large saucepan filled with water to a boil and season it with plenty of salt. Line a baking sheet with a kitchen towel.

While the water is heating, peel the potatoes, cut them in half lengthwise, and then cut each half into roughly wedge-shaped pieces about ¼ inch thick. Add the potatoes to the boiling water, turn down the heat to a simmer, and cook for 3 to 6 minutes, until just cooked but still firm. Drain well and scatter the pieces over the towel-lined pan to cool and dry.

Fill a wide, deep sauté pan about one-third full with oil and place over medium heat. When the oil is hot, working in batches, scatter the potatoes in the oil so they are mostly submerged and fry for 2 to 3 minutes, until golden brown, adding more oil as needed. Using a slotted spoon, lift out the potatoes and divide them among 2 to 4 plates, then season with salt.

When all of the potatoes are fried, pour off the oil into a heatproof dish, leaving a layer about ¼ inch deep in the pan, and return the pan to the stove top. Working quickly, heat the pan over medium-low heat, add the chorizo, and let it weep into the oil for about 30 seconds. Using the slotted spoon, lift the chorizo out of the oil, shaking off the excess oil into the pan, and scatter it over the potatoes, dividing it evenly.

CONTINUED

"Messy eggs" with rough-cut potatoes

CONTINUED

Raise the heat to medium. Crack the eggs into the pan two at a time and fry them in the chorizo-infused oil as directed for fried eggs on page 116. (To achieve the lacy golden edges that are a Basque signature, use the slotted spoon to poke at and perforate the egg whites to create air bubbles.)

Drape the eggs over the chorizo-topped potatoes. Just before serving, use scissors to cut open the yolks, or let the diners cut them open themselves. Serve immediately.

"Green eggs and ham" with peas and red onion

HUEVOS VERDES

Didn't all of our dads seem to have at least one specialty when we were growing up? When I was young, my dad made this dish and maybe one other one, both of them Basque. This is one of the first things I learned to cook for myself, and it is how I learned to use a knife, because my dad, who is a little particular, will not touch raw onions or garlic. Today, my kids are big egg eaters and, as I once did, they sit on the counter while we cook eggs together.

Think of the *jamón* here as a condiment. In the Basque Country, it's frequently used like salt or other seasonings, so that dishes like this one are considered vegetarian, a quirk that never fails to provoke strong reactions in unsuspecting vegetarian tourists. | SERVES 1

2 thin slices jamón serrano

Extra-virgin olive oil, for frying

1 small red onion, diced small (about ⅓ cup)

Kosher salt

¼ cup frozen shelled English peas, barely thawed

1 or 2 eggs, at room temperature

Maldon salt, for finishing

Stack the jamón slices and halve them. Restack them and roll them together into a tube. Cut the tube crosswise into thin ribbons. Set aside.

Heat a generous amount of oil (about 2 tablespoons) in a small nonstick frying pan over medium heat. When the oil is hot, add the onion to the pan and season with salt. Turn down the heat to medium-low and cook the onion for 3 to 5 minutes, until soft and sweet. Add the peas and another pinch of salt and cook for about 30 seconds, until warmed through. Add the jamón and sweat for a few seconds.

Make a well in the middle of the onion mixture and break 1 egg into it. Season the egg white with kosher salt. Dip the spatula in a bit of the hot oil before making contact with the egg, and then begin to chip away at the viscous white parts of the egg near the yolk. The egg white will begin to bubble and sputter, creating craters that grip the peas. When the white has cooked through, shake the pan to free the ingredients from the bottom. Use a spoon to baste the yolk with a little of the extra hot oil, warming it through.

Slide everything from the pan onto a plate. Finish the yolk with Maldon salt and serve immediately.

Smothered zucchini with soft scrambled eggs

PISTO A LA BILBAÍNA

Pisto is a ratatouille-like stew (see page 205), but when Basques talk about *pisto a la bilbaína*, or *pisto* Bilbao style, they're referring to a dish that marries scrambled eggs with a thick vegetable stew. Here, as with all scrambles, the eggs and garnish are partners—one is no more important than the other. Do not overmix them in the pan. As the eggs set in the stew, you want to create a marbled effect that delivers silkiness, body, and textural variety. | SERVES 4

2 tablespoons extra-virgin olive oil

1½ cups Basque Ratatouille (page 205)

8 eggs, at room temperature

Kosher salt

2 tablespoons chopped fresh flat-leaf parsley

Thinly coat a nonstick frying pan with 1 tablespoon of the oil and place over low heat. Add the ratatouille and heat gently. While it warms, in a bowl, lightly beat the eggs with a pinch of salt. Be careful not to overbeat the eggs; you want striations of yolk and white.

When the ratatouille is warm, using a heat-resistant rubber spatula, push it to one side of the pan. Raise the heat to high and add the remaining 1 tablespoon oil to the empty side of the pan. Pour the eggs over the oil and let them set for 10 seconds. Using the spatula, swirl the eggs and incorporate the vegetables into them just until the mixture takes on a marbled appearance, letting the eggs set slightly as you work. Cook the eggs for 2 minutes longer, until they are gently but uniformly cooked.

Transfer the mixture to a warmed plate, where the residual heat will finish cooking the eggs. Top with the parsley and serve.

Soft scrambled eggs with mushrooms

REVUELTO DE SETAS

Extra-virgin olive oil, for cooking

2 cups fresh wild or domestic mushrooms (ideally porcini), diced or sliced, depending on type

Kosher salt

1 clove garlic, chopped

1 tablespoon chopped fresh flat-leaf parsley

6 to 8 eggs, at room temperature

When you prepare this dish, make sure the mushrooms aren't bathing in their juices when you add the eggs or you will end up with a watery concoction. And remember, you don't want the eggs to take on any color. | SERVES 4

Very lightly coat a nonstick frying pan with oil and place over medium-high heat. When the oil is hot, add the mushrooms and let them cook, untouched, for 25 seconds. Stir, add a pinch of salt, and then add the garlic and a little more oil and cook, stirring occasionally, for about 3 minutes, until the garlic is no longer raw and the juices from the mushrooms have evaporated. Stir in the parsley.

In a bowl, lightly beat the eggs with a pinch of salt. Using a heat-resistant rubber spatula, push the mushrooms to one side of the pan and add a touch more oil. Pour the eggs into the empty side of the pan. Tilt the pan toward you and push the eggs up. Repeat this process twice, and then drag the mushrooms into the mix to create a marbled effect. Cook for 1 to 2 minutes, until the eggs are just barely set. Transfer to a warm plate and serve.

Sweet soft scrambled eggs with flowering garlic chives and shrimp

REVUELTO DE AJETES

Revueltos are an elegant craft in the Basque Country, and calling them scrambled eggs seems an injustice: they can anchor lunch and dinner menus and communicate the commitment to simplicity, modesty, and seasonality that is at the core of being Basque. Although they frequently include mushrooms, one of the most iconic combinations partners the eggs with garlic scapes, called *ajetes,* and small tender shrimp, or *gambas.* The Basques cut *ajetes* into 1-inch pieces, boil them like green beans until tender, and then sometimes put them up in brine for use when the spring season is over. We use garlic scapes when they're in season, but more often we create an *ajetes*-inspired dish from what's available in our neighborhood: we live on the border of Chinatown, where one of our favorite spots is Great New York Noodletown. It was there one night that we discovered the wonderful flowering garlic chive. Cut into 1-inch pieces, this sweet, crisp-stemmed vegetable carries all the promise of spring and none of the caveats of the garlic scape, which can be stringy and woody. | SERVES 4

½ cup extra-virgin olive oil, plus more for sautéing

1 medium to large shallot, minced

Kosher salt

2 teaspoons finely grated fresh ginger

½ teaspoon finely grated garlic

2 cups cut-up flowering garlic chives, in 1½-inch pieces

6 to 8 medium shrimp, peeled, deveined, and butterflied

4 eggs, at room temperature

¼ teaspoon sugar

Lightly coat the bottom of a nonstick frying pan with oil and place over medium heat. When the oil is hot, add the shallots and a pinch of salt and sauté for 1 to 2 minutes. Add the ginger and cook for another minute. Add the garlic and garlic chives and season with salt. Sauté the garlic chives until they are bright green and tender, about 1½ minutes, then raise the heat to high, add the shrimp, and sear for about 30 seconds per side.

When the shrimp start to curl up, lightly beat the eggs with a pinch of salt and the sugar. Be careful not to overbeat the eggs; you want striations of yolk. When the shrimp are just pink and done, add the eggs. Tilt the pan toward you, then use a spatula to push the egg halfway up the pan, letting the raw egg pool and fill the bottom of the pan. Repeat this process two more times. When the egg is nearly cooked through, transfer it to a warmed plate, where it will continue to cook in the residual heat. Serve immediately.

5 | Buscando Bakalao

FINDING COD

Fish is the absolute hallmark of Basque cooking. It is front and center from the *pintxos* bar to the family restaurant, from the home to the temple of fine dining. The Basques don't cook fish; the fire does that. Instead, they control the fire—the *sua*—until the perfect point has been reached. Ask any Basque and he or she will wax on about achieving that critical point: *"el punto esta muy conseguido"* is the highest compliment a fish cook can get.

When I talk about finding cod, I'm talking about a very specific salt cod of the highest quality—the kind of cod that, until I met Eder, I had no idea even existed; the kind that is so flavorful, tender, and altogether transcendent that it can induce a spiritual epiphany. It certainly did for me. With Eder's help, I saw the light and became a true believer in this modest ingredient's exquisite potential. What can I tell you? I found cod.

Although many kinds of fish are central to the Basque diet, cod occupies its own sanctified realm. The Basques have been seafarers for centuries. During the Middle Ages, they fed Europe's appetite for whale meat and built a thriving maritime economy in the process. Their ability to travel great distances was thanks in part to cod, which they salted and preserved for their journeys. Because of its low-fat content, it lasted longer than other kinds of salted fish and was said to have better flavor, too.

Salt cod also provided a lucrative business opportunity for the deeply religious Basques, who consumed fish on Fridays and throughout Lent. As cod became an increasingly prized commodity during the Middle Ages, fishermen throughout Europe competed for it, traveling farther and farther afield to find new stocks to plunder. But the Basques were able to remain above the fray thanks to a secret source they refused to divulge to anyone. It wasn't until the sixteenth century that the mystery was solved: a French expedition arriving on the shores of Canada's Gaspé Peninsula found a thousand Basque fishing boats anchored there. Some even believe that the Basques may have landed in North America long before Columbus did.

I'm so convinced of cod's inexorable link to Basque culture that I'll even go so far as to say it *looks* like it belongs in Basque Country. Think about it: the cod's speckled gray body is plain but intricately detailed, a totem for the outward plainness but innate exquisiteness of all Basque cooking. Cod is a humble, unassuming fish, yet astoundingly bountiful in all the ways it can be used: every bit of it, from its head to its tail, its bones to its bladder, can be turned into food, and a method exists for cooking every thickness of its neutrally flavored, delicate meat, from the fat loins that get thrown on the grill to the skin that gets transformed into gelatinous sauces and cracklin'. No culture has mastered every nook and cranny of the cod as Basque culture has. Any cook who embraces cod can become a member of its cult, and learning how to make *bakalao* (*bacalao* in Spanish), or salt cod, according to Basque tradition will help you understand why this humble fish inspires the kind of devotion more often found in a church or football stadium. In many ways, cod dishes, with their deceptively subtle textures and colors, showcase the principle that underlies Basque cooking: you can create bold strokes of genius using fewer strokes overall.

Discovering really good salt cod is a little like falling in love with someone, and like true love, cod is a precious commodity that shouldn't be taken for granted. Although some stocks are recovering after years of overfishing, cod still must be handled and prepared in a way that honors its relative rarity. Cooking fish and seafood the Basque way will give you the skills to do this, and it will help you develop techniques that can be put to work on much more than food that swims.

But before you embark on your journey, here are a few things to keep in mind. First, if you don't live in the Northeast, you will likely have to special order cod or salt cod. Luckily, it's easy to do either online or through your fishmonger, and you can store it in your freezer. You can also sometimes find high-quality salt cod already soaked and ready to go.

At Txikito, we make our own salt cod from day-boat cod, which is easy to obtain in New York and generally of good quality, with white flesh and a clean flavor. Nowadays, most cod is sold without its head, which means you have to develop a good relationship with your fishmonger if you want to buy a whole fish or if you just want to be sure that the whole fillet you are buying is of good quality. If the cod is being sold headless, make sure it is firm and looks wet; pass up fish with dry scales. Push the flesh with your finger (or ask the fishmonger to do it): the impression you make should spring back, a good indication that the fish is fresh and firm. It should also smell clean, so don't be shy about asking your fishmonger if you can smell it. (That's how you develop a relationship.) If the head is still attached, look for clear eyes and pink to red mucus-free gills. Headless or not, the skin should glisten, as if the fish were just pulled from the water.

Mastering fish and seafood cookery takes a lifetime, but, as the saying goes, practice makes perfect. In this chapter, you will learn the difference between cooking clams and cooking mussels and between cooking cod and cooking oily fish like tuna and sardines. You will also discover how to tease great results from different cooking mediums and heat sources, and to use recipes as a jumping-off point for wider exploration.

For example, if you make your own salt-cured cod, take time to think about all the ways you can use it. The recipes in this book are inspired by Basque traditions, but you should ask yourself if you might substitute salt cod in your favorite crab-cake recipe or whip it into mashed potatoes. Can you make white fish salad or a pasta sauce with it or use it in fried rice? How about grating dried salt cod over polenta? My hope is that the recipes in this chapter will inspire you to cook not only with salt cod but also with other abundant, more sustainable fish in both Basque ways and in your own ways.

Why, you may be wondering, is a chapter called "Finding Cod" not just about cod? Because the relationship you build with cod will be reflected in your approach to other fish and shellfish. Indeed, all of Basque cuisine is defined by the Basques' proximity and relationship to the sea. Hopefully these recipes, which draw on thousands of years of Basque experience, will capture your imagination as they have mine.

Home-cured tuna

BONITO EN CONSERVA

We buy amazing fresh bonito, skipjack tuna, tuna, and mackerel from Alex and Stephanie Villani's Blue Moon Fish stall in the Union Square Greenmarket. Fish in the tuna family are migratory, so they may come into season in your area once or twice a year. Take advantage then, as you will have access to smaller, less overfished varieties. (Buying whole fish is a great way to guarantee the fish's quality and get a much cheaper price.) Whether you buy whole fish or loin, buy larger pieces to ensure a succulent end product. | MAKES AT LEAST 4 POUNDS

4 to 5 pounds skinned whole loins of bonito, skipjack tuna, or mackerel, or filleted albacore, bluefin, or yellowfin tuna, bloodlines removed

Kosher salt

Extra-virgin olive oil, to cover

Cut the fish into 1-inch-thick steaks (your fishmonger can do this, too), or if you're using a smaller variety, just cut the whole fillet into large pieces. Place the fish on a large plate or a baking sheet, salt it generously, and refrigerate for 25 minutes. Remove from the refrigerator and scrape off the salt.

Bring a large saucepan of lightly salted water to a low simmer over medium-high heat. Submerge the fish in the simmering water, turn down the heat to low, and cook gently for about 25 minutes, until the fish is just cooked through but still juicy. The fish is done when you can just barely separate the layers of cooked fish with a fork. Using a slotted spoon or spider, transfer the fish to a large plate or baking sheet and let cool to room temperature.

Remove any remaining bloodlines and place the fish in jars or plastic containers. Add oil to cover and let cure for 2 days in your refrigerator before eating. Your patience will pay off.

If you want to can the fish properly, you must sterilize the jars before filling them. Seal them with canning lids, and process the jars in a pressure canner. You can find the directions on how to can tuna safely on the website of the United States Department of Agriculture (USDA). Because we make this in season to use in season, we don't bother canning the tuna. We have found that we can store it, covered in oil and capped, for up to 1 week in the refrigerator.

Quick salt-cured cod

BAKALAO

Bakalao is such a versatile and pragmatic ingredient that it can serve as a metaphor for the Basque people, whose brutishness, material ambition, and adaptability have meant that they are among the longest surviving cultures in the world. Following cod to faraway seas says as much about their tenacity and need for adventure as it might about their simple love of fish. Most of the cod we get at Txikito is not exactly the same species that Basques prize the most, but it is what we have come to know from head to tail and is ever present in our cooking.

To avoid unwanted scales on the cod flesh, be sure to always work with the cod skin side down, so any errant scales are touching the cutting board. Once you have removed the skin from the fillet, rinse the cutting board thoroughly before placing the cod flesh on it.

| MAKES 5 TO 7 POUNDS SALT COD

2 to 3 cups kosher salt

1 scaled skin-on whole fresh cod fillet (8 to 12 pounds)

Line a baking sheet, cutting board, or surface large enough to accommodate the length of the cod fillet with parchment paper. Sprinkle one-third of the salt over the parchment paper and place the cod, skin side down, on the salt. Sprinkle the remaining two-thirds of the salt directly onto the cod flesh, piling it up more aggressively on the thicker parts (the loin), and more lightly on the thinner parts (the tail and belly). Don't be shy with the salt. The cod must be visibly covered with it even in the "lightly coated" parts. Cover the cod with parchment paper or plastic wrap and apply even pressure with a few heavy items, such as 5-pound bags of rice or gallon containers of water. Allow the cod to cure for 2¼ hours at room temperature.

Uncover the cod and check the flesh. It should be notably tight and its surface should be a bit leathery. The salt will have extracted enough water from the fish that it will weigh about 60 percent less. Rinse off the salt and pat the fish dry.

To separate the cod into smaller pieces, place the fillet, horizontally and skin side down, on a cutting board. Using a sharp knife, cut off the rear section of the loin that includes the tail by making a vertical cut from the top of the fillet to the bottom about 4 inches from the tip. You will probably have to run the knife through a second time to make sure you have cut all the way through the skin. This tail piece will be triangular. The remaining larger, thicker piece has a natural seam running across it latterly separating the top thicker loin from the sloping and thinner belly section. Square, or more specifically, "rectangle," this section off by trimming the thinnest parts of the belly off (reserve that meat for another use). Cut the thicker loin section into 2-inch portions (or leave the loin whole if you have a specific plan for it). Wrap the pieces individually in airtight plastic and freeze overnight or up to 2 months.

You should now have 2 pieces to work with: the reserved triangular tail piece and the smaller, thinner piece that was the bottom of the fish—the belly—which will have bones and membrane still attached. Remove and discard the skin from the tail piece; reserve the flesh. Slowly run your knife under the bones and membrane on the belly to separate the flesh; discard the skin and membrane. Remove the vertical pin bones by cutting along them in a straight line with your knife, taking care to leave as little flesh as possible on them, and discard them. Using your hands, pull the belly flesh and tail meat into ¼-inch pieces. This flaked belly is called *migas*.

Pack the *migas* into one or more small containers so that they can be tightly sealed. For best results, freeze overnight or up to 2 months. Once defrosted, refrigerate for up to 3 days.

Salt-baked fish

PESCADO A LA SAL

Local bluefish is plentiful in New York, and I think it is the ideal fish for this recipe. That said, any fish of similar size will do, such as New Zealand snapper, Japanese *madai* (red seabream), or even branzino. Smaller fish will cook a little faster. Salt baking makes fish exceptionally moist, and the steam that gets trapped under the salt crust makes the flavor more delicate. Because the presentation is so dramatic, the fish needs no more adornment than a thread of your best olive oil.

The popularity of salt baking in the Basque country is no surprise, given that the Basques so capably commodified salt in tandem with their commercial cod fishing and preserving activities. Covering fish to cook it, whether in salt or clay or under the lid of a Dutch oven, is also decidedly Basque, as all of these techniques promote the pure flavors of the fish.

My favorite way to serve any leftovers is flaked over tomato slices and thinly sliced sweet onion and drizzled generously with oil. It's a magical combination. | SERVES 6

1 (5- to 6-pound) whole fish (see headnote), with head intact, gutted, scaled, and rinsed

2½ pounds (7½ cups) kosher salt

2 teaspoons fennel seeds

6 bay leaves, crumbled

1 tablespoon dried dill

Extra-virgin olive oil, for drizzling

Preheat the oven to 500°F. Bring the fish to room temperature. In a large container, combine the salt, fennel seeds, bay, and dill and mix well. Starting with about 3 cups, add enough water until the mixture is the consistency of damp sand for building a sand castle— in other words, barely wet and packable. If you add too much water and it begins seeping out, add more salt until you have the correct consistency. Set the salt aside to self-saturate for a minute or two.

Using aluminum foil, cover a roasting pan or baking sheet large enough to accommodate the fish on the diagonal. Place one-third of the salt mixture on the pan in a diagonal line and pat it with your palm until it is the width of the fish. Lay the fish on the diagonal salt bed, then cover it with the remaining salt mixture, piling and patting along the sides and being careful not to get any salt in the cavity of the fish.

Roast the fish for about 35 minutes, until the salt crust is firm and the fish is cooked. (Because it is so moist in there, it's hard for the fish to overcook.) Remove the pan from the oven. Using the back of a chef's knife, strike at the salt crust near the head of the fish, then lift off the salt in slabs and discard. Invite your family or guests to watch you as you do this, as it's quite exciting.

Serve the fish immediately so it doesn't dry out, being careful not to let the flesh come into contact with any salt that may have come loose from the crust. Use 2 spoons to separate the meat from the bones and reassemble it, bone-free, on a platter. Don't worry if it breaks a little. (Note: The skin usually gets picked up with the salt when you lift off the crust, but if the skin sticks to the flesh, serve the flesh skin side down so people who don't like gelatinous skin can skip it.) Top the fish with a drizzle of amazing olive oil.

Plaza Nueva salt cod salad

BAKALAO CRUDO AITXIAR

GARLIC CRUMBS

2 cups extra-virgin olive oil

15 cloves garlic, minced

Kosher salt

TOMATO PULP

2 large plum tomatoes

Kosher salt

2 cups garlic oil, reserved from making garlic crumbs

3 tablespoons garlic crumbs

Pinch of red pepper flakes

1 teaspoon high-quality blanco tequila (optional)

SALAD

Tomato pulp

8 ounces quick salt-cured cod flakes (page 142)

4 canned piquillo peppers, cut lengthwise into ribbons and stored in their own juices

3 tablespoons extra-virgin olive oil

¼ teaspoon red pepper flakes (optional)

⅛ teaspoon nigella seeds

Remaining garlic crumbs (about 3 tablespoons), for garnish

Maldon salt, for finishing

CONTINUED

This salad is inspired by one served at Aitxiar, a little bar in Bilbao's Plaza Nueva. Like most Basque *pintxos* bars, Aitxiar specializes in one thing; in this case it is *tako de bakalao con pimientos de Alegría*, or raw salt cod with Alegría peppers, a little-known hot pepper from Rioja that is generally spicier than most Basque palates will tolerate. I love it. This dish is great at summer's end when both peppers and tomatoes are abundant, and it makes an excellent home for your frozen salt cod *migas*, or flakes.

Give yourself permission to improve your tomatoes by adding the smallest pinch of sugar. If you are unfamiliar with nigella seeds, they are small black seeds with a mild, nutty flavor, and they are widely used in Sephardic, Middle Eastern, and Indian cooking. Look for them in Middle Eastern and Indian markets and online.

The golden garlic crumbs and garlicky tomato pulp are flexible components that you'll find yourself using again and again in both Basque and other recipes. The garlic crumbs can be sprinkled on white rice and tomato salads and add crunch and complexity to raw fish dishes and raw and cooked shrimp dishes. Leftover tomato pulp is bread's best friend: add a thread of good olive oil and some sliced sweet onion to the equation and let the sopping begin. | SERVES 4 TO 6

To make the garlic crumbs, place a small fine-mesh strainer over a heatproof container. Line a plate with paper towels. In a 2-quart saucepan, combine the 2 cups oil and garlic and gently warm over medium-low heat, stirring the garlic with chopsticks or a small wooden spoon to separate the pieces. Do not take your eyes off the garlic, as it can burn easily, turning acrid. When the garlic is a light gold, immediately pour the mixture into the strainer. Reserve the oil for garlicky tomato pulp.

Spread the garlic crumbs on the towel-lined plate and season with salt. The crumbs can be made up to 2 days in advance and stored in an airtight container at room temperature. You should have about 6 tablespoons garlic crumbs.

Plaza Nueva salt cod salad

CONTINUED

To make the tomato pulp, cut the tomatoes in half lengthwise, scoop out and discard the seed sacs, and grate each half on the medium-coarse holes of box grater, collecting the pulp on a plate and discarding the skins. Season the tomato pulp lightly with salt.

In a small saucepan, warm the garlic oil over medium-high heat. Add the tomato pulp and stir for about 1 minute, just long enough to heat the mixture. Stir in the garlic crumbs, pepper flakes, and tequila, and cook for 1 minute more. Remove from the heat. Let cool completely before using. The tomato pulp can be made up to 2 days in advance and stored in an airtight container in the refrigerator for up to 2 days.

To make the salad, bring the tomato pulp to room temperature, then divide it among 4 to 6 plates.

Arrange a layer of the cod over the tomato pulp and then scatter the piquillo peppers over the cod and drizzle with the piquillo juices. Drizzle with the oil and garnish with pepper flakes, nigella seeds, garlic crumbs, and a little salt.

Mussels with white beans

MEJILLONES Y POCHAS EN SALSA VERDE

This light stew of white beans and bouchot mussels is a Txikito signature. When I first encountered *pochas*, a creamy white bean typical of Navarra, I envisioned a salad or a blond stew. It turns out they are often served smothered with quail in a rich dark sauce. I think the lightness of this preparation is more respectful of the bean and reflects the general approach to cooking at the restaurant. Here, the beans take the place of the potatoes commonly found in dishes made with *salsa verde*, which, along with *salsa pil pil*, *salsa tinta*, and *salsa bizkaína*, is one of the most important sauces of Basque cuisine. When making the sauce, be sure to cook off the alcohol before adding the beans, or the dish will be too acidic. This warm stew can be enjoyed all year long. | SERVES 4

2 pounds large bouchot mussels

2 tablespoons extra-virgin olive oil, plus more for finishing

3 cloves garlic, thinly sliced

2 flat-leaf parsley sprigs, left whole, plus ½ bunch, chopped, for finishing

¼ cup dry white wine

¼ cup manzanilla sherry

3 cups cooked white beans, preferably pochas or other heirloom thin-skinned, white- or green-fleshed shelling beans, drained

Kosher salt

½ teaspoon lemon juice (optional)

Extra-virgin olive oil, for finishing

Cook the mussels as directed on page 161, reserving the mussel meats and 1 cup of the mussel stock. If using chilled reserved mussels, bring them to room temperature while preparing the beans.

In a heavy saucepan, heat the oil over medium-low heat. Add the garlic and cook, stirring, for no more than 1 minute, until just opaque. Add the parsley sprigs and cook until they wilt, then add the white wine and sherry and simmer for about 1 minute to cook off the alcohol. Add the beans and the 1 cup mussel stock and cook for 4 to 5 minutes, until warmed through.

Remove from the heat, remove and discard the parsley sprigs, fold in the mussels and almost of all of the chopped parsley, and then warm through gently over medium-low heat to avoid overcooking the mussels. Taste. Stir in salt and lemon juice if needed. Top with a little more chopped parsley and a thread of olive oil. Serve in warm bowls.

Grilled sardines, Basque port style

SARDINAS SANTURZI

The women who traditionally carried sardines to Bilbao from the port town of Santurzi were known as the *sardineras*. Each day they would trek some eleven miles along the Nervión River, which runs through Bilbao to the Cantabrian Sea, carrying large baskets of sardines on their heads to sell. Images of these women engaged in their taxing hike are depicted in paintings and murals all over Bizkaia (Vizcaya, or Biscay) Province, where eating sardines grilled on grapevines is a real treat. I have run this trail in an annual race, and it is grueling.

There is nothing better than simply grilled sardines in season. They are a social food—you don't eat one, you have an afternoon's worth—and they arrive crusted in a bloom of evaporated seawater. | SERVES 4

1 cup kosher salt

10 cups room-temperature water

8 impeccably fresh Mediterranean, Greek, or American sardines, rinsed, scaled, and optionally gutted

¼ cup extra-virgin olive oil

Japanese or Maldon smoked sea salt, for finishing (optional)

Grilled bread, for serving

Make a brine by combining the kosher salt and water in a large bowl or other vessel and then stir to dissolve the salt. Add the sardines to the brine and let stand for 15 minutes. Remove the fish from the brine, discard the brine, and pat the fish on both sides with paper towels (several times if needed) until thoroughly dry. Rub the sardines on both sides with the oil.

Lightly oil an 8-inch wire-mesh strainer and place it directly on top of the burner on a gas stove. Turn the burner on and allow the screen to heat for about 15 seconds. Place 4 oiled sardines on the screen and then immediately lift the screen about 1 to 2 inches above the flame to prevent burning the sardines excessively. Return the screen to the burner and cook the fish for 1 minute on the first side. Then, using tongs, carefully flip the sardines and cook on the second side for 30 seconds longer. Expect some flames and crackling from the oily sardine juices that fall on the fire, and when flare-ups occur, pull the screen away until the flames die down, then move the fish back to the heat source. When the fish are ready, transfer them to a platter. Repeat until they are all cooked.

Sprinkle the sardines with smoked salt and serve immediately with grilled bread for soaking up their juices.

Rice with cockles

ARROZ CON TXIRLAS

2 pounds cockles or manila clams

4 tablespoons extra-virgin olive oil, plus more for finishing

2 cloves garlic, smashed

1 dried red guindilla pepper, or small pinch of red pepper flakes

2 flat-leaf parsley sprigs plus ¼ cup loosely packed fresh flat-leaf parsley leaves, coarsely chopped, for finishing

¼ cup dry white wine

¼ cup manzanilla sherry

About 2 cups mussel stock (page 161) or fish stock (page 28), or as needed

½ Spanish onion, minced

Kosher salt

1 cup Bomba rice

I used to like going to the fish market around Christmastime with Eder's maternal grandmother, Eulalia. The authoritative Basque matriarch would take an elevator from Bilbao's Casco Viejo, where she lived, to Begoña, the neighborhood that towers high above the city. "Better fish at better prices," she would say. "Of course she was right," Eder would later say, "because she is a woman." Eulalia's fish lady was a well-known secret, betrayed by the lines that formed around the block. She had an incredible variety of fish and other sea critters, and everything she sold was pristine.

We would eat her clams raw. I remember that when I would bring my knife close to the plate, they would close around the blade so I could lift them out and pry them open in one motion. I had never seen such active clams.

This dish always makes me think of the heady ocean-infused perfume that rises when cockles or clams and parsley are mixed together. Salty and clean is the only way to describe it. In the Basque Country, you don't need to buy parsley for your fish. Because fish is never eaten without parsley and is rarely eaten with anything more than that, parsley comes courtesy of the fishmonger. When we finished shopping, Eulalia and I would take the elevator back to the street, return home, place a sprig of parsley in Eulalia's figurine of San Pancracio (Saint Pancras) for luck, work, and money, and then get cooking. | SERVES 4

In a large bowl, soak the cockles in cold water to cover for 5 minutes. Drain and repeat three times, until they cockles are free of sand. Set aside.

Heat a heavy 3-quart stockpot over medium heat and add about 2 tablespoons of the oil, or just enough to cover the bottom. Add the garlic and pepper and cook for about 30 seconds, until the garlic turns light gold. Add the parsley, cockles, white wine, and sherry and simmer for about 2 minutes to cook off the alcohol. Cover and steam, checking frequently to see if the cockles have opened (even a crack

CONTINUED

Rice with cockles

CONTINUED

means a cockle is open). This should take from 1½ to 2 minutes from when the pan was covered. Using tongs, transfer the cockles as they open to a bowl. Discard any cockles that failed to open after 3 to 4 minutes. Strain the cooking liquid through a fine-mesh strainer and reserve.

Cover the cockles with a clean kitchen towel. Combine the strained cooking liquid with enough stock to total 2½ cups.

Heat a saucepan over medium-low heat and add the remaining 2 tablespoons oil, the onion, and a pinch of salt. Sweat the onion for 8 to 10 minutes, until sweet and translucent. Add the rice, stir to coat, and cook for 1 minute, stirring constantly. Add the stock mixture, raise the heat to medium-high, and bring to a simmer. Turn down the heat until the rice is barely percolating and cook, uncovered and without stirring, for about 13 minutes, until the rice is tender but firm. Remove from the heat and let rest, uncovered, for 2 minutes.

Fold the cockles and chopped parsley into the rice and transfer to a serving dish. Finish with a thread of oil and serve immediately.

Anchovies, Bermeo style

ANCHOAS ESTILO BERMEO

Bermeo, another tiny port and fish-processing hub in Basque Country, is the inspiration for this recipe. This is a fish recipe, but it is also a condiment par excellence. The olive oil is as central to this preparation as the anchovy: my favorite part of eating this dish is when the fish are gone and all that remains is the flavorful oil, deliciously polluted with vinegar droplets, anchovy fat, and soggy golden garlic, begging to be mopped up with a chunk of warm baguette. Called *untar*, this ritual mopping is almost a national pastime in the Basque Country, where plates are often shared at the dinner table at home or in casual restaurants. If *untar* is not your thing, use the leftover juices to make a delicious vinaigrette for dressing romaine hearts or warm potatoes. Whatever you do, don't throw the juices away. | SERVES 4

½ cup kosher salt

5 cups warm water

1½ pounds fresh anchovies

3 cups extra-virgin olive oil

4 cloves garlic, thinly sliced

¼ teaspoon red pepper flakes

⅓ cup low-acid sherry vinegar

Baguette or country bread, for serving

Make a brine by combining the salt and water in a bowl and then stir to dissolve the salt. Rinse the fish under cold running water, gently massaging away the scales with your thumb and pointer finger, then push your finger into the belly and pull out the viscera. Rinse the fish again to clean—but be gentle as these fish are fragile. When they are all clean, place the anchovies in the brine and let stand for 10 minutes. Remove the anchovies from the brine and set aside. Discard the brine.

Make a refrito by heating the oil in a heavy saucepan over medium heat. Add the garlic and cook for about 40 seconds, until golden brown. Add the anchovies and immediately remove the pan from the heat.

Swirl the pan to coat the anchovies evenly with the hot oil. Add the pepper flakes and return to the heat for a moment to cook the anchovies just through (you are not frying them crisp). Finish with the vinegar.

Serve directly in the cooking pan or transfer to a cazuela, pouring the fish and oil together. Serve with plenty of bread for mopping up the flavorful oil.

Basque fisherman's stew

"MARMITAKO"

This famous Basque fisherman's stew is named after the *marmita*, the heavy pot in which it is cooked. I find the dish excessively rich. Even though I like all of its components and concede that they definitely flatter one another, I've never been able to embrace it, which presents a conundrum because Eder loves it. Over the years I have made at least ten versions of the stew, none of them traditional, and I have liked them all. This recipe reflects our style at Txikito: it's a leaner, cleaner *marmitako*-inspired dish whose luxury comes from buying the best fish and saving the liquor of roasted peppers—a nuanced dish that still honors tradition. | SERVES 4

5 red bell peppers

3 green bell peppers

½ cup plus 5 tablespoons extra-virgin olive oil

Kosher salt

2 or 3 russet potatoes

2 cups canola oil

Pinch of Hondashi or other packaged instant dashi

Pinch of ground cayenne pepper

2 pounds skin-on fatty tuna belly

1 tablespoon chopped fresh flat-leaf parsley

Preheat the oven to 500°F. Line a baking sheet with parchment paper. Cut the stem end off of each bell pepper, then seed the peppers. In a large bowl, toss the peppers with 3 tablespoons of the olive oil and some salt to coat evenly. Stand the peppers, cut side down, on the prepared baking sheet and roast, rotating the pan back to front at the halfway point, for 20 to 25 minutes, until the skins char and the flesh is tender. Transfer the peppers to a large plastic container, cover with an airtight lid, and let cool for at least 1 hour.

Transfer the peppers and any juices from the container to a colander placed over a large bowl and let stand for about 5 minutes to allow all of the juices to drain. Move the peppers occasionally to free any juices trapped inside. You should end up with about ⅔ cup juice, or liquor. Reserve the pepper flesh for another use, such as Roasted Red Peppers with Oil-Cured Anchovies (page 92), or serve the green ones with oil-poached cod or Open-Faced Sandwich of Jamón, Anchovy, and Roasted Pepper (page 56).

Peel 2 potatoes, rinse them, and cut them lengthwise into quarters. Cut the quarters crosswise into ⅛-inch-thick slices. You should end up with 2 cups potato slices. If you're short, cut up another potato. In a large saucepan, combine the potatoes, the canola oil, and the ½ cup olive oil, adding a bit more of each oil if the potatoes are not covered. Add enough salt to season the vegetables, not the oil. Place over low heat and cook gently for 30 to 40 minutes, until the potatoes are tender. Carefully drain the potatoes into a fine-mesh strainer, capturing the oil in a heatproof container. Set the potatoes aside. Let the oil cool, then cover and reserve for another use.

In a small saucepan, combine the pepper liquor with the dashi and cayenne pepper and simmer over medium-low heat for about 3 minutes, until the mixture thinly coats a spoon. Remove from the heat and cover with aluminum foil while you cook the tuna.

Preheat the oven to 300°F. Using a sharp knife and long, smooth cuts, remove the skin from the tuna. If a bloodline is visible, trim it away, wasting as little flesh as possible. Slice the tuna with the grain into ¼-inch-thick slices, cutting on the diagonal to maximize the number of slices.

Place 4 ceramic ovenproof plates in the oven and preheat them for 10 minutes. Meanwhile, lightly season both sides of each tuna slice with salt, then brush on both sides with the remaining 2 tablespoons olive oil.

Remove the plates from the oven, divide the tuna slices evenly among them, and return them to the oven. Cook the tuna for 3 to 4 minutes, until cooked through but still very moist. The tuna should still look light pink in the center.

While the tuna is cooking, sauté the potatoes in a nonstick frying pan over high heat for 2 to 3 minutes, until heated through without browning.

Divide the potatoes evenly among the 4 plates, arranging them next to the tuna in an attractive fashion. Spoon the pepper liquor over the tuna and then sprinkle the parsley over both. Serve immediately.

Mussels poached in vinaigrette

MEJILLONES EN ESCABECHE

3½ pounds large bouchot mussels

BASIC ESCABECHE

1 cup extra-virgin olive oil, plus more if needed

2 leeks, white and light green parts only, finely diced

Kosher salt

1 red onion, finely diced

1 carrot, peeled and finely diced

2 lemon thyme sprigs, or 10 fresh rosemary needles

½ teaspoon coriander seeds

½ teaspoon black peppercorns

1 jalapeño chile, halved lengthwise and seeded, or unseeded if you like heat

½ cup sugar dissolved in ½ cup water

½ cup seasoned rice vinegar

½ cup champagne vinegar

2 teaspoons sherry vinegar

Sweet Spanish paprika, for dusting

Dill sprigs, for garnish (optional)

This is one of the ways at Txikito that we imitate foods that are often canned in Spain. *Escabeche* describes a technique for flavoring and preserving fish and meat by poaching it gently in a vinaigrette. Toasted baguette slices spread with mayonnaise are an outstanding accompaniment to this dish. Try the green peppercorn mayonnaise on page 23. | MAKES 2 POUNDS

Cook the mussels as directed on page 161 and refrigerate until needed. Reserve the stock for another use.

To make the escabeche, heat the oil in a large, heavy saucepan over medium-low heat. Add the leeks and a pinch of salt and sweat for about 7 minutes, until wilted. Add the onion, carrot, and a little more salt and sweat for about 5 minutes, until tender.

Meanwhile, gather together the lemon thyme, coriander seeds, and peppercorns in a cheesecloth bundle tied with kitchen string. Add the bundle, chile, sugar water, and rice, champagne, and sherry vinegars to the pan, raise the heat to high, and bring to a boil. Turn down the heat to a simmer and cook for 3 to 5 minutes longer, until the vegetables lose their crunch but keep their body. Taste and adjust the seasoning with salt if needed. If you want to lessen the acidity of the mixture, add more oil.

Place the mussels in a heatproof bowl. Pour the escabeche mixture through a fine-mesh strainer held over the bowl. Let the mussels cool in the escabeche for 10 minutes, then cover and chill well. Remove the chile and the cheesecloth bundle from the strainer and discard. Transfer the vegetables to a bowl, cover, and refrigerate until serving.

To serve, bring the mussels and vegetables to room temperature and top the mussels with the vegetables. Dust with paprika and drizzle with a thread of olive oil and add a few dill sprigs for appearance and flavor. Serve on mayonnaise-swathed toasts or with cocktail forks.

CLEANING AND COOKING MUSSELS

Mussels are inexpensive, sustainable, delicious, and a great choice for anyone looking for a lean protein with less cholesterol than other shellfish. We like bouchot mussels, which are grown in the sea on ropes hung from poles, for their reliable sweetness and plump bodies. If you cannot find them, PEI mussels are a good substitute. Make sure that whatever mussels you buy are alive and that you use them as soon as possible after purchase. Unlike clams, mussels want to be cooked and will open wide when they're done. Avoid those that barely open. You want a good-quality wine here, too, one that you would actually drink.

Rinse the mussels thoroughly under running cold water. Remove their beards by pulling on the ropy fibers that protrude from their shells. Place a large, heavy saucepan over high heat and pour in half of a 750 ml bottle of wine. Bring the wine to a simmer and cook for 20 seconds to cook off some of the alcohol. Add 1 pound of the mussels, cover, and steam for 30 seconds. Uncover and check for open mussels and pull out any you find one at a time with tongs, or in batches with a slotted spoon. Discard any mussels that failed to open after 2 to 3 minutes.

Add a splash more wine if too much has evaporated (it should be at least ½ inch deep), bring to a simmer, and then add another pound of mussels and cook them as you did the first pound. Repeat until all of the mussels are cooked. Once the cooking is finished, strain the cooking liquid through a fine-mesh strainer (or a regular strainer lined with a dampened double layer of cheesecloth) into a container and set aside.

Spread out the mussels on 1 or 2 large baking sheets and chill them in the refrigerator for about 30 minutes, until cool enough to handle. Pull the mussels carefully out of their shells and discard the shells. Check each mussel for any remaining beard and tug lightly to remove if necessary. If not using the mussels right away, store them in their strained stock in the refrigerator. They will keep for up to 2 days.

If you have cooked 3½ pounds mussels for the *escabeche* recipe on page 160, you should have about 2 cups picked mussels and about 2 cups stock. If you have cooked 2 pounds mussels for Mussels with White Beans (page 151), you should have a generous cup picked mussels and about 1 to 1½ cups stock. If you are making a dish that doesn't use the stock, such as the *escabeche* recipe, reserve it for another use, like the Rice with Cockles (page 155). It will keep in the refrigerator for up to 1 day or in the freezer for up to 3 months.

Chinatown-style periwinkles

CARACOLILLOS "BARRIO CHINO"

2 pounds periwinkles

½ cup extra-virgin olive oil

4 cloves garlic, minced

2 tablespoons finely chopped fresh ginger

2 jalapeño chiles, finely chopped

⅓ cup loosely packed chopped fresh cilantro

From our earliest days together, Eder and I enjoyed going to restaurants, where we were constantly discovering new and interesting foods. One night after returning from a trip to the Basque Country, we went to Congee Village, a Chinese restaurant on the Lower East Side that is still one of my favorite places. It was after Christmas and we had spent December eating all manner of seafood: long hours had been passed chatting over periwinkles we freed from their shells with needles Eder's grandmother kept stuck in a cork in a dining room drawer. As we ordered razor clams and congee, we saw a mountain of periwinkles go by, accompanied by the blur of the waiter's tartan vest. "*Caracolillos!*" we said simultaneously. We summoned the server, who was convinced that we would not like them and recommended the lamb chop instead. But we insisted. He obliged, and our version of stir-fried periwinkles as a New York Basque dish was born.

I can pick periwinkles forever; my hunger for them is what we call *un vicio* in Spanish. In English, the closest definition is a relentless, single-minded quest to enjoy something fully until it's gone. I can't stop eating periwinkles until all that remains are empty shells. My five-year-old daughter, Maayan, is equally obsessive about eating them. She does a mama proud.

Buy your periwinkles in Chinatown if possible because they are cut at the ends. That means that if you suck on the cut side first and then turn the periwinkles and repeat the sucking at their natural opening, they free themselves without a pick. They are usually in high demand, so the stock rotates often, ensuring freshness. Periwinkles should smell like the ocean. If you notice an off smell, that means there is a bad one or two in the mix and you must smell them one by one to find the stinky needle in the haystack. | MAKES ENOUGH FOR 5 NORMAL PEOPLE (OR FOR JUST ALEX AND MAAYAN)

Rinse the periwinkles and then soak them in cold water for 1 minute, agitating them to remove any grit. Change the water three to five times to ensure proper cleaning, then drain well in a colander. Bring a large, heavy saucepan of salted water to a boil and add the

CONTINUED

Chinatown-style periwinkles

CONTINUED

periwinkles. Allow the water temperature to recover, but remove from the heat before it reaches a boil again. Leave the periwinkles in their cooking water for about 1 hour, until cooled to room temperature. If you will not be using them immediately, store them in their cooking liquid in the refrigerator for up to 2 days.

Line a colander with a kitchen towel. Using your hands, scoop out the periwinkles from the cooking liquid, being careful not to grab any sand that may be at the bottom, and place them in the towel-lined colander.

Heat a large sauté pan or wok over high heat. When it is hot, add the oil, garlic, ginger, and chiles all at once and sauté until the mixture is hot and aromatic. Add the periwinkles and toss them a few times to coat them with the oil and seasonings. Transfer them to a bowl and sprinkle with the cilantro. If they have not been cut on one side, serve with little pins to pick the flesh out of the shells.

Grilled head-on shrimp

LANGOSTINOS A LA PLANTXA

Head-on shrimp, or *langostinos*, are a ubiquitous treat throughout the Basque Country, but when we first started serving them at Txikito, some people asked us to serve them with the heads off. We politely refused, insisting that the head holds the riches of the shrimp. In time, most people came around. The shrimp make an easy and amazing dish to serve at a dinner party: your guests do the work and they leave the table happy.

If these shrimp are so easy, why do we include a recipe? Because we hope that if you do it our way, you will brine your shrimp every time, even when you're only planning to boil and peel them. Be sure to buy the freshest shrimp or highest-quality frozen shrimp available to you. | SERVES 2

½ cup kosher salt

2 tablespoons sugar

3 cups water

3 cups ice cubes

8 large head-on shrimp

3 tablespoons extra-virgin olive oil, or as needed, plus more for drizzling

Juice of ½ lemon

Maldon salt, for finishing

Make a brine by combining the kosher salt, sugar, and water in a bowl or other vessel and then stir to dissolve the salt and sugar. Add the ice to the bowl, then add the shrimp and let stand for 20 minutes. Remove the shrimp from the brine and pat them dry with paper towels.

Heat a griddle over high heat until very hot. In a bowl, toss the shrimp gently with the oil, coating evenly. Lay the shrimp flat on the hot griddle, making sure each shrimp has as much contact as possible with the surface. Allow the griddle to recover its heat and then turn down the heat to medium. If more oil is needed to prevent scorching, add it now. Cook the shrimp for 2 minutes on one side, turn them over, and cook on the second side for 1 minute, until red juices begin to ooze out.

Finish the shrimp with the lemon juice and then divide them among 4 plates. Finish with a drizzle of oil and a sprinkle of Maldon salt.

Tempura-fried soft-shell crabs in escabeche

NÉCORAS DE CONQUISTA

There were a couple of ways that I ensured Eder would fall in love with me. One was by being a quick learner, and the other was by bringing him crabs. In the Basque Country, the locals eat every type of crab they can find, but they don't have soft-shell crabs. I knew Eder would be wildly happy when he tried one and think I was a genius, so I made him a couple for lunch one day. *"Es bestial!"* he said. That's a compliment. It means that something is brutally good.

I have to give props to my mom, Susana, for all the *escabeche* I make. This is one of things she, not Eder, taught me, and the style of my *escabeches*, with their emphasis on leeks, is very much her influence. As for the jalapeños, I just need them.

To make the vegetables in *escabeche* and their liquid, you will need to make the basic *escabeche* recipe in Mussels Poached in Vinaigrette (page 160). But instead of finely dicing the vegetables as that recipe calls for, julienne them. | SERVES 6

Basic escabeche (see Mussels Poached in Vinaigrette, page 160)

6 small soft-shell crabs

Canola oil, for frying

½ cup cornstarch

½ cup all-purpose flour

Kosher salt

1 cup seltzer water, ice-cold

¾ cup thin mayonnaise (page 23)

Sweet Spanish paprika, for dusting

Make the basic escabeche as directed, but julienne the vegetables (long, thin ribbons) rather than finely dicing them. You can also increase the amount of chile, if you want more heat. Measure out 1 cup julienned vegetables and 6 tablespoons escabeche liquid for this recipe. Reserve the remaining vegetables and liquid for another use.

Using a good pair of kitchen scissors, remove the face of each crab by cutting across the front of the crab, just behind the eyes and mouth parts; it should come off in a single piece. Lift one side of the top shell and pull out and discard the gills. Repeat with the other side of the top shell. Turn the crab over to expose its underside and pull off the apron (triangular on a female crab and longer and thinner on a male crab) by lifting first, then pulling.

Pour the oil to a depth of 2 to 3 inches into a 3-quart stockpot or a deep fryer and heat to 365°F. While the oil is heating, in a deep bowl, stir together the cornstarch, flour, and 1 teaspoon salt. Whisk in the seltzer, a little at a time, until the batter is the consistency of heavy cream.

Working with 1 crab at a time, hold the crab by a pincer and submerge it completely in the batter, then lift it out and let the excess batter drip off. Lower the crab into the hot oil slowly and confidently; do not drop it in. A good pair of tongs or tweezers is great for this task. Working quickly, add more crabs, being careful not to crowd the pan. Soft-shell crabs can spatter as they fry, so as you work, stand back a bit to avoid burns. Fry the crabs for about 1½ minutes, until lightly golden on all sides. Using the tongs, lift them out of the oil and blot them dry with paper towels.

Sprinkle the crabs with salt, then split each crab in half lengthwise. Place 2 tablespoons of the mayonnaise on each plate. Top the mayonnaise with 1 split crab and 2½ to 3 tablespoons of the escabeche vegetables. Pour 1 tablespoon of the escabeche liquid over each crab. Dust the crabs with paprika and serve immediately.

Campfire trout

TRUCHA A LA NAVARRA

Trout is a mainstay of Navarran cooking, as is the use of *jamón* as a condiment. Here, I use *jamón* slices to protect the tender fish from drying out, with the added benefit of basting the trout with the salty, savory taste that is a trademark of Spanish ham. This dish is usually served with diced *jamón* in the *refrito* (frying oil), but when I first heard about it, I immediately pictured it as the campfire-style trout of my midwestern upbringing. The first time I made it splayed open and each loin topped with *jamón*, Eder thought it was hilarious. It is a true signature of Txikito and outsells even our most rarified seafood dishes. The high notes of a great vinegar make all the difference here, and changing the vinegar each time you cook the trout can be a good way to bring variety to a dish that promises to become a family favorite. | SERVES 4

2 (1- to 2-pound) whole butterflied trout (ask your fishmonger to do this)

Kosher salt

⅔ cup extra-virgin olive oil, plus more for searing

4 slices jamón ibérico

6 large cloves garlic, thinly sliced

1 dried guindilla pepper or árbol chile

3 tablespoons coarsely chopped fresh flat-leaf parsley

1 to 2 tablespoons Garnacha wine vinegar, sherry vinegar, or balsamic vinegar

Preheat the oven to 400°F. Season the trout inside and out with salt and coat the skin side with oil. Heat a cast-iron frying pan or other ovenproof frying pan over medium-high heat. Add enough oil to coat the bottom of the pan lightly, and when the oil begins to smoke, add 1 trout, skin side down and splayed open. Cook, shaking the pan back and forth constantly to ensure the fish doesn't stick, for about 1 minute, until you know the skin is free and won't stick.

Working quickly, lay a slice of jamón on each fillet of the trout, then cook for 1 more minute. Slide the fish onto a large baking sheet and repeat the previous steps in the frying pan with the second fish and the remaining jamón. Bake the trout for 4 to 6 minutes, until the flesh is firm but still pink when you peek under the jamón (cooked medium).

While the trout are baking, combine the ⅔ cup oil and garlic in a small saucepan and warm over medium-high heat for 35 to 40 seconds, until the garlic is barely golden. Remove from the heat and add the pepper, parsley, and a pinch of salt.

Serve the trout family style, adding a splash of vinegar to each fish and spooning the garlic oil over the top.

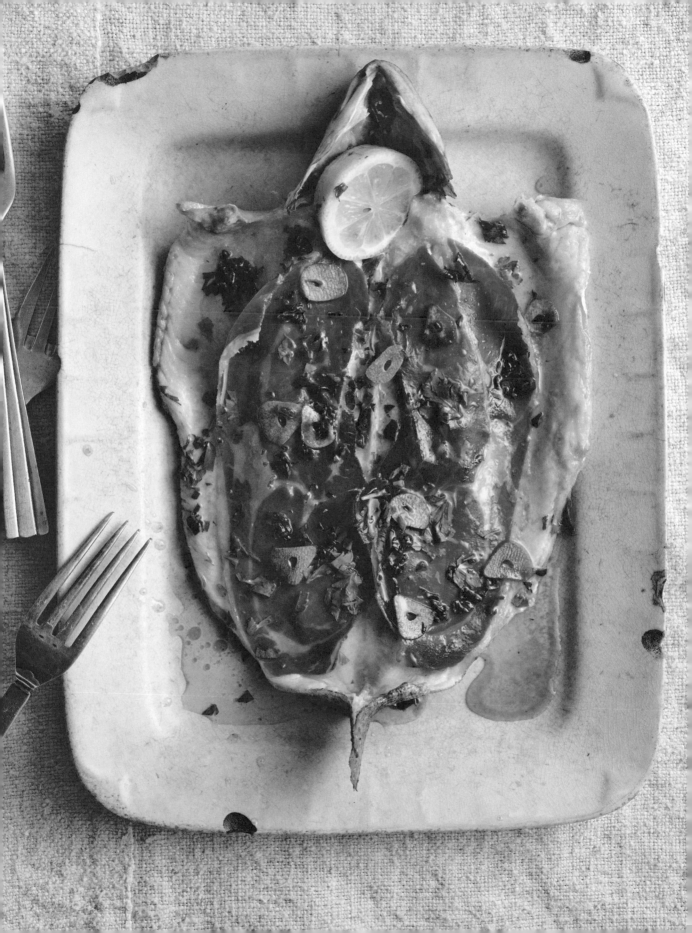

Squid in its ink

TXIPIRONES EN SU TINTA

Squid in its ink, or *txipis tinta*, as the Basques affectionately call it, is the black pearl of Basque cuisine. Shiny and completely opaque, a proper ink sauce should be as black as night, rich and sweet from slow-cooked onions, and disorienting in its richness.

When Eder was a child, this was the dish that made him want to be a cook. I remember that when he taught me how to make it, I ended up splattered with ink, with black beauty marks on my temples and with dark lines in the cracks of my rough kitchen hands. Still, every time I make this sauce I feel the excitement of discovering Basque cooking.

One of the keys to making the sauce is to taste and then retaste it. If it is too sweet, it will lack complexity. If it isn't sweet enough, it will lack that elusive quality redolent of both earth and sea. But don't give up—or serve it—until you've tweaked it to perfection. | SERVES 4 TO 6

SQUID

4 pounds whole medium-size squid, or 2 pounds cleaned squid

4 cups squid ink sauce (page 31)

Extra-virgin olive oil

RICE

2 tablespoons extra-virgin olive oil

½ cup minced Spanish onion

1 teaspoon kosher salt

2 flat-leaf parsley sprigs

1 clove garlic, smashed

1½ cups Bomba rice

3 cups water

CONTINUED

If using whole squid, clean the squid as directed on page 172, cutting the bodies into rings. Leave the tentacles whole. (You can simmer the wings to make a tasty stock for the rice.) Cover and refrigerate the squid until needed. If you have purchased cleaned squid, cut as directed for the cleaned whole squid.

To cook the squid, pour the sauce into a saucepan and bring to a bare simmer over medium-low heat. While it is warming, heat a large frying pan over medium heat and coat it with oil lightly. When the oil is hot, working in batches, add the squid and sauté for about 45 seconds, until cooked through. Transfer to a large bowl.

When all of the squid has been sautéed, transfer it to the simmering sauce with any juices it has released and braise gently for 20 to 40 minutes, until tender but still snappy, or what I call squid's "second point of tenderness."

While the squid braises, cook the rice. In a saucepan, combine the oil, onion, and salt and sweat the onion over medium heat for about 4 minutes, until translucent. Raise the heat to medium-high, add the parsley and garlic, and stir for about 2 minutes, until the garlic

Squid in its ink

is golden and the parsley is wilted, being careful not to let the onion brown. Add the rice and stir to coat with the oil. Add the water (or squid wing stock) and bring to a boil. Turn down the heat to a simmer, stir the rice once, cover, and then turn down the heat to low and cook for about 12 minutes, until the rice is tender.

Remove from the heat and let rest, uncovered, for 1 to 2 minutes. Stir the rice with a fork to release the excess steam. Place a small scoop of rice on each plate and pool the squid and sauce around the rice. Finish with a bit of olive oil, if you'd like. Eder's aunt simmers free-range eggs in leftover sauce to dazzling effect. So don't waste any leftovers.

CLEANING SQUID

Rinse the squid with cold running water. Working with 1 squid at a time, hold the head with one hand and the body with the other and gently pull the head from the body. Cut off the tentacles from the head just below the eyes and discard the head and the attached innards. Remove the beak from the base of the tentacles and discard the beak. Set the tentacles aside.

Gently pull off the "wings" near the base of each squid body, or tube, and then peel off the thin colored skin covering the wings and set them aside. Insert your index finger into the tube and pull out the plastic-like "quill" and any remaining innards. Peel off and discard the skin covering the outside of the tube until the tube is completely white. Rinse the tubes inside and out, the wings, and the tentacles thoroughly under cold running water.

Depending on the recipe, the squid bodies will either be cut into rings or snipped with scissors, scored, and then cut into squares. Cover and refrigerate the tentacles, wings, and bodies until needed.

Chilled Dungeness crab with Sichuan pepper salt and green peppercorn mayonnaise

BUEY DE MAR

Eating simply boiled seafood at room temperature is a Basque tradition. Here, Eder and I add just enough flavor to make it fun without masking the natural perfection and sweetness of the crab. My friend Henry Doane in Madison, Wisconsin, made the best crab cakes I've ever eaten. When I first tasted them, I was thrilled to realize that what I thought were capers studding the cakes were actually green peppercorns. Twenty years later, that light-bulb moment still informs my cooking, and green peppercorns remain my go-to secret weapon for crab cakes.

| SERVES 4 AS A MAIN COURSE OR 8 AS A STARTER

¼ cup kosher salt

2 tablespoons Sichuan peppercorns

1 star anise pod

4 live Dungeness crabs, about 2 pounds each

2 cups green peppercorn mayonnaise (page 23)

In a small dry pan, toast the salt and Sichuan peppercorns over medium heat, shaking the pan often, for about 30 seconds, until just aromatic. Transfer to a spice grinder, let cool, and grind to a fine powder.

In a large pot, combine the pepper-salt mixture with enough water to cover the crabs. Add the star anise and bring the water to a boil over high heat. Add the crabs head first, and when the water returns to a boil, turn down the heat to a simmer and cook the crabs for about 20 minutes, until they turn red. Transfer the crabs to 1 or 2 baking sheets and cool at room temperature for 20 minutes. Cover and refrigerate until serving or for up to 6 hours.

To clean and crack each crab, turn the crab on its back and lift up and remove the "apron" (triangular flap). Turn the crab belly down and lift off the top shell. Drain off the liquid from the shell, then scoop out any golden crab butter and reserve for true crab lovers. Remove and discard the exposed gills and mandible. Using a cleaver or heavy knife, cut the crab body into quarters, capturing any juices to fold into the mayonnaise. Crack the legs gently with a mallet, the back of the cleaver, or crab or nut crackers. Serving crabs is a messy job, so I recommend that you cover your table with newspaper or an oilcloth and then serve the crabs and mayonnaise family style, saving some of the top shells for serving the mayonnaise.

Salt cod in pil pil sauce

BAKALAO AL PIL PIL

3 cloves garlic, thinly sliced

3 cups extra-virgin Arbequina or other delicately flavored Spanish olive oil, or as needed

4 (4-ounce) pieces skin-on quick salt-cured cod (page 142)

½ teaspoon water

¼ teaspoon kosher salt

½ dry red árbol chile or guindilla pepper, thinly sliced or crumbled

This elusive, iconic Basque dish is a lesson in food science and sauce making. When done well, it is also the most elegant dish I have ever seen or tasted, but when prepared without care or with less than extraordinary ingredients, it can easily be off-putting. You must watch, listen, and learn from your mistakes with this dish. You will become one with it only when you have made it a dozen times and have learned your way around everything that can go wrong with it. But don't worry: you can make all kinds of things from broken *pil pil*. I have made a career of it.

With only three main ingredients, this dish is monochromatic, delicate, and minimalist. Before you begin, there are a couple of things you need to know. First, this dish is not served hot. It is served warm, which is when food is at its height of flavor, making it the ideal temperature for this delicately flavored sauce and neutral fish. Second, this dish is all about gelatin conservation and retention. That means you cannot cook the cod on heat that is too high or the gelatin will break down, or on heat that is too low or the gelatin inside the fish will not weep into the oil, which you need to have happen to *realizar*, or "realize," the sauce, as the Basques like to say. Fortunately, if you fail to control the heat properly, you can usually turn your mistake into a new dish. For example, if your cod is cooked at too high a temperature and becomes overly flaky, or you oversimmer the sauce and destroy its gelatin, you can always pour off the excess oil, combine the remains with the cod flakes, and stuff the mixture into green peppers. | SERVES 4

Line a small plate with a paper towel. In a 3- to 4-inch-deep pot or pan large enough to accommodate all 4 pieces of the fish in a single layer, warm the garlic and 1½ cups of the oil over medium-high heat and stir for about 45 seconds, until the garlic turns lightly golden and crispy. Using a slotted spoon, transfer the garlic to the paper-lined plate.

Add the remaining 1½ cups oil to the pan to cool the oil in the pan slightly, then nestle the cod pieces in the oil skin side up so they are

CONTINUED

Salt cod in pil pil sauce

CONTINUED

completely submerged, adding oil if needed. Place the pan over low heat and poach the cod for about 8 minutes, until barely cooked. The heat should be consistent, and you should see the fish purging little globules of gelatin into the oil. The fish is ready if it flakes slightly when prodded with the tip of a spoon. Using a slotted spatula, gently transfer the fish to a plate and tent with aluminum foil to keep warm.

Let the oil cool for 5 minutes, then pour almost all of it into a large heatproof measuring cup. At the bottom of the pan you will see a milky substance that beads in the small amount of remaining oil. This is the gelatin; pour that magic juice into a small bowl and add the water and salt.

Carefully transfer the cod pieces to 4 warmed plates. Add the juice that seeped out of the fish onto the plate to the pan juice in the bowl. Slowly add the warm oil to the pan juice mixture, whisking vigorously to form an emulsion, until you have an opaque, yellow, shimmery sauce with the viscosity of a velvety Chinese cornstarch-based sauce. You may not need all of the oil. The remainder can be recycled into mashed potatoes or mayonnaise or, if you become obsessed, you can use it in your next batch of pil pil.

Top the cod generously with the pil pil sauce and garnish with the reserved garlic chips and a slice or two of chile. Serve warm.

Poached monkfish with garlic soup

RAPE EN ADOBO CON SOPA DE AJO

1 cup kosher salt

10 cups water

2 (1¼-pound) boneless monkfish loins (or a little bigger), trimmed of any silver skin

3 cups fish stock (page 28) or water

5 flat-leaf parsley sprigs, plus chopped parsley, for garnish

4 dried choricero or guajillo peppers, tops trimmed off and seeds shaken out

3 tablespoons plus 2 teaspoons sweet smoked Spanish paprika

½ cup plus 6 tablespoons extra-virgin olive oil, plus more for drizzling

6 cloves garlic, thinly sliced

8 (1-inch-thick) slices day-old baguette, cut on the bias

Country bread, for serving

This recipe contradicts something that Eder taught me a long time ago. "French and American cooks are always treating fish like meat," he would say. "Basque cooks would never do that." Perhaps this recipe is borne of my American inclinations, though I would argue that in this particular case, the fish is meat. Monkfish, called *rape* (pronounced rah-pé) in Spain, is popular in soups in the Basque Country, where it is also called *sapo*. In this recipe, I treat it like the Paprika-Marinated Pork Loin Roast on page 226 and serve the soup, which is a variation on the garlic soup on page 192, underneath.

The recipe yields eight servings. You can slice one loin and chill the other for later use, as it will keep well in the refrigerator for up to 4 days. Or, you can make the recipe ahead to serve for a special occasion; its dramatic presentation makes it a great dinner-party dish. | SERVES 8

Make a brine by combining the salt and water in a large bowl or other vessel and then stir to dissolve the salt. Add the monkfish to the brine and let stand for 30 minutes. Meanwhile, begin preparing the remaining ingredients.

To make the soup, in a saucepan, combine the stock, parsley sprigs, and choricero peppers and bring to a bare simmer over medium-high heat. Turn down the heat to medium and simmer for 5 minutes. Remove from the heat and let steep for 20 minutes.

Strain the stock through a fine-mesh strainer into a large bowl, leaving the solids behind to settle at the bottom of the saucepan. Remove the peppers from the pan and, when cool enough to handle, use a spoon to scrape out their pulp into a bowl. Discard the skins.

Add 2 teaspoons of the paprika and ½ cup of the oil to the chile pulp and whisk to combine. Add 3 cups of the strained stock, mix well, and keep warm. (Or, let cool, cover, and refrigerate for up to 1 day.)

Line a plate with paper towels. In a small saucepan, heat 3 tablespoons of the remaining oil over medium-low heat. Add the garlic

CONTINUED

Poached monkfish with garlic soup

CONTINUED

and cook, stirring, for about 40 seconds, until golden brown and crisp. Using a slotted spoon, transfer the garlic to the towel-lined plate. Raise the heat to medium, add the baguette slices to the oil remaining in the pan, and toast, turning once, for about 2 minutes total, until golden on both sides. Set the bread aside with the garlic chips.

To finish the monkfish, fill a large rondeau or deep saucepan halfway with water and heat the water to 140°F. Remove the fish from its brine and pat dry. In a small bowl, mix together the remaining 3 tablespoons each oil and paprika until thoroughly combined. Rub half of the mixture evenly onto each piece of the fish and tightly wrap each piece in plastic wrap. Wrap each piece in a second layer of plastic wrap, holding both ends of the plastic wrap and rolling the fish forward so it resembles a large wrapped candy or sausage. The tapered end of the loin should now appear to be about the same thickness as the thicker end of the loin. Wrap each piece of the fish in aluminum foil, sealing securely.

Place a rack in the bottom of the rondeau. Place the fish packets on the rack and top them with a large, flat plate to keep them from floating in the water. Cook for 45 minutes. Check the temperature of the water occasionally to make sure it is consistently 140°F. Remove the packets from the pan and let cool for 20 minutes at room temperature.

To serve, carefully unwrap the fish, reserving the juices that drip out of the packets. Using a very sharp knife, slice each loin into 4 large scallops, applying as little pressure as possible to avoid flaking the fish. Add the reserved juices to the soup a little at a time, tasting as you go, as the juices will increase the salt level.

Place a toasted baguette slice in the bottom of each bowl. Place the fish on top of the bread and top with a few garlic chips and some chopped parsley. Pour the warm soup around the bread. Drizzle each serving with oil and pass the country bread at the table.

Butterflied bream

BESUGUITO A LA ESPALDA

Basques like bream (*besugo*) and hold it in the highest regard. Here in the United States, its closest available cousin is the Japanese snapper, or *tai*. American restaurants use lots of daurade, which is great, but we like porgies for their value, abundance, and sustainability. We encourage you to make the most of your local fish; when making this dish, you want a firm, white-fleshed fish of extreme freshness. *A la espalda* means "butterflied" and is the most common way to eat grilled fish in the Basque Country. Juicy and unadulterated, it makes an ideal pairing for a great *refrito de ajo*. | SERVES 4

2 (2-pound) whole porgies or daurades or small to medium Japanese snappers, scaled and butterflied by your fishmonger

Kosher salt

⅔ cup extra-virgin olive oil, plus more for searing

6 large cloves garlic, thinly sliced

3 tablespoons coarsely chopped fresh flat-leaf parsley

1 to 2 tablespoons Garnacha wine vinegar or sherry vinegar

1 guindilla pepper or dried árbol chile, thinly sliced or crumbled

Preheat the oven to 450°F.

Season the fish inside and out with salt. Coat the skin side with oil. Heat a cast-iron frying pan or other ovenproof frying pan over medium-high heat. Add enough oil to coat the bottom of the pan lightly and when the oil begins to smoke, add 1 fish, skin side down and splayed open. Cook, shaking the pan back and forth constantly to ensure the fish doesn't stick, for about 2 minutes, until the skin is lightly crisped. Slide the fish onto a large baking sheet and repeat the previous steps in the frying pan with the second fish, then slide it onto the baking sheet. Bake the fish for about 4 minutes; the fish should be white but it should not contract dramatically, and the center should be just firm.

While the fish are baking, combine the ⅔ cup oil and garlic in a small saucepan, place over medium heat, and heat for about 40 seconds, until the garlic is barely golden, about 40 seconds. Remove from the heat and add the parsley and a pinch of salt.

Serve the fish family style, adding a splash of vinegar to each fish and spooning the garlic-herb oil over the top. Garnish with the chile slices.

Hake fried in golden egg wash with sweet red peppers

MERLUZZA A LA ROMANA CON PIMIENTOS ASADOS

When I first encountered *a la romana*, I thought it was the most technique-deficient fish fry I had ever seen. "Why," I asked myself, "are the Basques hell-bent on frying something that won't become crispy?" But I have now turned 180 degrees on this dish, which renders delicate fish soft and luxurious and marries the Basques' love of eggs with their love of olive oil. | SERVES 4

3 roasted red bell peppers (page 38), cut lengthwise into 1/4-inch-wide ribbons

Canola oil, for coating

Kosher salt

1/3 cup extra-virgin olive oil, plus more for frying

4 cloves garlic, smashed

1 1/4 pounds skinless hake fillet, cut into 4 equal pieces

1/2 cup all-purpose flour

3 eggs

1 teaspoon sherry vinegar

Place the peppers and their juices in a small saucepan. Add the olive oil, 1/2 teaspoon salt, and 1 garlic clove and simmer over low heat for about 15 minutes, until the peppers are tender and sweet. Remove from the heat and let the pepper cool completely in the oil.

Season the fish with a moderate amount of salt. If you are working with pieces that are 1 1/4 inches thick or thicker, let them stand for 6 minutes. If you are working with the tail or thinner pieces, let them stand for 3 minutes. Pat the fish dry. Make sure it is at room temperature before proceeding to the next steps.

Pour the olive oil to a depth of 1 inch into a deep frying pan and heat over medium-low heat. The oil is ready if when you dip the handle of a wooden spoon into it, the oil sizzles around it. Do not allow the oil to reach its smoke point, as it would be too hot. Line a plate with paper towels. Spread the flour on a plate. Crack the eggs into a bowl, beat lightly, and season with salt. One at a time, coat the fish pieces evenly with the flour, then the egg, then carefully slip the fish pieces into the hot oil and fry for 1 to 1 1/2 minutes on the first side, until golden. Turn the fish over, add the remaining 3 garlic cloves to the pan, and cook the fish for 1 to 1 1/2 minutes longer. You want a golden, lacy omelet to form on the outside of each piece. Using the spatula, transfer the fish and garlic to the towel-lined plate and season the fish lightly with salt. Let rest for 2 minutes. Add the vinegar to the reserved peppers them, stir well, then divide the peppers with some of their oil evenly among 4 plates. Place the fish on top of the peppers and serve immediately.

6 | Putxero, Sopa, and Potaje

SOUPS AND STEWS FOR ALL SEASONS

In the Basque Country, stews aren't only eaten when it's cold outside. They're enjoyed all year-round as practical one-pot meals. The primal simplicity of their preparation—combine a bunch of ingredients in a pot, let them simmer, and you've got a meal—is echoed in how they're eaten: you're hunched over a bowl, pushing food into a spoon with a chunk of bread ripped from a loaf. The Basques hold these spoon foods in very high regard.

Included in this family of stew dishes are variations of stews, or *guisos*: *sopas*, *potajes*, *putxeros*, and *sulkakis*. The act of cooking is often described by the infinitive *guisar*, or "to stew." "*Que van a guisar?*" someone might ask when they want to know what's for dinner.

Sopas are mostly liquid, or sometimes passed through a food mill or whirled in a blender like *pure de verduras*, the pureed vegetable soup eaten almost daily around the Basque Country. *Zurruktuna*, a humble brothy garlic-fish soup with incredible depth of flavor, is another popular *sopa*. *Potajes*, on the other hand, are typically chunky and unblended. They often contain beans, and they sometimes include meat as a condiment or garnish to flavor the beans. *Garbanzos de vigilia*, a Lenten chickpea stew endowed with salt cod and Swiss chard, is an extremely tasty example of the form, as is *lentejas*, a warming, satisfying dish built on a lusty foundation of earthy lentils.

Beans, potatoes, or squashes are at the center of any good *putxero*, a chunky stew usually served with meat or fish, still in a supportive role as in a *potaje*, though a more generous one. For me, these stews provide yet another connection between the Basque Country and my Argentine heritage: *puchero* is the national dish of Argentina. Although the ingredients you use in Argentine *pucheros* differ slightly from what you find in their Basque Country cousins—Argentine versions often contain corn and are served in a pumpkin—they are essentially the same dish. I grew up eating *pucheros* all winter long in Minnesota, where my mom cooked up large batches and cleverly froze them on the back porch.

Putxeros (spelled *pucheros* elsewhere in Spain) are unique in that they are enjoyed throughout the country, not just the Basque Country, and they seem to be a legacy of Jewish Sabbath cooking. What distinguishes the Basque versions are their use of the choricero pepper, the quality and diversity of the beans, and the rigorous discrimination with which they're prepared, with every ingredient added in the correct order to achieve the desired textures and flavors.

Because *putxeros* usually rely on a tasty broth or other cooking liquid, they are often eaten in three stages: the broth or soup first, followed by the beans, and then finally the meat. *Alubias con sacramentos*, a red bean–based stew served with pickled green peppers and mixed meat, is a typical *putxero*, as is *garbure*, a Basque-style minestrone with lardons. The name *putxero* also refers to the pot used to produce the stew. Usually made from iron, they traditionally have three little legs and look like the pots used by cartoon hobos. In the past, railroad laborers would bring them to work for cooking their meals over charcoal fires. Nowadays, people haul their *putxeros* along on camping trips, even though they are heavy and unwieldy. But once you taste a *putxero*, you'll understand why people go through the hassle: rich, textured, and enormously satisfying, *putxeros* are comfort food for the ages. And despite their cold-weather suitability, they can be tailored to the seasons: when *garbure* is served tepid, for example, it makes a wonderful bed for warm or cold poached fish.

The last category of Basque stew is *sukalki*, a hearty braised meat dish that is usually made with beef, lamb, or veal shank. Here, meat is the main event and vegetables are used to make the sauce. Its name is a nod to the monumental importance of cooking in Basque culture: *sua* means "fire," and refers to the hearth. The Basques say that the hearth is the heartbeat of the family, and in many legends, the family shrivels if the fire goes out, so stoking the fire and long-cooking methods go together.

Old-fashioned simmering is easy for the stay-at-home cook or for a Sunday supper, but you can make even the longest cooking of these simmered dishes quicker than you think. How? With a pressure cooker, aka *olla a presión*. I'm a huge fan of this steam pressure–fueled appliance. Its powers to reduce cooking time are almost unparalleled, and the creaminess it imparts to beans is the stuff of legend. Most Basque homes have at least one pressure cooker; some even have a set of nesting pressure cookers.

I urge you to buy one: not only will you be able to cook rice in two minutes and lentils in seven, but you'll also be able to make all of the stews in this chapter with minimum time and effort and maximum flavor. If you are ready to invest in a pressure cooker, look for a medium-size one (six quart) rather than a larger one. The best and fanciest pressure cookers are Swiss, but you can find good-quality options in Chinatowns, too. That said, you certainly don't need a pressure cooker to make these recipes. You just need to give them your care and patience, to build a relationship with them like you would any other food, and they will repay you lavishly.

Lentils with chorizo

LENTEJAS CON CHORIZO

STEW

4 cups green lentils

1 (2-inch) chunk dry-cured chorizo or jamón end, or a combination

½ Spanish onion, unpeeled

1 head garlic, unpeeled, with the top cut off to expose the cloves

½ carrot, peeled

3 lemon thyme sprigs, or 2 regular thyme sprigs

Kosher salt

GARNISH

½ cup extra-virgin olive oil, plus more for finishing

¾ cup minced Spanish or red onion

1 large leek, white and light green parts only, minced

1 fresh bay leaf, or ½ dried bay leaf

Kosher salt

1 carrot, peeled and cut into small dice

1 cup minced dry-cured chorizo, jamón serrano, or jamón ibérico

½ teaspoon sherry vinegar

Lentils are Eder and our daughter Maayan's favorite thing in the world. (She actually wants them for breakfast.) This recipe will make them yours, too. Many Basques add a little potato to the lentils, but I prefer to bind them with the vegetables. Look for small greenish-brown Spanish Pardina lentils or slate green Le Puy lentils from France. | SERVES 6 TO 8

To make the stew, rinse the lentils and place them in a bowl. Add water just to cover and let stand for 5 minutes. Drain and discard the water.

In a saucepan, combine the lentils, chorizo, onion, garlic, carrot, and thyme. Add water to cover by 3 to 4 inches, season with salt, and bring to a boil over medium-high heat. Turn down the heat to a simmer that will cook the lentils and vegetables without reducing the liquid. Cook for about 15 minutes, until the lentils and vegetables are tender.

Meanwhile, prepare the garnish. In a small saucepan, combine the oil, onion, leek, and bay leaf, season with salt, and place over medium heat. Cook, stirring often, for about 10 minutes, until the onion and leek are translucent. Do not allow them to caramelize. Add the carrot and continue to cook for 5 minutes. Add the chorizo and cook for about 1 minute, until just warmed through. Finish with a splash of vinegar.

Remove the lentils and vegetables from the heat. Pick out the onion, carrot, garlic head, and thyme and discard the garlic and thyme. Peel the onion and place it in a blender with the carrot and some of the cooking liquid. Puree until smooth, then fold the puree into the lentils.

This dish can be served two ways: Fold the garnish into the lentils, taste and adjust the seasoning, and serve hot, drizzled with oil. Or, for a fancier presentation, divide the garnish among warmed individual bowls, piling it in the center, and then spoon the lentils around the garnish and drizzle with the oil.

Winter broth finished with manzanilla sherry

SALDA

8 cups double chicken stock (page 26)

Kosher salt

2 (½-inch-thick) slices Spanish onion, rings kept together

3 egg whites

2 tablespoons hand-crushed canned tomato, or 1 plum tomato, halved lengthwise, seeded, grated on the medium-coarse holes of a box grater, and skin discarded

1 cup diced jamón ibérico, for garnish (optional)

Cooked fresh or thawed frozen shelled English peas, for garnish (optional)

1 cup manzanilla or fino sherry

½ cup chopped mixed fresh herbs (such as flat-leaf parsley, lemon thyme, and mint)

Croutons (recipe follows), for garnish (optional)

On wintry, damp evenings and afternoons in the Basque Country, the fogged windows of bars and restaurants reveal signs propped on the sills. *Hay Caldo*! they say in Spanish. *Salda Dago*! they say in Basque. (We have broth!) Inside, double-handled mugs of warm broth are served to a colorful blur of people who peel off their layers as they enter and then settle into the warm, inviting surroundings. At the best places, the broth is dispensed from a beautiful samovar. I love this tradition. The bartender places the steaming cup before you, tops it off with a tipple of sherry or more commonly white wine, and the aromas flow. Then a small terrine of *pica tostes* (fried croutons) comes around; you can plop in a few, though I prefer not to. At Txikito, we serve this broth, also known as *caldito*, in the spring and winter. Its light elegance is a metaphor for the simplicity of Basque food and the good life. We clarify ours like a classic consommé to be both extra fancy and to show respect for the tradition. Although you don't have to clarify the broth, I think it's pretty magical to learn the principles of consommé. If you are a vegetarian, consider cooking some delicious garbanzo beans with leek and onion for another dish and stealing the broth for sipping, *salda* style, with a splash of sherry. | SERVES 4 TO 6

In a 4-quart pot, heat the broth to a bare simmer over medium-high heat and season to taste with salt. Meanwhile, without the use of any fat or oil, sear the onion slices on both sides in a dry cast-iron frying pan, pressing down on them to make sure each side makes full contact with the pan, for 3 to 5 minutes on each side, until black. Transfer to a cutting board and chop coarsely.

In a bowl, whisk the egg whites with a pinch of salt until foamy. Add the tomato and charred onion.

While whisking continuously, gradually add about 1 cup of the warm broth to the egg white mixture to temper the whites. Then add a second cup of broth, whisking until incorporated. Transfer the tempered egg whites to the rest of the broth, return the broth to the barest simmer, and stir gently, scraping the bottom of the pot, until the egg whites gather on the surface. Turn the heat down, making sure the broth doesn't begin to boil. The egg whites will clarify your broth and the onion will give it a sweet flavor and golden color.

Meanwhile, line a strainer with a damp coffee filter or wet paper towel and place it over a pot large enough to accommodate the broth.

When the onion is soft and the broth has turned golden, after about 15 minutes, using a slotted spoon or spider, carefully lift off the whites from the surface and discard. Strain the broth through the prepared strainer into the pot. Stir in the jamón and peas, place over medium heat, and heat the broth until piping hot. Add the sherry and herbs, stir well, and then serve in beautiful bowls or mugs with the croutons on the side.

Croutons | PICA TOSTES

MAKES 2 CUPS

Extra-virgin olive oil, for frying

2 cups cut-up crustless rustic white bread, in ½-inch pieces

1 tablespoon unsalted butter

Kosher salt

Line a plate with paper towels. Pour the oil to a depth of about ¾ inch into a small saucepan and heat over medium-low heat. When the oil is hot, add the bread all at once and stir for about 2 minutes, until light golden. Add the butter and stir until the pieces are an even light brown.

Using a slotted spoon, transfer the croutons to the towel-lined plate and season while still hot with salt. Let cool before serving. Discard the oil or use it to fry eggs.

Garlic soup with torn salt cod

ZURRUKUTUNA

This fish-enhanced garlic soup is the humblest soup in this chapter and also one of the most flavorful. It calls for *pan sopako,* a nearly burnt, hard bread that is made especially for thickening the garlic-and-water base, much like a ship's biscuit would. Revived by the broth and salt cod, this baked-to-be-stale bread is transformed into the Basque answer to chowder. At Txikito, in spring, we amplify its garlicky goodness with ramp greens; the rest of the year, we use Chinese garlic chives or flowering chives. It also benefits from the addition of a rich yellow pastured egg yolk, stirred in at the end for a velvety effect. It is a pantry meal par excellence, one that has inspired many an elevated dish at the restaurant, like the monkfish recipe on page 177. | SERVES 6 TO 8

½ cup extra-virgin olive oil

6 cloves garlic, sliced paper-thin

6 to 8 (1-inch-thick) slices day-old baguette, cut on the bias

½ cup thinly sliced Chinese garlic chives or ramp leaves

2 tablespoons plus 2 teaspoons sweet smoked Spanish paprika

1 tablespoon choricero pepper paste (page 39)

3 cups fish stock (page 28)

Kosher salt

2 cups torn quick salt-cured cod, in ¼-inch flakes (page 142)

6 to 8 eggs, at room temperature

Chopped fresh flat-leaf parsley, for garnish

Line a plate with paper towels. In a small saucepan, combine the oil and garlic over medium-low heat and cook, stirring, for about 40 seconds, until the garlic is golden brown and crisp. Using a slotted spoon, transfer the garlic to the towel-lined plate. Raise the heat to medium-high, add the baguette slices to the oil remaining in the pan, and toast, turning once, for about 3 minutes total, until medium-dark brown on both sides. Set the bread aside with the garlic chips.

Turn down the heat to low, add the garlic chives, and cook, stirring occasionally, for about 3 minutes, until wilted. Whisk in the paprika and pepper paste, mixing well. Stir in the stock and season with salt. Add the cod and poach for about 40 seconds, until white and flaky.

To serve, place a toasted bread slice in the bottom of each bowl. Pour the garlic broth around the bread and top the bread with some fried garlic. Working quickly, separate the eggs one at a time and place a yolk on each piece of toast. Discard the whites or save for another use. Ladle more broth over the top, garnish with parsley, and serve immediately.

Pureed leek and onion soup

PORRUSALDA

The Japanese and the Basques have a similar approach when it comes to food. Here, a rustic leek soup usually made with salt cod gets an elegant spin with daikon taking the place of potato and dashi the place of cod. Despite these Japanese flourishes, the soup is still very Basque in its celebration of a singular ingredient. | SERVES 6 TO 8

5 leeks, white and light green parts only

3 Spanish onions, cut into small dice

½ bay leaf

Kosher salt

⅔ cup extra-virgin olive oil, plus 3 tablespoons, for finishing

2 cups sake or mirin

1 cup peeled daikon, cut into ½-inch dice

1 tablespoon unsalted butter

4 cups Hondashi or other instant dashi, prepared according to package directions, or fish stock (page 28)

Score the leeks lengthwise, cutting through the top 3 or 4 layers. Remove the outer layers and set aside the hearts. Slice the outer layers lengthwise into narrow ribbons, then rinse well and transfer to a pressure cooker or saucepan.

Add the onions, bay leaf, a pinch of salt, and ⅓ cup of the oil to the sliced leeks, cover, and cook until the vegetables are meltingly tender but without color. This should take 6 minutes if using a pressure cooker and about 20 minutes in a saucepan over medium-low heat. Add the sake and simmer uncovered over low heat for 5 minutes. Add the daikon and cook over low heat until it has softened to a pale, mushy consistency, about 7 minutes.

While the soup is cooking, prepare the leek heart garnish: Cut the reserved leek hearts on the bias into 1-inch diamond-shaped pieces. In a small saucepan, heat ⅓ cup oil over medium-low heat. Add the leek hearts and salt them generously. Add the butter, cover the pan with a piece of parchment paper or loose aluminum foil, and braise over low heat for about 10 minutes, until tender.

Now, return to the vegetables. Remove and discard the bay leaf and let the vegetables cool slightly. Working in batches, transfer the vegetables to a blender and puree until very smooth. Pour the puree into a clean saucepan, place over medium-low heat, and whisk in the dashi. Heat until hot, then taste and adjust the seasoning with salt.

To serve, divide the leek hearts evenly among warmed bowls, placing them in the center. Ladle the hot soup around them and then drizzle with the remaining 3 tablespoons oil. Serve immediately.

Braised flat beans and potato stew

VAINAS Y PATATAS

I first had this dish on a misty day in Getxo, a seaside community in the Bizkaia region. While surfers were riding the waves outside, I was warm and happy indoors eating an amazingly tender and delicious two-tone army-green stew. I don't think Eder understood what a revelation this dish was for someone who had been eating al dente vegetables for way too long. It was so romantic to be enjoying that view with a new love and finding more and more things to love about his culture and landscape. Called *shirimiri* in Basque, that misty weather defines the maritime climate that makes stew eating so inviting year-round. Even light vegetable-based braises enfold you in a Basque hug.

Carola potatoes, with their golden, firm, creamy flesh, are a good choice here. Cut them into rough chunks with a paring knife. This allows the starch to be released and act as a secondary thickener. Flat, broad romano beans tend to be sweeter and more tender than green beans. But if you can't find them, green beans are an acceptable substitute. | SERVES 6 TO 8

1 pound fresh or frozen romano beans or fresh green beans, thawed if frozen

Kosher salt

6 good-quality boiling potatoes

¼ cup extra-virgin olive oil

6 cloves garlic, sliced paper-thin

2 teaspoons sherry vinegar, or more to taste

Chopped fresh flat-leaf parsley, for garnish

If using romano beans, trim and then cut them on the bias into large pieces. If using green beans, trim and then cut them on the bias into medium-size pieces.

Pour water to a depth of about 3 inches into a saucepan and season with salt. Peel the potatoes. Then, working over the water, use a paring knife to break off 2-inch chunks of potato, so that each potato is broken into about 6 pieces. Once you've worked your way through all of the potatoes, check to make sure they are almost covered with water, then place over high heat and bring to a boil. Turn down the heat to a simmer, add the beans, and season with a little salt. Cook for 12 to 20 minutes, until the vegetables are tender and the broth is foggy.

In a small saucepan, combine the oil and garlic over medium-high heat and cook, stirring, for about 40 seconds, until the garlic is barely golden. Carefully add the vinegar to the sizzling garlic oil and then immediately pour the mixture into the stew. Stir to mix well, garnish with parsley, and serve.

Pureed vegetable soup

PURE DE VERDURAS

Thick, warming *sopas* of pureed vegetables or legumes are the most common counterparts to *potajes* (chunkier, brothy vegetable stews like *vainas y patatas*). The names of these soups often begin with *crema de*, even though they contain no dairy, and instead owe their creamy consistency to a blender or a food mill. This soup makes a great beginning to a meal, particularly when sopped up with a heel of bread. | SERVES 6 TO 8

1 Spanish onion, cut into medium dice

6 tablespoons extra-virgin olive oil, plus more to coat and drizzle

Kosher salt

1 pound green beans, trimmed and cut into small pieces

1 butternut squash, halved, seeded, peeled, and cut into chunks

1 carrot, peeled and cut into chunks

6 cloves garlic, thinly sliced

Grated Roncal or other salty aged cheese, for garnish (optional)

In a large saucepan, combine the onion, 3 tablespoons of the oil, and a pinch of salt and sweat the onion over medium-low heat for about 15 minutes, until soft and translucent (without browning it). Add the beans, squash, and carrot and a little more oil to coat, season with salt, and sweat the vegetables for 6 to 8 minutes, until slightly softened.

Meanwhile, cut a circle of parchment paper slightly smaller than the diameter of the saucepan. When the vegetables have softened, add water to cover by 1 inch and more salt to balance the salt content of the cooking liquid and the vegetables. Raise the heat to medium and bring the water to a boil. Turn down the heat to a gentle simmer and cover the vegetables with the parchment to keep them submerged. Gently simmer the soup for about 40 minutes, until all of the vegetables are very tender.

Remove from the heat and pour into a strainer placed over a heatproof bowl. Transfer the vegetables in batches to a blender, pureeing until smooth and adding a little reserved cooking liquid if needed to reach your preferred consistency.

In a small saucepan, combine the remaining 3 tablespoons oil and the garlic and cook over medium heat, stirring, for 35 to 40 seconds, until golden brown. Remove from the heat and immediately pour into the blender with the last batch of vegetables. Whisk the batches together in a clean saucepan and heat over medium-low heat, stirring occasionally. Ladle into bowls and garnish with the cheese and a drizzle of oil.

Basque red beans with braised meats

ALUBIAS CON SACRAMENTOS

1 pound (2¼ cups) dried red beans, rinsed

1 large Spanish onion, unpeeled, ends cut off

1 leek, white and light green parts only

1 carrot, peeled

1 head garlic, unpeeled, top cut off

1 bay leaf

3 thyme sprigs

2 dried guajillo or choricero peppers, tops trimmed off and seeds shaken out, or 2 tablespoons choricero pepper paste (page 39)

1 small head Savoy cabbage, halved through the stem end

2 ounces jamón serrano or prosciutto ends

8 ounces pork belly, in one piece

1½ to 2 pounds baby back ribs, in one piece

Kosher salt

1 link (approximately 3 ounces) best-quality Spanish chorizo

CONTINUED

Every winter people go to Tolosa, a town in Gupuzkoa Province, to eat the new crop of dried red beans, which are served garnished with chorizo, blood sausage, and pork rib or belly. In the Basque Country, beans are a food fit for kings. At their best, they have thin skins, a creamy texture, and yield a sweet, dark liquor. The highest-quality beans can cost more per kilo than a fine cut of meat and are held in equal and sometimes higher regard. The best versions of *alubias de Tolosa* (beans of Tolosa) contain cabbage and, most crucially, are served with pickled green guindilla peppers, which are like Italian *peperoncini* but better.

At Txikito, we serve the meat and cabbage atop the beans, but at home we put the meat and cabbage on a platter and serve the beans on the side. We use *txistorra*, a thin rope–style fresh chorizo, but any good-quality dry cured or fresh Spanish chorizo will do (just fish it out when it's tender, or it will dry out). If you cannot find Spanish *morcilla*, or blood sausage, Argentine or Uruguayan blood sausage is a good substitute.

For the beans, we like Rancho Gordo's Rio Zape, Ayocote Negro, or Sangre de Toro, but scarlet runners also work well. Look for beans that are labeled "new crop" (from the current season) so they won't split and peel during cooking. I'm not a bean soaker, perhaps because I buy good beans that don't seem to need it. In the Basque Country, some cooks believe that beans that rest overnight after cooking provide better, more harmonious flavors. If you have a pressure cooker, this is a one-pot meal that you can make in an hour. If not, just let it bubble away gently as the recipe directs. | SERVES 6 TO 8

In a large stockpot, combine the beans, onion, leek, carrot, garlic, bay leaf, thyme, dried peppers or pepper paste, half of the cabbage, the jamón, the pork belly, and the ribs. Add 3 tablespoons of salt and water to cover by 6 inches. Bring to a boil over high heat, turn down the heat to a simmer, and taste and adjust the salt. Cook, skimming off any fat and impurities that rise to the surface, for about 1½ hours. Using a spider or 2 slotted spoons, remove the meats as they are done, being careful not to overcook them. The chorizo and blood sausage will take only 20 minutes to cook, so add them when the pork belly

Basque red beans with braised meats

CONTINUED

2 blood sausages (about 6 ounces total weight)

¼ cup extra-virgin olive oil

6 cloves garlic, sliced paper-thin

Pickled green guindilla peppers or peperoncini, for serving

and ribs are getting close to done. You know the ribs and belly are done if a bamboo skewer can be inserted without resistance but sticks a bit on the way out. Set the pork belly and ribs and both sausages aside to cool before cutting each into 6 to 8 pieces.

Continue to cook the beans, checking frequently and adding water as needed to keep them submerged. They may take as long as 3 hours total.

Meanwhile, bring a small saucepan of salted water to a boil. Cut the remaining cabbage half into narrow ribbons, add to the boiling water, and boil for about 10 minutes, until just tender. Drain well and set the cabbage aside on a plate. It can be served at room temperature or reheated.

When the beans are tender, remove and discard the cabbage, garlic, and jamón ends. Then remove the onion and carrot, peel the onion, and add the onion and carrot to a blender. Scoop out about 1 cup of beans from the pot and add to the blender along with about 1 cup of the bean broth. Puree until smooth. Return the puree to the rest of the beans; it will add body. If you have exceptional beans, you can leave them brothy and forego this step, simply discarding the onion and carrot. Continue to cook, stirring from time to time, for about 10 minutes, until the flavors are melded. Taste and adjust the seasoning with salt.

In a small saucepan, combine the oil and garlic over medium heat and cook, stirring, for about 40 seconds, until the garlic is just golden brown. Carefully stir half of the garlic and oil into the beans—it will sizzle—and pour the other half over the cabbage.

Serve the beans in warmed bowls and garnish with the reserved meats, pickled peppers, and cabbage. Or, serve the meats on the side, reheated in a little chicken stock in the microwave or in an aluminum foil–covered baking dish in a 300°F oven.

Lenten stew of chickpea and spinach with quick salt cod

GARBANZOS DE VIGILIA

CHICKPEAS

4 cups dried chickpeas, rinsed

1 head garlic, unpeeled, with the top cut off to expose the cloves

1 Spanish onion, halved

1 carrot, peeled and halved

Kosher salt

STEW

¼ cup extra-virgin olive oil

2 cloves garlic, thinly sliced

½ teaspoon sweet Spanish paprika

3 bunches spinach (about 1½ pounds), or young collards, stems trimmed and cut into narrow ribbons, or substitute 1½ pounds baby spinach

1 to 2 pounds quick salt-cured cod (page 142), torn by hand into small pieces

2 hard-boiled eggs (see page 115), peeled and chopped or sliced into thin wedges, for garnish (optional)

Every year around Lent, Eder's maternal grandmother, Eulalia, made great *garbanzos de vigilia,* a simple, mild stew that is a great illustration of the three-flavor rule: never emphasize more than three flavors at a time. In this case, that trio of flavors is sweet, creamy chickpeas, flaked salt cod, and freshly simmered greens. Since chickpeas are pretty much the entirety of this stew, you might wonder if you can use canned. You can, of course, but the whole point of this book is to get you cooking. You're welcome to substitute kale or even broccoli rabe for the collards and spinach. | SERVES 8

To cook the chickpeas, place them in a large saucepan or a pressure cooker and add the garlic, onion, carrot, and water to cover by 4 inches in the saucepan or 2 inches in the pressure cooker and season generously with salt. Place the saucepan over high heat until it boils, then reduce to a simmer. Cook, uncovered, topping off with hot water if needed. If using a pressure cooker, cover the beans, bring to full pressure, and then reduce the heat to medium-low. In both cases cook until the chickpeas are soft and creamy. This will take 60 to 65 minutes in the pressure cooker, or up to 3 hours on the stove.

Remove and discard the garlic. Remove the carrot, onion, ½ cup of the chickpeas, and about 1 cup of the liquid, transfer to a blender, and puree until smooth. Return the puree to the remaining chickpeas, stir well, and then taste and adjust the seasoning with salt. Remove from the heat. The chickpeas can be cooked up to 2 days in advance. Let cool, cover, and refrigerate until needed.

To make the stew, combine the oil and garlic in a large saucepan and heat over medium heat, stirring, for 35 to 40 seconds, until the garlic is just golden brown. Add the paprika and the cooked chickpeas and their liquid and bring to a simmer. Add the greens then fold in the cod. Serve in warmed bowls topped with the eggs.

White wine–braised rabbit

CONEJO A LA RIOJANA

3 pounds bone-in
rabbit legs, cut into
3-inch chunks

Kosher salt

Extra-virgin olive oil,
for frying

2 Spanish onions,
cut into 1-inch chunks

3 red bell peppers, seeded
and cut into 1-inch squares

1 bay leaf

1 green bell pepper,
seeded and thinly sliced
lengthwise

3 cloves garlic, minced

1 tablespoon sweet
Spanish paprika

¼ teaspoon cayenne
pepper

2 tablespoons
tomato paste

2 cups dry white wine

3 tablespoons chopped
flat-leaf parsley, plus
more for garnish

¼ cup diced dry-cured
chorizo (optional)

4 to 6 cups chicken stock,
homemade (page 26) or
store-bought

1 rabbit liver (optional)

1 teaspoon unsalted
butter (optional)

Everyone knows about Rioja's great wines, but when it comes to cooking *a la riojana*, it usually involves both wine and peppers. An unoaked Viura like an Ostatu white is great for a braise like this one, but any dry white wine you like will work. Whichever bottle you choose, be sure to sip while you cook.

This rabbit dish is warm and cozy but not too heavy. If you can't find rabbit, chicken thighs are a great, everyday substitution (use a couple of chicken livers in place of the rabbit liver). No matter which meat you use, remember that patience and care are the keys to any braise or stew, which should percolate along without ever reaching a hard boil.

I like to serve this stew with confit potatoes, but you can substitute your favorite mashed potato recipe. I recommend, however, that you replace any butter in the potato recipe with olive oil. | SERVES 4 TO 6

Season the rabbit generously with salt. Pour oil to a depth of about ¼ inch into a large, heavy enameled saucepan or Dutch oven and place over medium heat. When the oil is hot, in batches, add the rabbit, brown well on both sides, and transfer to a plate. Each batch should take about 8 minutes. If at any point you notice the browned bits left in the oil between batches are starting to burn, quickly pour off the oil into a heatproof container (discard when cooled), add ½ cup water to the saucepan, return the pan to the heat, and loosen any remaining bits with a wooden spoon or spatula. Reduce the liquid to a syrup. Pour the bits over the browned rabbit, wipe out the pan, add fresh oil to the pan, and continue browning the remaining meat.

In a food processor, combine the onions and red bell peppers and pulse about 15 times, until chopped but not watery. Drain the mixture in a strainer.

CONTINUED

White wine–braised rabbit

Wipe out the saucepan, pour in oil to a depth of about ¼ inch, and place over high heat. Add the onion and pepper mixture and sweat, stirring occasionally, for about 5 minutes, until dry. Add 1 teaspoon salt and the bay leaf, turn down the heat to medium-low, and cook, stirring occasionally, for about 15 minutes, until the mixture is soft and sweet. Add the green pepper and garlic and cook for 5 to 10 minutes, until wilted. Add the paprika and cayenne pepper, cook for 1 minute, and then stir in the tomato paste and cook for 2 minutes.

At this point, the mixture should have a nice marmalade-like consistency. Raise the heat to high, add the wine, and cook for about 8 minutes, until the alcohol cooks off and the wine is reduced by half. Turn down the heat to medium and nestle the browned rabbit pieces in the onion-pepper mixture. Scatter the coarsely chopped parsley and chorizo over the top. Pour in enough stock to almost cover the meat, then season with salt. Bring the stock to a gentle simmer, cover, and braise the rabbit, being careful not to let the liquid boil, for 45 to 60 minutes, until a skewer inserted into the thickest part of the meat goes in without resistance but still clings to the meat on the way out. Let the rabbit rest in the sauce off the heat for 45 minutes. Just before serving, heat the stew through gently.

Blend the rabbit liver and butter using a mortar and pestle, or finely chop the liver and butter and press them through a fine-mesh strainer.

Transfer the rewarmed rabbit pieces to a platter. Add the liver-butter mixture to the sauce remaining in the pan and heat gently, stirring, for 5 minutes, until thickened.

Pour the sauce over the rabbit, sprinkle with chopped parsley, and serve.

Basque ratatouille

PISTO

Pisto is the Basque version of ratatouille, a deeply flavorful stew of vegetables that peak in late summer and early fall. Hearty and healthy, it's incredibly versatile, as much a sauce as a stew: mix it with eggs and you have *pisto a la bilbaína* (page 130), with cod and you have *ajoarriero*, and with *bakalao al pil pil* and you have *bakalao Club Ranero*. It also makes an excellent partner for lamb. When I was a child, my mom often stuffed zucchini with a similar filling, so that's what we do at Txikito. | SERVES 6 TO 8

2 cups diced Spanish onion

Leaves from 5 marjoram sprigs

1 dried guindilla pepper or bird's-eye chile, or ⅛ teaspoon cayenne pepper

Extra-virgin olive oil, for cooking

Kosher salt

1 cup diced red bell pepper, in ¼-inch dice

1 cup diced green bell pepper, in ¼-inch dice

4 pounds zucchini (about 3 medium to large), halved lengthwise, then cut crosswise into ¼-inch-thick half-moons

2 tablespoons choricero pepper paste (page 39)

1 cup hand-crushed canned plum tomatoes and their juices, or ½ cup tomato sauce (page 36)

¼ teaspoon cayenne pepper or red pepper flakes

Preheat the oven to 500°F.

In a large saucepan, combine the onion, marjoram, chile, about 3 tablespoons oil, and ½ teaspoon salt and sweat the onion over low heat, stirring occasionally, for about 20 minutes, until soft, sweet, and translucent.

Meanwhile, in a large bowl, toss the red and green peppers and the zucchini with 3 to 4 tablespoons oil and 1 to 1½ teaspoons salt, making sure to salt the zucchini aggressively. Spread the vegetables on a large baking sheet and roast, stirring once at the halfway point, for 15 to 20 minutes, until lightly charred. Let cool slightly.

Once the onion is soft and sweet, add the peppers and zucchini to the saucepan, adding a little more oil (up to a tablespoon) if needed. Cook for 2 minutes. Turn up the heat to medium, add the pepper paste and tomatoes, and continue to cook, stirring often, for about 30 minutes, until the acid has cooked out of the tomatoes and the mixture is dark and sweet. Add the cayenne and serve immediately.

Braised beef shank with pickled guindilla and herb gremolata

ZANCARRÓN CON QUIQUIRIMICHI DE GUINDILLA VERDE

6 to 8 (1½- to 2-inch-wide) pieces crosscut beef or veal shanks

Kosher salt and freshly ground pepper

Extra-virgin olive oil, for browning and sweating

2 large carrots, peeled and cut into chunks

2 large leeks, white and light green parts only, cut into chunks

1 large Spanish onion, cut into chunks

1½ cups dry white wine

10 flat-leaf parsley sprigs

6 to 8 thyme sprigs

1 cup hand-crushed canned plum tomatoes, with their juices

¼ cup plus 1 whole piquillo pepper (you can use scraps for the ¼ cup)

8 cups water or chicken stock, homemade (page 26) or store-bought

Basques like gelatinous, tough, flavorful cuts that benefit from long simmering. When we make *zancarrón* at Txikito, we often use beef rather than veal shank because we find it is more flavorful and affordable. But veal feels kind of special if you are cooking for a party. There are many Basque recipes for hearty meat stews, or *sulkalkis*, that call for cubed boneless shank, and if you prefer boneless shank, it will work here and will cook a little faster. But you'll miss out on some of the flavor and texture benefits that come with cooking with bones and marrow.

I became proficient in making osso buco while living in Milan in the 1990s. It was there that I also learned about *gremolata*, the lemony herb condiment traditionally served with the shank dish. Since then, I have always finished deeply flavored stews with chopped herbs and often a little lemon zest. I call this particular topping *quiquirimichi* (one of the few words I know in Quechua, a language native to the central Andes), because it's fun to say and I created it to mimic the condiment we put on *locro*, an Argentine stew my mom makes expertly. My kids love this type of dish with rice, but I prefer to serve it with olive oil–infused mashed potatoes. | SERVES 6 TO 8

When you buy the shanks, ask you butcher to tie them off so they don't lose their marrow during braising.

Generously season the shanks with salt and pepper. Pour oil to a depth of ⅛ inch into a large, heavy enameled saucepan or Dutch oven and heat over medium-high heat. When the oil is hot, in batches, add the shanks, sear well on all sides, and transfer to a large plate. Each batch should take about 4 minutes per side to brown.

Preheat the oven to 325°F. Add the carrots, leeks, onion, and enough additional oil to coat the vegetables—about 1 tablespoon—to the pan, season with salt, and sweat over medium heat for about 15 minutes,

CONTINUED

Braised beef shank with pickled guindilla and herb gremolata

CONTINUED

QUIQUIRIMICHI

1 red bell pepper, seeded and minced

1 green bell pepper, seeded and minced

6 green onions, white and light green parts only, thinly sliced

3 tablespoons coarsely chopped fresh flat-leaf parsley

3 tablespoons minced pickled green guindilla peppers

¼ cup extra-virgin olive oil

3 tablespoons habanero vinegar (page 37)

½ teaspoon sweet or hot Spanish paprika

Kosher salt

until the vegetables are soft, sweet, and translucent. Be sure to scrape the bottom of the pan for any good crispy bits from searing the meat. Raise the heat to medium-high, add the wine, parsley, and thyme, and cook for about 7 minutes, until the alcohol cooks off and almost all of the wine has evaporated. Add the tomatoes and the ¼ cup piquillos and season with salt. Cook, stirring occasionally, for 12 to 15 minutes, until the acid has cooked out of the tomatoes and the mixture has a marmalade-like consistency.

Nestle the seared beef shanks in the mixture and add the water or stock and a little more salt. Cover, transfer to the oven, and cook for 2½ to 3 hours, until the meat is tender but not completely falling apart.

Meanwhile, make the quiquirimichi. In a bowl, combine the bell peppers, onions, parsley, guindilla peppers, oil, vinegar, paprika, and a pinch of salt. Mix well, then taste and adjust the seasoning with vinegar and salt if needed. (The quiquirimichi can be made up to 2 days in advance and refrigerated.)

Using a slotted spatula, carefully transfer the shanks (removing the ties) to a large plate. Strain the liquid through a fine-mesh strainer, reserving both the solids and the liquid. Add about 1 cup of the solids and the whole piquillo to a blender and puree until smooth. Return the puree to the pan with the unblended vegetables, stir well, and bring to a simmer, skimming off any impurities that float to the surface. Return the meat to the sauce to rewarm it, letting it rest over very low heat for 15 minutes before serving. Or, you can let the shanks and sauce cool completely, cover, and refrigerate for up 1 day and then reheat before serving.

Serve the beef shanks with some of their braising liquid and garnish with the quiquirimichi.

Braised tongue in tomato española

LENGUA ESTOFADA CON TOMATE

2 tablespoons
extra-virgin olive oil

2 large carrots, peeled
and chopped

2 large leeks, white and
light green parts only,
chopped

1 large Spanish onion,
chopped

1½ cups dry red wine

1 large or 2 small
beef tongues, at room
temperature

Kosher salt

2 cups tomato sauce
(page 36)

2 tablespoons choricero
pepper paste (page 39)

3 Carola or russet
potatoes or your favorite
farmers' market variety,
peeled and held in water

1 cup frozen shelled
English peas (optional)

Chopped fresh flat-leaf
parsley, for garnish

Tongue does not have to be a polarizing ingredient! Here's the thing: It's a muscle, not an organ. It doesn't taste funky. It's not texturally challenging. It's inexpensive. Its results are impressive. It is, simply put, the most well-exercised—and tastiest—meat you can buy for your money. And like all braises and things that take a little time, the Basques love it.

When I was growing up, my mom made great tongue stews that my friends thought were weird. Today, my kids love them. Txikito's version is half *salsa española* and half *tomate frito*, putting it somewhere between the versions cooked by my mom and cooked by Eder's mom. *Española* is a ubiquitous Basque sauce that I have only just recently come around to. For a long time, I found the thick brown sauce, which is made by simmering together beef broth and cooked vegetables, to be too unrefined, and I didn't like that it relied on spent vegetables for body. I began to appreciate it more once I began to think of it as gravy, which opened up a world of ideas for how to thicken sauces with pureed vegetables. Both *española* and *tomate frito* are Basque *amatxu* (mother) and *amama* (grandmother) sauces. The sauce I use here gets its texture and freshness from a healthy amount of *tomate frito*. Stirring in fresh or frozen peas adds a little color and is typical of many Basque stews.

If you're preparing the stew in a pressure cooker, brown the mirepoix and reduce the wine, and then add the tongues, cover with salted water, and cook for about 60 minutes. | SERVES 6 TO 8

Preheat the oven to 325°F. Select an ovenproof pot large enough to accommodate the tongue(s) snugly and place over medium-high heat. Add the oil and then the carrots, leeks, and onion and cook, stirring occasionally, for approximately 8 minutes, until the vegetables are browned. Pour in the wine, raise the heat to high, and cook for 8 to 10 minutes, stirring frequently, until the alcohol cooks off and the wine is reduced by one-third. Remove from the heat.

Cut a circle of parchment paper slightly smaller than the diameter of the pot. Nestle the tongue(s) in the vegetables and add water just to cover the tongues. Aggressively season the water with salt (the amount will depend on the size of your pot), starting with at least 2 tablespoons.

Cover with a parchment paper "lid," transfer the pot to the oven, and cook for 2½ to 3 hours, until a skewer inserted in the thickest part the tongue goes in without resistance but is still gripped by the meat on the way out. Passing this test will ensure that the tongue is tender but not stringy.

Remove the pot from the oven. Using tongs, transfer the tongue(s) to a cutting board and let cool slightly. While still warm, peel off the skin to expose the meat. It should come off easily. Strain the contents of the pot through a fine-mesh strainer into a bowl and set the solids aside. Skim off any fat and impurities from the broth, then measure 4 cups and reserve. Store any remaining broth in the freezer for another use.

Place 1 cup of the tomato sauce in a clean saucepan and warm gently until heated through. Meanwhile, in a blender or food processor, combine the reserved solids, the 4 cups broth, the pepper paste, and the remaining 1 cup tomato sauce and puree until smooth. Fold this puree into the tomato sauce warming in the saucepan.

Remove the peeled potatoes from their water and, using a paring knife, break them into ½-inch chunks. Add the potatoes to the sauce, bring to a simmer over medium heat, and cook for about 12 minutes, until the potatoes are tender when tested with a fork.

While the potatoes are cooking, slice the tongue(s) across the grain into ½-inch-thick slices. When the potatoes are tender, add the tongue slices and the peas to the pan, bring to a simmer, and heat through. Serve warm, sprinkled generously with parsley.

7 | Txokos, Asadores, Sagardotegis, and Ferias

GATHERING THE BASQUE WAY

Although *pintxos* bars provide some of the Basque Country's most popular gathering spots, they're hardly the only places where people congregate. Given the monumental importance of eating and drinking to Basque culture, it comes as no surprise that institutions and events designed for these purposes are everywhere. Like most people, the Basques use food as an excuse to socialize, viewing it as sustenance for both body and community. This weaving together of food, drink, stories, and song—often accompanied with a *trikitrixa* (a diatonic accordion)—is best reflected by four distinct feasting traditions: *txokos*, *asadores*, *sagardotegis*, and *ferias*.

Txokos

Txokos are Basque gastronomic societies of men who regularly gather to snack and cook elaborate traditional menus. A popular fixture of Basque society, they're often made up of men from the same *kuadrilla*, or group of friends, and can be either large and formal or smaller and more casual. Although on the surface they're a little like civilized frat houses, their importance in Basque culture cannot be overstated: through recipes and song, these *txokos* have helped keep alive the Basque language, which is the core of Basque identity. Even during the darkest days of Franco's dictatorship, when the Basque language and culture were banned, *txokos* were closed-door clubs where, amid all of the eating and accordion and tambourine playing, Basque was secretly but freely spoken.

The most popular theory on the origin of these men-only gastronomic societies is that they were meant to provide an antidote to the matriarchal and matrilineal character of Basque families. *Txokos* have evolved a bit in recent years: although women still cannot cook or clean in traditional *txokos*, they are increasingly invited to join in for the meal and drinks. *Txokos* are a truly collaborative experience: members pay a membership fee, split costs equally, and jointly rent or buy a gathering space. Rarely does every member attend every feast. Instead, smaller groups organized around family, friends, or fellow members who are available that day come together. The menus are typically seasonal and focus on *materia prima*, or the best-of-the-best ingredients: the rare fish caught early that morning, the *percebes* (goose barnacles) plucked from the rocks, or a mushroom dish compliments of a member who hit a milk-cap jackpot while foraging that day. Whatever is cooking at a *txoko*, however humble the ingredient, it's meant to showcase the cook's special abilities.

Most *txokos* are located on the street level and have well-equipped kitchens, along with well-stocked bars where you're allowed to help yourself as long as you abide by the honor system and record your drink on a board. Membership dues cover basic pantry items, and alcohol is always left over from one festivity or another.

Asadores and sagardotegis

The word *asador* is used to describe a style of restaurant where the menus are focused primarily on fire-cooked meat and seafood. *Asadores* are extremely common in the Basque Country, both in the interior, where they focus more on meats, and near the coast, where seafood straight from the port is the specialty. These restaurants range from extremely casual cider house–type places to expensive white-tablecloth steak restaurants and fish grills specializing in wild catch and ocean views.

Asadores usually fall into three categories: fish based, meat based, and chicken based. Meat-based *asadores* include, but aren't limited to, cider houses, which specialize in the *txuletones*, or big rib eyes, preceded by salt cod omelets and washed down with hard cider dispensed from large wooden barrels. *Asadores* that serve chicken are known as *cerveceras*; they're similarly specialized, but in rotisserie chicken and beer. Although each type has its specialty, *asadores* are united in cooking food over natural wood, or vines, which are known as *cepas* or *sarmientos*. Don't be fooled by the simplicity of their menus: you'll pay top dollar for the absolute best meat and seafood. *Asadores*, which are often festive, especially in their most casual iterations, are regarded as a great way for people to get together, usually in larger groups.

Given the quality (and cost) of the food, *asadores* are seen as occasion-worthy destinations, which is why families and groups of friends often plan their visits months in advance. *Kuadrillas* typically reunite at a cider house. Although they may see one another every weekend in their towns, a cider-house trip is a seasonal excursion, much like chasing great beans during bean season or traveling to a mussel festival in a port town.

My favorite *asadores* are fish based: where else can you taste so many exquisite kinds of seafood? Menus typically start with bivalves and crustaceans and then move on to whole wild turbot, rockfish, monkfish, or *cogote* (the head and neck of the fish). They're all about the pure product, so they are invariably seasoned with nothing more than salt and grilled to perfection.

Wine is the champion beverage at a fish-based *asador*, along with the post-dessert gin and tonics served tableside from chic carts. They make the perfect ending to a long, leisurely lunch that often comes with a view of the port at which your meal arrived. The most famous fish *asador* is Elkano.

The most rarified and famous contemporary *asador* is Extebarri, which is owned and operated by Victor Arguinzoniz. A quiet place located in the little village of Axpe, where the golden natural light seems streamed out of a fairy tale,

it is a boutique experience that combines the steak house and fish models. At the restaurant, you will find Victor cooking the simplest and most pristine ingredients with very little help. He uses his own milk, tomatoes, chorizo, and anchovies; keeps live elvers; and cooks nearly everything on grills. By experimenting with different woods and natural charcoal, he creates the most astonishing yet naked flavors I have ever tasted. He moves the grills up and down like a puppeteer, giving each ingredient a personality so nuanced that even the familiar tastes better than you have ever experienced it. The food's nakedness is also its Basqueness.

A close cousin of the *asador*, the *sagardotegi*, or cider house, is usually open during cider season from January to April. Cider was originally pressed by individuals or families for their own consumption, but as people gradually came to trade it for meat, cider houses evolved to serve the dual function of producer and grill restaurant. Cider houses tend to be remote and require traveling. Once you're there, you sit side by side at long, picnic-style tables where you're served giant dry-aged rib-eye steaks cooked rare and sliced, piquillo peppers, salt cod omelets, cheese, and, of course, plenty of cider.

Cider houses are less-expensive alternatives to the meat-based *asadores* that serve comparable or finer steaks and boast a great wine list. Young people and families populate cider houses, which are fun and joyful places where food and singing are plentiful. It's customary to fill your cider glass by getting down on bended knee, tapping the cider barrel, and yelling "*txotx*!" In the Basque Country, even the simple act of drinking cider is imbued with centuries of ritual and tradition.

Ferias

Ferias are the Basque equivalent of what an American harvest festival might look like: small-town events usually timed to coincide with a particular harvest. They take the form of large, multigenerational street parties where revelers gather to eat standing up, which is pretty much the only time they'll do so, unless they're at a *pintxos* bar.

Some *ferias* focus on just one type of food, such as sardines, stews, or mussels. There's one for *morcilla* and one for *alubias* (beans). Regardless of what food they are celebrating, *ferias* usually attract out-of-towners, who come to partake of the specialty. The *aldeanos* (locals) will often vend artisanal products like homemade jam-filled *gâteaux basque*, preserves, and charcuterie, and farmers will sell their livestock and vegetables. There's traditional dancing and music, and many people wear traditional clothing. The crowds at *ferias* tend to be mixed. You'll see young guys with multiple piercings mingling with older women dressed in lace-up espadrilles, crinoline-lined peasant skirts, and shawls.

The main food protagonist of the *feria* is the *talo*, a thin, pliable, neutrally flavored corn-flour disk pockmarked from dry griddling without fat until it is an aromatic envelope designed to hold everything from house-cured pork, bacon, or chorizo to chocolate bars or Idiazábal cheese. But the most popular accompaniment is *lomo adobado* (page 226), a workhorse recipe of the Basque repertoire.

Garden snails in bizkaína sauce

CARACOLES EN SALSA BIZKAÍNA

2 Spanish onions, cut into small dice

¼ cup extra-virgin olive oil

1 bay leaf

Kosher salt

4 cloves garlic, minced

2 cups diced bacon, in ⅛-inch dice

2 cups thinly sliced dry-cured spicy chorizo

¼ teaspoon red pepper flakes, or ⅛ teaspoon ground cayenne pepper

3 cups sweet pepper sauce (page 32)

15 ounces canned snails (drained weight) from about 3 cans, liquid reserved

Baguette, for serving

Basques love *caracoles*, or garden snails, as much as they love *caracolillos*, or periwinkles (see page 163). They buy them in net bags, purge them, and then cook and anoint them with amazing sauces. Fortunately, in the United States you can buy them cleaned and ready to go. All they need is a quick braise.

Basques eat snails directly out of the shells: they pick them up with their fingers or with a special instrument at fancy places, suck out the tasty sauce, and use a pick or needle to remove the earthy meat. They then sop up the delicious sauce with chunks of soft baguette. The sauce used is a variation of *salsa bizkaína*, my favorite thanks to the bacon, onion, chorizo, and red pepper flakes it contains. It's ideal served with snails. This stew is wonderful on its own, but it is also great spooned over polenta or stirred into a simple risotto. Calculate a dozen snails per person, and plan on serving them with plenty of bread to sop up the sauce.

A note on buying snails: You can buy canned wild Burgundy snails online or at gourmet stores. They usually come in counts of three dozen large snails (5 ounces drained) per tin. | SERVES 6 TO 8

In a saucepan, combine the onions, oil, bay leaf, and ½ teaspoon salt and sweat over low heat for about 10 minutes, just until the onions soften. Raise the heat to medium, add the garlic and bacon, and cook, stirring occasionally, for 8 minutes, until golden. Add the chorizo, turn down the heat to low, and cook for 3 minutes. Add the pepper flakes and the pepper sauce and simmer for 2 minutes. Add the snails and one-third of their liquid, raise the heat to medium, and bring to a boil. Turn down the heat to low and braise for about 20 minutes, until the flavors are mingled and the snails are tender but still a little snappy.

Remove the pan from the heat and let the snails rest for 5 minutes. Divide the snails among small bowls and serve with bread.

Cider house–style prime dry-aged rib-eye steak

TXULETÓN

1 (1½- to preferably 2-inch-thick) center-cut dry-aged rib-eye steak, chine and cap on (2½ to 3 pounds)

Kosher salt and freshly cracked pepper

Canola oil, for brushing

Beef (and even veal) in the Basque Country often comes from older animals and has a profoundly meaty flavor. There is a renewed interest in indigenous breeds like the Pirenaica and the Terreña, gorgeous animals that graze in the mountains and are fed apple pulp left over from cider making. These animals have a naturally diverse diet and get plenty of fresh air and exercise.

If you are unable to get a dry-aged rib eye, buy the best steak you can and salt it aggressively to pull out even more of its water content. Salting also draws the water-soluble proteins to the surface, which makes for a better sear. American butchers tend to remove the chine bones and cap from steaks, so make sure to call ahead and specify exactly what you need. Try to get a piece of meat with a lot of personality, something tender that has been fed a good diet. And when you're cooking it, err on the side of medium-rare over rare. The best-tasting meat I have had in the United States is organically fed Angus raised in New York State, but perhaps you can find something similar, raised by someone doing the right thing, near where you live, too. I always prefer grass-fed and grain-finished beef. Do not use previously frozen meat.

The best part about this very Basque cut is that the outer muscle gets more cooked and the eye stays rare, so there is something for everyone in terms of doneness.

I prefer a cast-iron frying pan to cook this thickness of steak. You will get an amazing sear and won't have to worry about flare-ups. And by searing and then cooking at a low temperature, you control the cooking better. Thick steaks require tinkering to get optimal results. Here is a good way to do it at home. | SERVES 6 TO 8

Bring the meat to room temperature if it has been refrigerated. Coat the rib eye with a layer of salt. Don't be shy here: this is a thick, fatty cut, so use about 2 tablespoons on each side. Let the meat sit for 7 minutes and then brush off the excess salt and crack on pepper, massaging it into the meat (and on the sides as well). Brush the steak on both sides with a thin layer of oil (this helps it conduct the heat more evenly).

CONTINUED

Cider house–style prime dry-aged rib-eye steak

CONTINUED

Meanwhile, preheat your oven to 200°F and get your cast-iron pan ripping hot on the stove top over high heat.

Prepare a sheet pan with a metal cooling rack on it. Place the steak on the cast-iron pan and press gently so all of the meat is in contact with the surface. As the meat contracts, it will release itself from the pan, indicating it is ready to turn or move. Sear it on one side for approximately 2 minutes, until deep mahogany in color. Place the steak, seared side up, on the rack and allow the cast-iron pan to recover its heat. Wipe the pan clean with a paper towel. Place the unseared side of the steak into the cast-iron pan, and once again hold the meat to the pan to ensure contact. Sear to a deep mahogany, 1 to 2 minutes. Transfer the steak to the cooling rack and let rest for 10 minutes. At this point it is well seared, and the meat is cooling on the outside and coming to room temperature or a little above internally. After 10 minutes, transfer the sheet pan with the steak to the low oven. Cook the steak until a probe inserted in the middle reads 130°F, about 7 minutes for thinner steaks and 8 to 9 minutes for thicker ones. Tent the steak with foil, then let it rest for 2 minutes.

To serve, cut away the outer muscle and crosscut the meat against the grain into ½-inch slices. Separate the eye from the chine and rib bone, and slice that similarly. Present with the bone—someone like me will go to town on it.

Cider house cod omelet

TORTILLA DE BAKALAO

This omelet is part of the cider-house grill experience, and it is ubiquitous in the Basque Country beginning in January, when the cider barrels are tapped for a traditional *txotx*. The *txotx*, which is most typical in the Guipuzkoa region, is a tradition where friends gather at *sidrerías* or *sagardotegis* to drink directly from the barrel. Each time the barrel is tapped, they call "*txotx!*" which is the signal for everyone to get up and fill their glass with two more fingers of cider. The first time I saw one of these omelets, I was surprised to see a classic rolled French-style variation. This is an oddball dish to eat before a steak, which is when it is typically served, but it works beautifully. | SERVES 1 TO 3

3-ounce piece quick salt-cured cod (page 142)

Extra-virgin olive oil, for poaching and cooking

3 eggs, at room temperature

Kosher salt

½ dried guindilla pepper or árbol chile, thinly sliced into rings or crumbled

2 tablespoons thin mayonnaise (page 23, optional)

Handful of Blistered Shishito Peppers with Sea Salt (page 105, optional)

Place the cod in a small saucepan and add oil to cover. Place over low heat and poach gently for 7 to 10 minutes, until the flesh flakes when prodded with the tip of a spoon. Using a slotted spatula, transfer the cod to a plate. Let the oil cool, then strain through a fine-mesh strainer and reserve for another use.

When the fish is cool to the touch, break it into pieces, being careful not to crumble it too small or massage it into a pulp.

Thinly coat the bottom of a nonstick frying pan with about 1 tablespoon oil and heat over medium-high heat. While the oil heats, lightly beat the eggs with a pinch of salt. Be careful not to overbeat the eggs; you want striations of yolk and white. When the oil is hot, add the beaten egg to the pan. Dip a spatula in a bit of the hot oil to prevent the egg from sticking to it, and then tilt the pan toward you. Use the spatula to push the egg halfway up the pan, letting its raw parts pool and fill the bottom of the pan. Repeat this process one more time and then scatter the poached cod on top of the egg. Reduce the heat to low. At this point, the egg should be set on the bottom but still moist on top. Using a rubber spatula, free the egg from the bottom of the pan, rolling the egg away from you, and then roll it out of the pan and onto a plate. Scatter the crumbled or sliced guindilla over the top and then top with the mayonnaise, and shishitos. Serve immediately.

Paprika-marinated pork loin roast

LOMO ADOBADO

It isn't elegant or even particularly gourmet, but in a cuisine that doesn't fall victim to culinary fashion, this dish is a mainstay. In our family, it's a recipe we return to again and again, as both kids and adults like it. It gives and accepts flavor, and can be thickly cut, served in thin slices like Canadian bacon, or roasted in one piece to juicy pinkness. If you don't have time to roast it in one piece, cure the whole thing and cut it into slices, cooking them like boneless pork chops, which is very common in the Basque Country. | SERVES 6 TO 8

1 cup kosher salt

10 cloves garlic

½ cup water

1 (5-pound) boneless Berkshire or Kurobuta pork loin roast, with fat cap intact if possible

¼ cup hot Spanish paprika

¼ cup sweet Spanish paprika

⅓ cup extra-virgin olive oil

In a food processor, combine the salt and garlic cloves and pulse until you have a rough paste, about 15 times, then add the water, a little at a time, pulsing to form a thick but smooth paste. Rub the paste onto the pork roast, covering evenly, and cover and refrigerate for 30 minutes.

Rinse off the paste and pat the pork dry. In a small bowl, stir together the hot and sweet paprikas, then stir in the oil to make a paste. Smear a thin layer over the pork loin and wrap the loin in plastic wrap. Refrigerate overnight.

The next day, let the pork loin come to room temperature. Preheat the oven to 450°F. Unwrap the loin and scrape off any excess paprika paste to keep it from burning. Place the loin in a baking dish or roasting pan with a rack, place in the oven, and immediately turn down the heat to 300°F. Roast for 45 minutes to 1 hour and 20 minutes, until an instant-read thermometer inserted into the center of the loin registers 145°F. The timing will depend on the thickness of the cut.

Let the meat rest for 10 minutes, tented with foil, then slice and serve immediately.

I will be honest: *goxua*, or Basque desserts and sweets, are typically so monochromatic in appearance that I considered calling this chapter Beige is the New Basque. Basque children grow up without the expectation that sweetness comes in myriad flamboyant colors; instead, they understand that it often wears the plainest disguise.

What Basque desserts lack in looks they more than compensate for in flavor. Eggs, milk, and sugar are the basis for most sweet treats: think puddings, custards, frozen terrines, soft buns, puff pastry layered with cream, and cakes made with yogurt or cheese. Fruits and nuts are also common players, with quince jam, or *dulce de membrillo*, an after-dinner accompaniment to such cheeses as Idiazábal or Roncal, one of the most famous uses for fruit.

Basque bakeries are filled with plain, rustic pastries in varying shades of golden brown that are displayed like fine jewels. Everything is kept behind glass, with none of the help-yourself tradition found in many bakeries in the United States. Instead, Basque bakeries are proudly old-school: everything is sold by the pound and weighed by the clerks, who then wrap the purchase in tissue paper or put it in a bag sealed with a gold sticker. That kind of presentation has inspired the work Eder and I do at our restaurants: at our tapas bar, El Quinto Pino, for example, we serve our *uni panino* in a beautiful glassine bag.

Basque bakeries also differ from their American counterparts in their selection, or relative lack thereof: instead of the American one-size-fits-all model, where you'll find a hodgepodge of bagels, muffins, cakes, and cookies under one roof, Basque bakeries are highly specialized. You might buy your *bollos* (soft buns) at one place, your *gâteau basque* at another, and so on.

Religious symbolism is intertwined with a number of Basque desserts. The strong current of Catholicism that runs through Basque culture can be tasted in the excess of yolks that endow many sweets: Catholic nuns traditionally made egg yolk–rich treats and sold them to raise money for their convents and to help the poor and then used the leftover whites for starching their habits. Fewer orders make the sweets today, but they can still be found in some areas. Flan is an obvious example of an egg yolk–rich dessert, as are *yemas*, or candied egg yolks, and *tocinillo de cielo*—a thick custard dessert made from just egg yolks and sugar. At Christmastime, sweets are especially pervasive: *turrón* (nougat), fruit compote, and *polvorones* or *harinados*, the confectioners' sugar–dusted cookies found on every family table, round out the variety of sweets that prevail from December until Easter.

But the Basques do not view dessert as something that requires a special occasion: sweets are very much woven into everyday life, often as a midafternoon snack. Indeed, eating a pastry as a snack, like going to a bakery, is a ritual. Rather than gulping down a pastry on the run, a Basque will typically sit down and savor it slowly with a fork and knife.

These days, the Basque love of dessert doesn't usually extend to making sweets at home, especially elaborate ones. That's what the bakeries are for. However, some home cooks use powdered mixes to make flans and junkets (milk-based rennet-set custards) that they sometimes turn into layered desserts. Also, yogurt is as much a dessert to Basques as baked goods are and is often offered as an option in restaurants.

Many of the desserts in this chapter should be viewed as including components that you can mix and match. These are superflexible recipes that will help you learn to think in terms of versatility: make them once, absorb them into your repertoire, and then keep coming back for more, no matter what the occasion.

Seared croissant with honey butter and orange marmalade

CROISSANT A LA PLANTXA

One person's lifeless, dry croissant is a Basque café's beyond-delicious invention. I saw my first *croissant a la plantxa* in Bilbao when my now *prima politica* (Basque cousin-in-law) Idoia ordered one with her coffee at a posh café near her office. I still remember how completely floored I was when it arrived at our table in its golden gorgeousness, and I can even recall the thoughts that raced through my reeling brain: What? A buttery pastry refried in butter and dusted with sugar? You're going to eat it with a knife and fork like it's a pork chop? This is a snack? Oh my God, this is the most over-the-top midafternoon snack I have ever seen!

Breakfast for dessert, dessert for breakfast, and unapologetic midafternoon snack—the *croissant a la plantxa* fits all of these roles perfectly. And incidentally, it will also make you look absolutely brilliant in front of your friends and children. | SERVES 4

HONEY BUTTER

¾ cup unsalted butter, at room temperature

¼ cup honey

1 teaspoon kosher salt

2 vanilla beans, split lengthwise

4 day-old croissants, split lengthwise

Unsalted butter, for frying

Confectioners' sugar, for dusting

Orange marmalade, for serving

To make the honey butter, put the butter, honey, and salt in a bowl. Using the tip of a knife, scrape the seeds from the vanilla bean halves into the bowl, and then stir to mix thoroughly. If your butter is soft, you can do this easily with two forks or a small rubber spatula or palate knife.

Heat 1 teaspoon butter in a large nonstick frying pan over medium-low heat. Add the croissants, cut side down, and cook for about 2 minutes, until nicely browned on the first side. Flip the croissants and brown for about 2 minutes on the second side.

Transfer the croissants to individual serving plates, placing 2 halves, cut side up, on each plate. Dust with confectioners' sugar and accompany with the honey butter and marmalade. Store any leftover honey butter in an airtight container in the refrigerator for up to 3 days and bring to room temperature before serving.

Basque-style yeast buns

SUIZOS Y BOLLOS DE MANTEQUILLA

3 tablespoons unsalted butter

½ cup whole milk

2 tablespoons granulated sugar, plus more for sprinkling

1 egg, whisked

1 teaspoon pure vanilla extract

1 teaspoon orange blossom water (optional)

2 teaspoons active dry yeast

1½ cups all-purpose flour

¼ teaspoon kosher salt

1 egg white mixed with 1 tablespoon water, for egg wash

4 tablespoons unsalted butter, at room temperature; ¼ cup crème fraîche; and ⅓ cup confectioners' sugar, if making bollos de mantequilla

Suizos and *bollos de mantequilla* are my favorite members of the Basque sweets repertoire. The soft white yeast buns—*suizos* are round and plain, and *bollos* are oblong and filled with whipped butter and sugar—also remind me of my childhood trips to Argentina, where *pan de leche*, a sweet, tender, milk-rich yeast roll, was my pick at the bread shop near my grandmother's house. I can't overstate how much I love these Basque buns: As soon as I land in Bilbao, I head straight for the airport café to eat one. On my flights out of Bilbao, which often leave at 6:00 a.m., I repeat the ritual, always with a *cortado* (espresso with a little warm milk). The *bollos* have a way of erasing any memory of a bad meal or other unpleasantry, so that the only thought in my mind as I fly home is that everything is amazing and delicious in the Basque Country—even the airport cafés. Here, I've added the faint exotic aroma of orange blossom water, which you can find at health food stores and Middle Eastern markets. But feel free to omit it or to use grated orange zest in its place. | MAKES 9 BUNS

In a heavy saucepan with a lid, melt the butter over low heat. Add the milk and granulated sugar and heat gently, stirring until the sugar dissolves. Remove from the heat. Stir in the egg, vanilla, and orange blossom water, mixing thoroughly.

Check the temperature of the mixture with an instant-read thermometer; it should register between 110°F and 115°F. Sprinkle the yeast over the mixture and let stand for a few minutes until the yeast begins to bubble. Add the flour and mix with a wooden spoon until a sticky dough forms. Stir in the salt.

Cover the saucepan with its lid and place in a warm, draft-free place. A turned-off oven is a good spot. Let the dough rise for 1 hour, until it doubles in size. The time will vary depending on the ambient temperature, so be patient.

Punch down the dough and use your hand to roll it around the bottom of the saucepan for a few minutes. Replace the lid and return

CONTINUED

Basque-style yeast buns

the saucepan back to the rising space. Let the dough continue to rise for another 30 minutes.

Deflate the dough and roll it around the bottom of the saucepan again, this time folding it and throwing it down so that the dough ball essentially "cleans up" all of the extra bits that have stuck to the sides of the pan. You will notice that the dough is easier to work with and doesn't stick as much as it did before. This is an indication that it is ready to knead. Continue to work the dough around the saucepan until it is fairly smooth and forms an elastic ball.

Butter a 9 by 13-inch baking pan. Lightly dust a work surface with flour and transfer the dough to it. Using as little additional flour as possible, knead the dough until it is a smooth, supple ball. Divide the dough into 9 equal portions and form each portion into a tight ball by using your palm and fingers to roll the dough against the work surface. Working with 1 ball at a time, press the ball flat and then fold the sides into the center. Tuck the two short ends under to make a perfect oval and then flip the bun over to hide the seam. Using a paring knife, score the bun with a lengthwise slash and place it in the prepared pan. Repeat with the remaining 8 balls, then cover the pan with plastic wrap and let the buns rise for 1 hour, until doubled in size.

Preheat the oven to 350°F. Brush the buns with the egg wash and sprinkle generously with granulated sugar. Bake for 15 minutes, until the buns have puffed up and turned golden brown. Remove from the oven. The fresh-baked rolls are very delicate, so allow them to rest for at least 20 minutes in the pan on a wire rack before removing them. Let cool completely before serving.

To serve bollos de mantequilla, in a bowl, whip together the butter, crème fraîche, and confectioners' sugar until pale, light, and smooth. Cut each bun in half lengthwise and fill with the whipped butter mixture.

Breakfast yogurt cake

MAGDALENAS DE YOGUR

1½ cups all-purpose flour

1 tablespoon baking powder

½ teaspoon kosher salt

1 cup full-fat plain Greek yogurt or crème fraîche

½ cup extra-virgin olive oil

Grated zest of 1 lemon

3 eggs

1 cup sugar

1 cup fresh whole huckleberries or diced rhubarb

2 tablespoons cornstarch

Part of the tea cake family, this yogurt cake is a plain and delicious treat often eaten at breakfast or as an afternoon snack. If neither huckleberries nor rhubarb is in season, substitute your favorite berries. | MAKES ONE 8½ BY 4½-INCH LOAF CAKE OR 8 TO 12 INDIVIDUAL CAKES

Preheat the oven to 350°F. Butter an 8½ by 4½-inch loaf pan or 8 to 12 baba au rhum molds (2 to 3 inches deep). Line the pan or molds with parchment paper.

In a bowl, stir together the flour, baking powder, and salt. In a separate bowl, whisk together the yogurt, oil, and lemon zest.

In a stand mixer fitted with the paddle attachment, combine the eggs and sugar and beat on medium speed until pale and fluffy. On low speed, add the oil and yogurt mixture and beat just until combined. Using a rubber spatula, gently fold in the flour mixture just until thoroughly combined. Do not overmix.

In a bowl, toss the huckleberries with the cornstarch to coat evenly. Scatter the berries evenly over the batter, then fold in gently just until evenly distributed. Transfer the batter to the prepared pan or molds.

Bake for 20 to 25 minutes for individual molds or 45 to 50 minutes for a loaf pan, until a cake tester or toothpick inserted into the center comes out clean. Let cool for 10 minutes, then unmold and let cool completely on the rack. Store for up to 3 days in an airtight container.

Red wine–poached cherries with crème fraîche flan

FLAN DE YEMA CON CEREZAS ITXASSOU

CHERRIES

1½ cups red wine

2½ cups sugar

Peel of ½ lemon, in wide strips

½ cinnamon stick

Pinch of kosher salt

2½ pounds black or dark cherries, pitted if you like

FLAN

2 whole eggs

4 egg yolks

Pinch of kosher salt

½ cup plus 1 tablespoon sugar

½ teaspoon pure vanilla extract

1 cup whole milk

1 cup crème fraîche

Found throughout the French Basque Country, Itxassou cherries are famous primarily for the role they play in jams and in desserts like *gâteau basque*. These cherries are better on day two or three, so make them up to a week ahead of time—if you can resist the urge to devour them.

You can pit the cherries or not. If you decide to leave the pits in, let your diners know. They lend a magnificent almondy undertone to the compote, but they can also cause a trip to the dentist. Be careful not to overcook the cherries, too. They can go from raw to overcooked quickly, so test them continually as they simmer. | SERVES 6

To make the cherries, in a saucepan, combine the wine, 1¾ cups sugar, lemon peel, cinnamon stick, and salt and bring to a boil over medium-high heat, stirring well. Turn down the heat to medium and simmer for 5 minutes, until the alcohol cooks off and the sugar is completely dissolved. Be careful not to reduce the syrup too much: this is fruit in red wine, not a conserve.

Add half of the cherries and simmer for no more than 8 minutes, until tender but still intact. Stir in the remaining cherries off the heat. Chill the cherries, submerged in the liquid, for up to 1 week.

Line the bottom of a baking dish or a roasting pan with a kitchen towel and place 6 (4-ounce) ramekins in the pan. To line the ramekins with caramel, in a small, heavy saucepan, melt the remaining ¾ cup sugar over medium-high heat, whisking continuously so sugar clumps break up and caramelize evenly as you go. As the sugar begins to melt, turn down the heat to medium-low and continue to stir until the melted sugar is a uniform blond, about 2 minutes. Remove the pan from the heat and let the sugar continue to color off the heat for 1 to 2 minutes, until it is dark gold (putting it on and off the flame as needed). Then, working quickly, pour the hot caramel to a depth of ¼ inch into each ramekin. As it cools, it will harden

CONTINUED

Red wine–poached cherries with crème fraîche flan

CONTINUED

to a hard-candy-like consistency but will loosen up again when the custard is baking. Set the baking dish holding the ramekins aside.

Preheat the oven to 300°F. Place a fine-mesh strainer over a bowl and set aside. (Be sure to line the molds with caramel and turn on the oven before beginning the next step.)

To make the flan, in a bowl, whisk together the whole eggs, egg yolks, salt, about half the sugar, and the vanilla until blended. In a small saucepan, combine the milk, crème fraîche, and the remaining sugar and bring to a simmer over medium heat, stirring to dissolve the sugar. Remove from the heat. Whisk about ½ cup of the hot milk mixture into the egg mixture to temper the eggs, then whisk in the remaining milk mixture about ½ cup at a time until all of it has been incorporated. Pass the mixture through the strainer. Divide the custard evenly among the caramel-lined molds.

Pour boiling water into the baking dish to reach two-thirds of the way up the sides of the molds, taking care not to splash any water into the flans. (A teakettle is the best way to do this.) Cover the top of the pan loosely with aluminum foil, making sure that steam can still escape from the sides, and then very slowly and carefully move the baking dish to the oven.

Bake for 45 to 50 minutes, opening the foil once or twice to release steam, until the flans are just set. Carefully remove the pan from the oven and then remove the flans from the pan. Let cool completely and chill well before serving.

To unmold the flans, slide a small knife around the inside edge of each ramekin, pulling the blade gently toward you to create an air gap. Invert a shallow bowl over the mold, flip the mold and bowl, and lift off the mold. Serve each flan with ½ cup of the chilled cherries.

Pedro Jimenez ice cream with orange zest

HELADO DON PEDRO

We add Pedro Jimenez sherry or dark rum to a rich and creamy ice cream base to make this ice cream. Orange zest brings out the flavors in the sherry or rum. The combination reminds me of my maternal grandfather, a gourmand who loved a similar dessert and would have loved the Basque Country, so I named this eggy ice cream after his favorite dessert. I recommend making the base a day ahead so that it has time to chill thoroughly. Adding the alcohol to the ice cream when it is semifrozen in the ice cream maker helps reduce the freezing time.
| MAKES 1 QUART

1 cup whole milk

¾ cup heavy cream

⅓ cup sugar

¼ teaspoon kosher salt

4 egg yolks

¼ teaspoon orange zest

3 tablespoons Pedro Jimenez sherry or dark rum

Prepare an ice bath. Nest a metal or glass container in the ice bath and have a fine-mesh strainer handy.

In a saucepan, combine the milk, cream, sugar, salt, and orange zest, place over medium heat, and bring to a simmer, stirring to dissolve the sugar. While the milk mixture is heating, in a bowl, whisk the egg yolks until blended. When the milk mixture is hot, remove it from the heat. Whisk about ½ cup of the hot milk mixture into the egg yolks to temper them, then whisk in another ½ cup. Return the tempered mixture to the saucepan and whisk over medium-low heat, tilting the pan occasionally to make sure the egg yolks are not curdling, until the yolks begin to cook slightly and the mixture thickens enough to lightly coat the back of a spoon. Remove from the heat and pour through the strainer into the container resting in the ice bath. Stir the custard immediately to cool it down, then cover and chill overnight.

Transfer the chilled base to an ice cream maker and churn according to the manufacturer's instructions. When the ice cream has thickened and is almost ready—it will have the consistency of soft serve—add the sherry and continue to churn until frozen. Transfer the ice cream to an airtight container and place in the freezer for 2 to 3 hours, until frozen hard. The ice cream will keep for up to 2 days.

Basque cake

GÂTEAU BASQUE

DOUGH

3 eggs

1 cup sugar

¾ cup plus 2 tablespoons unsalted butter, at room temperature

Grated zest of ½ lemon

½ teaspoon pure vanilla extract

¼ teaspoon pure almond extract

¼ teaspoon baking powder

2¼ cups all-purpose flour

PASTRY CREAM

2¼ cups whole milk

½ cup sugar

1 cinnamon stick

Zest of 2 lemons, in wide strips

6 egg yolks

⅓ cup cornstarch

½ teaspoon kosher salt

1 tablespoon all-purpose flour

1 tablespoon sugar

1 cup dried cherries, plumped in ¼ cup hot water and drained (optional)

Pastel vasco, euskal pastela, and *gâteau basque* are all names for this magical, custard-filled cake, which is so beloved throughout the Basque Country that entire bakeries are dedicated to its production. Until recently, I think the cake was better known than the region. It's a common attraction at festivals, where it's often sold filled with homemade cherry jam. Not a cake in the traditional sense, its magic lies in the buttery, shortbread-like crust that encloses its pastry cream filling. This dough is easiest to work with when it is cold, firm, and pliable and impossible to work with effectively otherwise. This recipe takes time and patience, but it is well worth it if you carefully follow each step. It calls for a 9-inch springform pan, but I recommend that you purchase a 9-inch round silicone mold at least 1½ inches deep, as it will make all the difference during the cooking and freezing steps.
| MAKES ONE 9-INCH CAKE

To make the dough, in a stand mixer fitted with the paddle attachment, cream together the eggs and sugar on medium speed until pale and fluffy. Add the butter, lemon zest, vanilla and almond extracts, and baking powder and beat just until combined.

Using a rubber spatula, add the flour in 3 equal additions, mixing just until combined after each addition. Divide the batter evenly between 2 pastry bags fitted with a ¼-inch plain tip. Place the bags in the refrigerator for about 1 hour, until the batter is firm but still pliable.

To make the pastry cream, line a 13 by 18-inch baking sheet with plastic wrap and set aside. In a small saucepan, combine the milk, ¼ cup of the sugar, the cinnamon stick, and the lemon zest and warm gently over medium-low heat until the milk is barely simmering. Remove from the heat and cover with plastic wrap. Let steep for about 1 hour, until cooled to room temperature. Pour the cooled milk through a fine-mesh strainer into a larger saucepan, place over medium-low heat, and bring to a bare simmer.

CONTINUED

Basque cake

While the milk is heating, in a bowl, whisk the egg yolks until blended, then whisk in the remaining 1/4 cup sugar, the cornstarch, and the salt. When the milk is hot, remove it from the heat. Whisk about 1/2 cup of the hot milk mixture into the egg mixture to temper the eggs, then whisk in the remaining milk mixture about 1/2 cup at a time until all of it has been incorporated. Return the combined mixtures to the saucepan, place over medium-high heat, and bring to a boil, whisking constantly. Reduce the heat to medium-low, then continue to cook, whisking constantly, for 5 to 7 minutes, until the mixture is thick and creamy. Using a rubber spatula, spread the pastry cream onto the plastic wrap–lined baking sheet. Lay a second sheet of plastic wrap directly on top of the cream to prevent a skin from forming. Let cool, then refrigerate for about 2 hours, until well chilled.

You can use a 9-inch springform pan or a 9-inch round silicone mold at least 1 1/2 inches deep. If using the pan, butter it. If using the silicone mold, you can skip this step. (If using a silicone mold, make sure you keep the bottom of the mold as flat as possible.) Remove a pastry bag of batter from the refrigerator and pipe a thin layer of batter onto the bottom of the pan, starting from the center and working outward to make a snail-shell spiral. Be careful not to pipe too much of the batter; the thickness of the layer should not exceed 1/4 inch. Return the piping bag to the refrigerator to allow the batter to firm up again. Using a small offset spatula, smooth out the batter on the bottom of the pan, making sure the thickness is uniform. Put the pan in the freezer for about 10 minutes, until the layer firms up.

Return the pan to the work surface and remove the same pastry bag from the refrigerator. You are now going to build up the sides of the cake by piping the batter against the sides of the mold and using the offset spatula to smooth it out. The sides can be thicker than the bottom, but make sure the sides are a uniform thickness (about 1/3 inch) throughout. Also, be sure to pipe the batter to the top edge of the pan. The easiest way to do that is to pipe the batter to the top of the pan and then level it out against the lip with the offset spatula.

By the time you reach the top, you should have used up all of the batter in the first piping bag. Return the pan to the freezer for about 1 hour, until the batter is frozen.

Remove the pastry cream from the refrigerator and lift off the top sheet of plastic wrap. Using a paring knife, cut out an 11-inch disk. Remove the pan from the freezer and dust the frozen batter layer on the bottom with the flour and sugar. Transfer the disk of chilled pastry cream to the pan and gently press it onto the bottom and halfway up the sides with your fingertips or the offset spatula. Scatter the cherries evenly across the pastry cream, pushing them in gently. Save any extra pastry cream for another use.

Remove the remaining bag of batter from the refrigerator and return the pan to the work surface. Pipe the batter evenly over the pastry cream and cherries and then smooth the surface with the spatula. Return the pan to the freezer for at least 3 hours or up to overnight, until the top layer is frozen.

Position a rack in the upper third of the oven and preheat the oven to 350°F. Place the frozen pan on a baking sheet, place the baking sheet on the bottom of the oven, and bake for 20 minutes. Transfer the baking sheet, rotating it back to front, to the top oven rack and bake for about 40 minutes longer, until the top is a nice golden brown.

Remove from the oven and place the pan on a rack set over a baking sheet. Let cool for about 10 minutes. If using a springform pan, run a knife around the sides, release and lift off the pan sides, and slide the cake onto the rack. If using a silicone mold, tip the cake out of the mold onto the rack and turn upright. If when you unmold the cake, the bottom looks too pale or is not sufficiently crisp, do not despair: pop the cake back into the oven on the rack (upside down) and baking sheet and bake for 7 to 10 minutes, until the bottom is browned.

Let cool completely on the rack before flipping and cutting into wedges to serve.

Pear and patxaran sorbet

SORBETE DE PERA Y PATXARAN

Patxaranes (*endrinas* in Spanish), or sloe berries (aka blackthorn berries), grow wild in Navarra, where they make excellent wines and families often concoct their own artisanal liqueur or digestif. The sloe berries have an incredibly plummy aroma, and, when mixed with anise liqueur, create a great little something to sip after dinner. Look for *patxaran* liqueur at any good liquor store (in Spanish, it's *pacharán*). It has a great shelf life and is absolutely delicious on the rocks or chilled in the freezer and served in a shot glass. This sorbet is refreshing and pretty; I recommend serving it in glasses or jars to showcase its charms. Feel free to substitute sloe gin or arak for the *patxaran*. The result will be different but fabulous. | MAKES 1½ QUARTS; SERVES 8 TO 10

¾ cup water

1 tablespoon agave nectar

1 tablespoon lemon juice

½ cup sugar

¼ teaspoon salt

5 large, soft ripe pears, such as Bosc or D'Anjou, peeled, halved, cored, and cubed

¼ cup patxaran liqueur, chilled

Set a fine-mesh strainer over a mixing bowl. In a blender, combine the water, agave nectar, lemon juice, sugar, and salt and blend for 30 seconds. Add the pears and puree until smooth. Pass the puree through the strainer, pressing against the pulp with a rubber spatula to force all the puree through. Cover and refrigerate for at least 1 hour, until well chilled.

Transfer the sorbet base to an ice cream maker and churn according to the manufacturer's instructions for about 5 minutes. Add the liqueur and continue to churn until frozen. Transfer the sorbet to an airtight container and place in the freezer for at least 2 to 3 hours before serving. It will keep for up to 2 days prior to serving. After that, melt and re-spin for best texture.

Walnut semifreddo with salted chocolate sauce

CORTE DE INTXAURSALSA CON TXOKOLATE

SEMIFREDDO

⅔ cup chopped walnuts

1⅓ cups sugar

3 cups whole milk

2 cups heavy cream, cold

1 cinnamon stick

4 strips lemon zest

1¼ teaspoons kosher salt

4 egg yolks

2 egg whites

½ teaspoon cream of tartar

CHOCOLATE SAUCE

8 ounces bittersweet chocolate (68 to 72 percent cacao), chopped

⅓ cup whole milk

1 cup heavy cream

3 tablespoons glucose syrup or agave nectar

1 vanilla bean, split lengthwise, or ½ teaspoon pure vanilla extract

½ teaspoon kosher salt

¼ cup hot water

Maldon salt or fleur de sel, for serving

Raspberries or blackberries, for serving (optional)

As plain in appearance as it is sophisticated in flavor, this lemon-and-cinnamon-scented walnut cream is among the most iconic of Basque desserts. I freeze it into a terrine, to create a very adult sundae. | SERVES 8

To make the semifreddo, in a food processor, combine the walnuts and ½ cup of the sugar and pulse until reduced to a medium-fine meal.

In a 2- to 4-quart saucepan, combine the milk, 1 cup of the cream, the cinnamon stick, the lemon zest, and 1 teaspoon of the kosher salt. Add the walnut-sugar mixture, place over medium heat and bring to a simmer. Heat, whisking occasionally, for 20 minutes, making sure the milk doesn't boil or scorch on the pan bottom and the sugar is completely dissolved. Remove from the heat, cover with plastic wrap, and let steep for about 30 minutes.

Remove the plastic wrap and reheat the mixture until warm. Meanwhile, prepare an ice bath in a bowl big enough to accommodate the base of the saucepan. In a small bowl, whisk together ½ cup of the sugar and the egg yolks until blended. Slowly whisk about 1 cup of the warm walnut mixture into the egg yolk mixture to temper the eggs, and then whisk in another 1 cup. Return the tempered egg mixture to the saucepan and cook over low heat, whisking continuously, for 1 to 2 minutes, until the egg yolks coat the back of a spoon. Do not allow the mixture to boil.

Remove from the heat, and while continuing to stir, quickly plunge the saucepan into the ice bath to halt the cooking. Stir occasionally until cooled, then remove and discard the cinnamon and lemon zest.

Transfer the walnut base to a container, cover, and refrigerate for about 2 hours, until well chilled.

Using a stand mixer fitted with the whip attachment, or a bowl and whisk, whip the remaining 1 cup cream until doubled in size and soft peaks have formed. Transfer to a bowl, cover, and refrigerate for about 1½ hours, until well chilled.

In the bowl of the stand mixer fitted with the whip attachment, whip together the egg whites, cream of tartar, and the remaining ¼ teaspoon kosher salt on medium speed until foamy. Add the remaining ⅓ cup sugar bit by bit, whipping until the mixture is stiff and glossy.

Have ready a 1-quart milk carton, cut open on one end to form a rectangular mold. Spoon the whipped cream into a large bowl. Fold in the walnut base and then the whipped egg whites, mixing in each component just until combined. Scrape the mixture into the mold and tap the mold on a countertop to remove any air pockets. (Put any extra in a separate container and freeze for another use.) Cover the mold with plastic and freeze until the semifreddo is firm, at least 8 hours or preferably overnight.

To make the sauce, place the chocolate in a heatproof bowl. In a small saucepan, combine the milk, cream, and glucose. If using a vanilla bean, use the tip of a knife to scrape the seeds into the pan. If using vanilla extract, add to the pan. Place over medium heat and heat until scalding hot. Remove from the heat, add to the chocolate, let stand for 1 minute, and whisk until the chocolate melts. Add the water to loosen the sauce and give it a shiny finish. Keep warm.

To serve, chill individual serving plates. Turn the frozen quart of semifreddo on its side. Using a serrated knife, cut crosswise into uniform slices 1 to 1½ inches thick. As you work, place the slices on the chilled serving plates. When all of the semifreddo has been cut, peel off the carton paper from each slice. Pour some warm chocolate sauce over each serving and finish with a pinch of Maldon salt and a spoonful of berries. Serve immediately.

Roasted banana puddin', Basque style

NATILLAS DE PLATANO ASADO CON GALLETAS

When Eder and I first dated, I lived near the famous Magnolia Bakery on Bleecker Street, where I would occasionally pick up banana pudding. The first time I took one to Eder, he declared it the most disgusting thing in the world—and then ate the whole thing. *Natillas* is a type of crème anglaise that the Basques like to scoop up with *galletas María* (Maria's cookies), the Spanish equivalent of Nilla wafers. Goya makes them, or you can find great versions at Japanese and Chinese groceries. | SERVES 6

1 medium-ripe banana, unpeeled

1½ cups whole milk

¾ cup heavy cream

½ cup sugar

⅛ teaspoon pure vanilla extract or vanilla bean paste

½ teaspoon kosher salt

4 egg yolks

3 gelatin sheets

Butter cookies, for serving

Preheat the oven to 450°F. Wrap the banana in aluminum foil, place in the oven, and roast for 10 minutes. Remove from the oven, unwrap, and let cool to room temperature. Peel the cooled banana, transfer to a blender, and puree until smooth. Transfer the puree to a saucepan, add the milk, cream, sugar, vanilla, and salt, and place over low heat. Bring to a gentle simmer, stirring to dissolve the sugar. Remove from the heat, cover with plastic wrap, and let steep for 1 hour.

Place a fine-mesh strainer over a bowl and pour the banana mixture into the strainer. Discard the solids and return the liquid to the saucepan. Bring to a simmer over low heat. While the liquid is heating, in a bowl, lightly whisk the egg yolks just until blended. In a second bowl, immerse the gelatin sheets in ice water for 5 minutes to soften.

When the banana liquid is simmering, remove from the heat. Whisk the hot liquid into the egg yolk mixture ½ cup at a time to temper. Return the tempered mixture to the saucepan and whisk over medium-low heat, making sure the egg yolks are not curdling, for about 5 minutes, until the mixture lightly coats the back of a spoon. Immediately remove from the heat to a cool surface and keep stirring for about 2 minutes to cool.

Lift the gelatin sheets from the water, wring gently, add to the warm banana custard, and stir until completely melted. Strain the custard through a fine-mesh strainer into a pitcher or bowl, and divide the custard among 6 ramekins or glasses. Cover and refrigerate for at least 1 hour. Serve chilled with butter cookies.

Sticky almond cake, Tate pastry shop style

TORTA DE ALMENDRA

Eder and I were married in the town of Markina. Or rather, we almost burned down the town with fireworks and festivities. Markina is home to Tate, an amazing bakery that still makes traditional desserts and candies that come wrapped in gorgeous boxes. The last time I was there I sampled an almond cake much like the one we make but more wonderful for the layer of sliced almonds that protected its tender center. Sweet and rich, it looks and tastes like it's hard to achieve, but it's unbelievably easy. This is a cake that you will return to again and again, one that is equally ideal for gifting or for chipping away at in your kitchen. | MAKES ONE 8½ BY 4½-INCH LOAF OR 9- TO 10-INCH TART

1 cup plus 1 tablespoon unsalted butter, cut into cubes, at room temperature

2 cups sugar

¼ teaspoon kosher salt

1 teaspoon grated orange zest

1 teaspoon grated lemon zest

¼ teaspoon pure almond extract

6 eggs

2 cups blanched almond flour

½ cup all-purpose flour

¼ cup apricot jam, mixed with 2 tablespoons warm water and strained to remove fruit lumps

1½ cups sliced blanched almonds

¾ cup superfine sugar

Preheat the oven to 325°F. Have ready an 8½ by 4½-inch loaf pan or a 9- or 10-inch silicone tart mold.

In a food processor, combine the butter, granulated sugar, and salt and process until creamy. Add the citrus zests and almond extract and process until mixed. Add the eggs, one at a time, pulsing after each addition until combined. Add the almond flour and pulse until combined, stopping to scrape down the sides of the processor bowl as needed. Pour the batter into a bowl and sprinkle the all-purpose flour over it. Using a rubber spatula, fold in the flour, making sure none of it has clumped together or is stuck on the bottom of the bowl. The finished batter should be smooth.

Pour the batter into the loaf pan or mold. Bake for 25 minutes, until the top is just set and a little firm to the touch. Carefully remove the cake from the oven and brush the top with the jam mixture. Scatter the almonds and the superfine sugar evenly over the surface. Return the cake to the oven and bake for 15 minutes longer, until a cake tester inserted into the center comes out with only a couple of crumbs attached to it and the center feels springy when lightly pressed with a fingertip. Be careful not to overbake or the cake will be dry. Let the cake cool completely in the pan on a wire rack, then remove from the pan and serve. Run a knife blade around the inside edge of the pan to release it if needed.

Grilled pound cake with candied fruit

PLUM CAKE A LA PLANTXA

8 ounces high-quality dried fruits (such as candied citron, grapefruit, and orange), diced

1 cup raisins or dried sour cherries (halve the cherries, if using)

1 cup brandy or dark rum (optional)

¾ cup plus 2 tablespoons unsalted butter, at room temperature, plus melted butter for grilling

1 cup granulated sugar

5 eggs, at room temperature

2¾ cups all-purpose flour

1 tablespoon baking powder

1 teaspoon kosher salt

Confectioners' sugar, for dusting, or Pedro Jimenez Ice Cream with Orange Zest (page 243), for serving

Before I ever met Eder's family, I received a care package from his aunt Madalen, a stellar baker. Inside the box was an aromatic fruit cake, wrapped in foil and about the length of a commercial Pullman loaf. It was a confection that only a true Brit or a food geek like me would choose over chocolate. When I finally got to meet the woman behind it, I realized that you can find this type of cake pretty much everywhere in the Basque Country. It is great when sliced the first day, but like all fruit cakes, it's a multitasking workhorse: you can douse it in booze and let it sit for a while, or brown it in a buttered pan, as we do, and serve it with ice cream. Never grilled pound cake before? You will always grill pound cake from now on.

I recommend baking the cake in a 8½ by 4½-inch loaf pan. If you're not using a loaf pan, be very careful about the baking time, as the cake will bake much faster in a shallower pan. Check for doneness every 10 minutes, and count on the cake being finished in 30 to 40 minutes, tops. | MAKES 1 LOAF

In a saucepan, combine the dried fruits, raisins, and brandy over low heat and bring to a simmer. Remove from the heat and let cool. Drain the fruits, reserving the fruits and liquid separately.

Preheat the oven to 275°F. Butter an 8½ by 4½-inch loaf pan. Line the pan with parchment paper, allowing it to overhang both long sides by about 2 inches.

In a stand mixer fitted with the paddle attachment, beat together the butter and granulated sugar on medium speed until the mixture turns pale yellow. Add the eggs and continue to beat until the volume increases and the texture is fluffy. (Alternatively, beat by hand in a bowl with a whisk.)

In a large bowl, stir together the flour, baking powder, and salt, then stir in the plumped fruits. Gently fold the butter mixture in two batches into the flour mixture just until combined. Do not overwork the batter.

Pour the batter into the prepared pan. Bake for 1 hour, until a cake tester inserted into the center comes out clean. Let the cake cool in the pan on a wire rack for 15 minutes. Using the parchment overhang, lift the cake out of the pan and place on the rack. Let cool completely before slicing.

To serve, slice the cake into ½-inch-thick slices. Brush both sides of each slice with melted butter. Heat a cast-iron frying pan over medium heat. When the pan is hot, in batches, add the slices and sear, turning once, for about 1½ minutes on each side, until golden brown.

Transfer to individual serving plates and dust with confectioners' sugar or a scoop or two of ice cream. Serve warm.

Goat's milk junket with honey and walnuts

CUAJADA CON MIEL

Cuajada is a delicious traditional Basque dessert that is one step away from cheese, curds, and whey. In the (very) old days, Basques would heat the milk for *mamia*, as they called it, in a *kaiku*, a vessel originally made from a tree trunk and later from clay. The heating and pasteurization were achieved with hot rocks, which gave the milk a burnt taste. The flavor and texture of *cuajada* will grow on you, so you may need to make this healthy, lean dessert several times before you appreciate how wonderful it is. Serve it in beautiful vessels: unmatched etched glasses, little ceramic bowls, or Weck jars. Jam or maple syrup makes a nice substitute for the honey. | SERVES 12

6 cups goat's milk or farm-fresh full-fat sheep's or cow's milk

2 tablespoons sugar

Pinch of kosher salt

8 rennet capsules, crushed

1 tablespoon water

Honey, for drizzling

Chopped walnuts, for garnish

In a saucepan, combine the milk, sugar, and salt and heat gently over low heat until it reaches about 110°F on an instant-read thermometer. Remove from the heat and let cool slightly.

In a small bowl, stir together the rennet and water, then whisk the rennet mixture into the milk mixture, working quickly (if you work too slowly, the mixture will set). Pour into small bowls or tumblers and let cool at room temperature without agitating. When the junkets are set, cover and chill until ready to serve. They will keep for up to 3 days.

Serve chilled, topped with a drizzle of honey and a scattering of walnuts.

Spice cookies

POLVORONES

These dusty cookies are popular around Christmastime in the Basque Country, when they are prettily wrapped in printed tissue paper that keeps them from crumbling. They're so delicate that before they are eaten, they are smashed, still inside their paper, and compacted to prevent them from breaking up when they are bitten into. *"Polvorón, polvorón, que estás en mis manos"* is a line from a song sung by and to children as the cookies are passed around the table and hidden in cupped hands. My kids play this game all year long whenever the cookies are available, and they love to guess who is hiding the cookie before prying open each other's hands to find the prize. I have used butter here, rather than the more common lard, but the cookies have the same dusty texture. | MAKES 20 COOKIES

½ cup plus 2 tablespoons semolina flour

½ cup all-purpose flour

5 tablespoons granulated sugar

½ cup plus 1 tablespoon unsalted butter, at room temperature

3 egg yolks, at room temperature

¼ teaspoon ground cinnamon

1 tablespoon grated orange zest

1 teaspoon kosher salt

½ cup finely chopped walnuts, or ¼ cup blanched almond flour

Confectioners' sugar, for dusting (optional)

Line a large baking sheet with parchment paper. In a bowl, combine the semolina flour, all-purpose flour, granulated sugar, butter, egg yolks, cinnamon, orange zest, and salt. Mix together with your hands or a wooden spoon, making sure the butter is evenly incorporated. Add the walnuts, mixing until the pieces are evenly distributed throughout the dough.

Shape the dough into 1-inch balls and arrange on the prepared baking sheet, spacing them about 1 inch apart and pressing down lightly so they do not roll around. Chill for 1 hour.

Preheat the oven to 325°F. Using the palms of your hands, crush the cookies into little disks; their edges will look slightly cracked. Bake the cookies for 30 minutes, until they are golden brown and have a crumbly shortbread-like consistency. Transfer to a wire rack or wooden cutting board and let cool completely.

Dust just the tops of the cookies with confectioners' sugar, or lightly coat the cookies completely with the sugar. Or, wrap the cookies individually in white tissue paper. They will keep in an airtight container at room temperature for up to 1 week.

Basque-style French toast with pineapple

TORRIJAS CON PIÑA EN PEDRO JIMENEZ

All fried food is big around carnival time in Spain, and *torrijas* are no exception. A slice of bread soaked in milk and fried in olive oil, they're typical of Lent and Holy Week. It's so simple that most people have the ingredients already on hand. Didn't buy a pineapple? Just use a grapefruit or any other citrus. | SERVES 4 TO 6

1 perfectly ripe pineapple

About 2 cups Pedro Jimenez sherry

1 cup whole milk

2 cups heavy cream

¼ cup plus 1 tablespoon granulated sugar, plus more for sprinkling on pineapple (optional)

1 cinnamon stick

Zest of 1 lemon, in wide strips

Pinch of kosher salt

4 to 6 (1-inch-thick) slices pain de mie or challah

2 eggs

Unsalted butter, melted, for frying

Confectioners' sugar, for dusting

Peel the pineapple, then stand it upright and quarter it lengthwise. Cut away the hard core from each quarter and then slice the quarters vertically into ⅛-inch-thick slices. Place the slices in a plastic container and add the sherry to cover completely. Cover the container and let the pineapple soak at room temperature overnight. You will have more pineapple than you need for this recipe. The remainder will keep in the refrigerator for up to 1 week or longer.

In a saucepan, combine the milk, cream, granulated sugar, cinnamon stick, lemon zest, and salt over medium heat and bring to a simmer, stirring to dissolve the sugar. Remove from the heat, cover with plastic wrap, and let steep for about 1 hour, until cooled to room temperature.

Pour all but ½ cup of the cooled milk mixture into a small, deep baking pan. Submerge the bread slices in the milk in the pan and let soak until most of the liquid has been absorbed.

Remove the bread slices and place them in a single layer on a baking sheet. In a shallow bowl, whisk the eggs until blended, then whisk in the reserved ½ cup milk mixture.

Warm a nonstick pan over medium-low heat with a little melted butter, tipping the pan to coat it. Dip the bread one slice at a time into to the egg mixture, shaking off excess egg, and sear until golden brown on each side. Continue working in batches without crowding the pan until all the bread is dipped and browned. Place the pieces on a sheet pan as you go.

Serve immediately, dusted with confectioners' sugar and garnished with the pineapple.

9 │ Bebidas

BEVERAGES

Basques love to imbibe, and the spirit of constant party, or *fiestuki*, as Eder says, is one of the culture's most exciting aspects for foreigners. They like to have fun and share their festive ways with anyone willing to come along for the ride, which can mean bar crawling, making wine, tapping a cider barrel, or sipping a gin and tonic or a rum and Coke. They have a lot to celebrate and a lot of different kinds of drinks to help them do it right. What follows is an overview of the most common and important alcoholic beverages consumed throughout the Basque Country, where the people are as devoted to the quality of what they sip as they are to what they eat.

Wine

In the past, when nearly everyone lived in the countryside, most Basques made their own wine, and those who didn't traded other foods and services for it with their friends. Families still do this, though they are generally enjoying far better wines today.

As with cooking, boat building, and many other pursuits in which they became expert and soon monetized, the Basques came to fine wine making through a combination of necessity and opportunity. They were not exactly living in the world's breadbasket, and the poor soils of Rioja Alavesa (the left side of the Ebro River) meant there wasn't much that could be grown there other than grapevines. Those same poor soils that did not allow other crops to thrive also meant that Rioja Alavesa was spared phylloxera, a deadly blight that destroyed most of the vineyards in Europe, especially in France, in the late nineteenth century. As a result, the ever-industrious, business-minded Basques began to make aged wines for the French, who quickly bought them up.

The Basques have a history of using carbonic maceration for red wines (fermenting the grapes in a carbon dioxide–loaded atmosphere before they are crushed), yielding young wines meant to be drunk as *vino joven* in the same year. That said, they also have a long and prestigious history of aging wine in both the barrel (notably American oak) and in the bottle, so that theoretically a wine that has been released is ready to drink. Overall, the reds and whites of the Basque Country make great food wines, while the rosés (*rosados*) are out of this world. As proof of just how good Basque wines are, the Basque Country boasts Denominación de Origen (D.O.) status (a government regulatory system that ensures the wines are from a specific geographical origin and have been produced according to certain practices that guarantee high quality) for three of its Txakoli wines, for the wines of Rioja Alavesa, and for its *cava*. There is also Navarra, where Basque culture prevails and so too does a great wine-making tradition.

Several tiers of wine exist, beginning with young table wines and ascending through various levels of aging, according to the D.O.'s guidelines on aging and varietals. A trio of categories, *crianza*, *reserva*, and *gran reserva*, denote the amount of barrel aging and bottle aging the wine has undergone (barrel aging can last from one to three years, and bottle aging takes anywhere from six months to six years). The standards differ for reds and whites, with whites subject to fewer requirements. These categories also correlate with the prestige of the plots and the age of the vines, which in turn dictate yield, quality, concentration, and ageability.

Some winemakers feel burdened by all of the rules applied to their work, so they opt not to participate in the D.O. regulation and instead make high-quality table wines their way. Faced with an ever-changing ecological climate and better access to modern methods, they have chosen to place greater emphasis on making wines with personality than on maintaining classical rules. Yet classical wine making still has its proponents, and I am thankful to those winemakers who have persisted and are making excellent wines.

Many Basque restaurants offer a mix of classical and modern wines, and most favor hyperlocal selections over an international list. At more informal restaurants (called *jatetxeas*) like Txikito, wines are almost always local: Rioja (Alavesa), Navarra, and Txakoli made by great makers from older vines, better properties, and with longer aging. Basque wine is arguably some of the best wine in Spain and perhaps the world. It's definitely some of the best value. Like Basque restaurants, Basque *bodegas* have attracted talented and committed artisans who are striking a balance between the past and the future on a quest to make life more delicious.

Txakoli

Txakoli is happy wine! Its bracing acidity forces you to smile and then other people want to have what you are having. It is a charismatic wine and it has really caught on Stateside. I like to think it's because of Txikito that we no longer have to tell people in New York how to pronounce Txakoli (which, by the way, is pronounced *cha-co-lee*). This typical Basque wine, which can be white, rosé, or very occasionally red, is zesty and fresh, though some bottles coming from the interior these days are getting rounder, riper, and more complex. But as a rule, Txakoli is very fresh and dry, making it pretty much the only thing Basques drink by the seaside. Low in alcohol and an ideal accompaniment for salty foods and fish, the wine is poured in the same way as cider (see page 271): held high above a glass tumbler and poured to a depth of about two inches.

The predominant grape varietals used in Txakoli are the indigenous Hondarribi Zuri and Hondarribi Beltza, though others sometimes play a role, too. Red Txakolis with D.O. status tend to be challenging because they often retain a green quality, along with some harsh tannins and acidity. I describe them as rustic, but not in the most positive way. They're also not particularly inexpensive, so I recommend instead seeking out whites and rosés, the latter of which are increasingly being produced as a festive option for spring, when all of the wines are released. If you want something more complex, try "sobre lias" styles or bottle-aged whites like K5.

The style of most Txakolis from Gipuzkoa is influenced by the strong cider culture there, so they tend to have residual carbon dioxide and are thus a little spritzy. The ones from Bizkaia, like Uriondo, which is one of my favorites, are less effervescent, and the ones from Álava can be still or slightly bubbly. All are low alcohol and perfect with delicate flavors and make a nice contrast to fatty foods, too. At Txikito, we always serve Txakoli in tumblers like we do cider—just two fingers full so it stays crisp and cool. We also pour it from above like cider, so it aerates when it hits the glass. "Newstyle" Txakolis can be poured more conventionally.

Navarra and Rioja

The Basques reign over two other very exciting wine regions, Navarra and Rioja, that are producing high-quality wines comparable to some of the world's best. Navarra is home to many grape varietals that are well known in Bordeaux, such as Chardonnay, Garnacha (Grenache), Merlot, and Cabernet Sauvignon. In addition, you'll find Tempranillo, the definitive Spanish grape; Viura, a fabulous, easy-drinking white grape; sweet Moscatel; and Graciano, a blueberry-like blending grape with impressive potential in the right hands.

I'm particularly fond of the Navarran Garnachas (Garnatxas); the rosés are some of the best on the planet and pair beautifully with food all year long. At Txikito, we try to showcase all of the styles of rosé, which can vary from light pink and mineral to hot pink with raspberry or cherry notes. The red Garnachas from Navarra's colder areas are extraordinary, boasting great acidity and balance along with structure and finesse. One of the very best is Vega Sindoa's El Chaparral, an incredibly affordable bottle made by Concha Vecino, the winemaker at Bodegas Nekeas. It was during a walk with Concha through the vineyards, where she showed me which grapes were in her wine, that I began to understand the patience required to make wine in such a cold climate, and how much complexity and risk go into each bottle. As Concha's El Chaparral (which typically retails for fifteen dollars) illustrates, Navarran wines are a great value relative to their Riojan and French cousins. They definitely deserve a try. Another great red Navarran Garnacha is Artazuri, and I also like all of the wines from Marko Real, especially the rosé.

Next door in Rioja, D.O. Rioja Alavesa is widely considered to produce the highest-quality wines in the Basque Country and, depending on whom you're talking to, all of Spain. Located north of the Ebro River and south of the Cantabrian Mountains, the region has a long gastronomic and viticultural history, and its wines have great character and elegance, from prestigious producers like Cune and Contino to the more humble but delicious wines I drink daily, such as Luberri and Marqués de Vitoria. The everyday *vino joven* that you see at local bars is fermented from whole grape clusters, stems and all, and goes through carbonic maceration, which results in fresh, fruit-forward wines that are lower in alcohol and designed not for aging but to be released and consumed either the year they are produced or shortly thereafter. I love these wines: they're casual, very balanced, and refreshing.

Rioja's predominant grapes are Tempranillo, a native grape of great elegance and unmistakable Spanish character. Although it's good on its own, it's often blended with Graciano and Mazuelo and sometimes Garnacha grapes, as well as a few other varieties. Personally, I'm a big fan of the blends: each grape has a function and can add a lot of complexity, finesse, hardiness, and balance to wine. Different varieties are often planted side by side in order to bring out the best in one another, and they do.

Although wines are theoretically released when they're ready to drink, styles have evolved to become more concentrated and favor higher alcohol content, making the once-reliable descriptors of age—*crianza*, *reserva*, and *gran reserva*—occasionally deceiving. That said, they remain fairly good indicators of what you can expect, as do prices and availability. My advice is

that you seek out Riojan wines, regardless of category, because they're generally pretty impressive. I especially enjoy wines from Bodegas Basilio Izquierdo, a boutique producer that makes the B de Basilio and Acodo whites and their red counterparts. These are small production wines that emphasize unique blends and are truly special.

I also like Contino wines, which are universally fabulous and quite expensive. The winery's white is complex, as is its new Garnacha. I like seeing the same level of quality wine making in an entry-level wine as in its tremendous Graciano and blended age-worthy wines.

Ostatu's white Viura is good year after year, and other great reds include those from Bodegas Muriel and Barón de Ley. And Basque winemaker Telmo Rodriguez is also producing beautiful bottles; I particularly like his white wine, which is a blend of many grapes, and his *grand reservas*. Telmo also makes wine outside of the Basque Country, and these Basque heritage wines often round out our list, along with a small rotating list of Irouléguys (French Basque wines) and wines from Latin American winemakers with Basque heritage.

Irouléguy

I like this unusual wine, which comes from the French side of the Basque Country. I'm a particular fan of the whites, which we have at Txikito. Their grapes—among them Petit Courbu, Gros and Petit Manseng, and Folle Blanche (also found in some Txakolis)—have bizarre flavors, often with discernible pineapple and herbaceous notes. There are some nice rosés, too. The reds, which are typically blends of Cabernet Franc, Cabernet Sauvignon, and the extremely tannic Tannant, are rough and rustic, with a certain iron-like quality. Because they can be pretty tannic, it's best to hang on to them for a while before drinking, or to seek out an older vintage, which you might be lucky enough to come across if you go combing for wine in unlikely places.

Sherry

Sherry is not a Basque product, but it is an incredibly popular beverage in the Basque Country. And like much of the olive oil consumed in the Basque Country, manzanilla sherry comes from the south of Spain, specifically Andalusia. It is a fortified wine that is blended from many vintages and goes through biological aging under a blanket of *flor*, a white mold unique to Jerez, where it is made. It then goes through oxidative aging as the *flor* dies off, which yields darker, more concentrated, nuttier styles like oloroso.

But Basques are most interested in manzanilla, the freshest style of sherry, from Sanlúcar de Barrameda. They drink the dry, pale sherry in large quantities; in fact, sherry *bodegas*, or producers, have sponsored some of the most important Basque bars, which boast glorious tile work that serves as an indirect advertisement for the brand.

Manzanilla is also the name for chamomile tea, so be clear if you are ordering one before 11:00 a.m. My father-in-law taught me to drink manzanilla before 3:00 p.m., and it has proven to be a good lesson. It is the perfect drink to accompany great Basque shellfish dishes like peel-and-eat shrimp, and is an ideal accompaniment to charcuterie, fried foods, and cheese. For something truly amazing, pour a tipple of manzanilla into a portion of consommé. I cook with sherry all the time at home and once opened, it will last for a few days in the fridge, which is something you can't say about most wines. My favorite labels for drinking and cooking alike are La Guita, La Gitana, and Valdespino Manzanilla Delicioso en Rama.

Hard cider

Hard cider is called *sidra* in Spanish and *sagardo* in Euskera—literally, "apple wine." Its history traces back to the Romans, who brought apples with them to the region. For centuries, *sagardo* was the predominant beverage for the Basques; the wine regions of Álava and Navarra were far from Gipuzkoa, the heart of the Basque Country's cider production, and so cider houses maintained a stronghold over the province. In time, Txakoli wine began to make inroads throughout Bizkaia and near the sea, though cider remains important to both the culture and the gastronomic identity of the area. Today, it's gaining popularity in the United States, as more and more farmers replace eating apples with cider apples in their orchards.

The most famous center of cider production is the town of Astigarraga, where cider is made in October and usually ready for drinking in January. You can drink it straight from the barrel through April, but bottles are consumed throughout the year. A visit to the cider house each season is mandatory among friends: the drink is synonymous with celebration, sharing, and gathering.

Basque cider is not sweet. It is made from dozens of cider-specific apple varieties that yield a crisp, refreshing beverage with a slight yeasty or cheesy quality. The best ciders have nuanced apple flavors with complex aromas and a clean finish. Although they take some time to get to know, they have a lot to say, and they say it particularly well as accompaniments to steak, cheese, and fatty and lean white meats. Until recently, we had a hard time getting proper

Basque cider for Txikito, so we've enjoyed seeking out newly minted East Coast producers who are making naturally carbonated ciders from "lost" or "foraged" heirloom apple varieties. Their work provides us with a window to the future of cider both here and in the Basque region. Although cider consumption has decreased in Spain, it is just peaking here in the States, and I'm looking forward to seeing how both Basque and local producers seize this moment. For domestic producers, try Farnum Hill, Shacksbury (which also imports English and Basque ciders under its name), and Aaron Burr; for imported Basque ciders, look for Petritegi from Gipuzkoa, and Bordatto from the French side.

Cider is served two fingers at a time in large, thin glass tumblers so it stays fresh and oxygenated. If it is being poured from a bottle, it is traditional to hold the bottle about two feet above the glass so that the cider is agitated as it hits the bottom of the glass, which brings out its aromas and spritzy quality.

Beer

Basques enjoy drinking beer, generally preferring simple lager-style varieties that are quaffable and not heavy. Although artisanal beer production is increasing in the Basque Country, until recently the artistry in beer was on the service side, left to bartenders who clearly have affection for their *zurritos*, or tiny beers, and *cañas*, or full glasses. I appreciate the pride they take in pouring the beer, because service is a huge part of what charms me about eating in Spain. Basques like a little foam on their beer, perhaps more so than Americans, so expect more than you are accustomed to. And a bartender will invariably tell you that the beer he or she is pouring is the best. When you taste it, you'll likely agree, especially if it has been beautifully poured in just the right amount and is cold.

Many craft beers are now being produced in Spain, but I know of only one, from Pamplona, that is available in New York. Our friend Kevin Patricio is currently producing craft beers in San Sebastián, and we are hoping to be able to serve his Basqueland Brew Project here someday. Until then, just be discerning about the beer you choose and make sure it doesn't overwhelm the food.

Other drinks

Clara

Blend beer with a lemon soft drink and you have a *clara*. Cousin to the shandy, this light, refreshing cocktail is especially Basque if made with Kas Limón or La Casera Gaseosa, two Basque soft drinks worth seeking out at your favorite Spanish food source online or in your area. If you get lucky, the art on the can of Kas will be by Basque artist Mikel Urmeneta.

Kalimotxo

This blend of Coca-Cola and red wine is the beverage of choice for young people at fiestas. It's a fun drink that can be embellished with aged rum, lime juice, and a cinnamon stick. The Coke has a corrective effect on bad, very acidic wines and goes well the with fruity carbonic-maceration wines. Make sure you drink this on the rocks.

Patxaran and licor de hierbas

Basques love a digestif, and herb-infused liqueurs (*licor de hierbas*) and anisettes infused with sloe berries (*patxaran*) are fabulous concoctions to add to your repertoire. Keep a couple of *chupitos*, or shot glasses, in your freezer and sip these beverages after dinner: both your stomach and your palate will thank you. These drinks will also inspire you to infuse your own liqueurs with aromas you like; at Txikito, we've used huckleberries and serviceberries.

Vermouth

This fortified wine is well loved in the Basque Country: white vermouth often appears in the form of a *marianito*, served on the rocks with olives and a lemon twist. Sweet or dark vermouth is typically served as a *vermút preparado*, served on the rocks with an orange slice and a couple of olives. I like both of these drinks, preferably paired with raw clams somewhere near the water. Whenever I serve vermouth on the rocks to a friend in the summertime, he or she always says, "Wow! This is my new summer drink!" Look for Atxa and Perucchi, two Spanish brands with very different flavor profiles.

Gin and tonic

The Basques have reinvented the gin and tonic as a luxury item. That makes me very happy, because I love this drink. I prefer mine to be classic, and at Txikito, the gin and tonic has been the subject of many conversations. We serve only one gin, one tonic, and always with lemon, not lime. When we first opened, I got a lot of flack for our exceptionally narrow cocktail list. Only having variations on vermouth, rum and Coke, and gin and tonic (and being a bit inflexible about how we made those) ticked off a few people. But I wanted people to drink in a different way—to look at an old drink with fresh eyes. I still don't think you need to make a gin and tonic with a million different gins or mixers. Just make one, but it must be a good one that you love, to share with someone you love. Make anything with love and flair, and it will be received in kind. And take a position: have a point of view about all things food and drink. That is the Basque way.

Rum and Coke

The principle I apply to the gin and tonic also goes for rum and Coke. Buy real, preferably cane-sweetened Coca-Cola in a bottle and good aged rum; my mother-in-law, Amaia, taught me to use aged rum in my rum and Coke. Serve the drink in a globe wineglass with big, clear ice cubes and a squeeze of lime. It is a seriously delicious cocktail. At Txikito we use Plantation 5-Year Grande Reserve. In Spain, these kinds of cocktails are consumed after dessert.

INGREDIENTS

In most cases, I recommend buying imported Basque or Spanish ingredients, either online or from a specialty store (see Sources, page 287). Imported Basque and Spanish goods are still a tremendous value, just like Basque and Spanish wine. That said, you can also use non-Basque ingredients you love in Basque ways. We always look for the best expression of an item; the quality trumps its provenance. What follows is a list of the most essential Basque pantry items.

Oil and vinegar

At Txikito, we use very few different oils but keep a large variety of vinegars on hand.

ARBEQUINA OLIVE OIL: Arbequina is a common olive cultivar. We use this oil for both cooking and finishing dishes. We're big fans of Romanico, a Catalan brand, and Abbae de Queiles, an organic brand grown on a small estate in Navarra. Both are a bit grassy and have a luscious mouthfeel.

SHERRY VINEGAR: We recommend imported Spanish sherry vinegar, and once you find one with a sweet complexity that you like, stick with it. Be careful that you do not pick up a bottle of cooking sherry, which is an easy mistake to make. (Don't use cooking sherry when I call for manzanilla or fino sherry, either.)

GARNACHA WINE VINEGAR: Not as acidic as sherry vinegar, this is a versatile red wine vinegar of very high quality that is ideal for *refritos* (seasoned oil-and-vinegar mixtures) that accompany vegetables, fish, and other foods and for many other uses. If you can't find it, substitute another red wine vinegar.

SEASONED RICE VINEGAR: Sweet and relatively mild, rice vinegar is made from fermented rice or rice wine. You can find it in the Asian foods aisle of most supermarkets. We like it for its low acidity and neutral sweetness.

CHAMPAGNE VINEGAR: Although you don't need to spend a lot of money for this vinegar, you do need to buy one that's actually from France. We buy a commodity French brand that is probably the cheapest imported variety available. If you can't find champagne vinegar, Chardonnay vinegar makes a fine substitute. Champagne vinegar is great for making quick pickles or for any dish in which you would typically use cider vinegar.

Chile peppers

Chile peppers appear in numerous Basque dishes; here is a rundown of the varieties used repeatedly in this book.

GUINDILLA: Sold fresh, dried, and pickled, the sweet-spicy guindilla is one of the most common peppers used in Basque and Spanish cooking. Typically on the mild side, it's grown in numerous red or green varieties that can range from about 1 to 6 inches in length. Its pickled form, which is similar in flavor to Italian peperoncini, is used most famously on the iconic Gilda pintxo (page 51).

GUAJILLO: Used widely in Mexican cooking, these mild to hot dark red peppers are typically sold dried. In this book, they're used primarily as a substitute for choricero peppers.

CHORICERO: Grown in Navarra, this bittersweet red pepper is extremely common in Basque cooking but difficult to locate in the United States. Typically sold dried, it is rehydrated to be used in pastes, sauces, and stews.

SHISHITO: Small, slender, sweet, and green (and red when it's mature), this Japanese pepper is similar to the Basque *pimiento de Gernika*—and much easier to find in the United States. "Shishito" was also the nickname of Félix Ibarguren, a famous Basque chef and cookbook author who sold a number of his books to Japanese chefs in the late nineteenth and early twentieth centuries.

PIQUILLO: Bright red and arrow shaped, the piquillo is an excellent roasting pepper beloved for its extremely sweet flavor and versatility. It's typically sold canned or jarred, and often stuffed with other ingredients.

PADRÓN: Native to Galicia, this small, green pepper has a mild flavor (though you'll find the occasional scorcher)

OSSAU-IRATY CHEESE: This compact, semifirm sheep's milk cheese hails from the French side of the Basque Country. Its flavor is fairly neutral, and while I love it on its own, it's also a terrific melting cheese for sandwiches, pastas, and croquettes.

BLEU DES BASQUES CHEESE: This sheep's milk blue cheese is exceptionally creamy for a blue when young and grows steadily more crumbly with age. Woven with delicate veins and not too salty, it's made in the Pyrenees on the French side of the Basque Country. It is ideal for using on salads and in other dishes where you want to add an earthy, rich element and savoriness.

IDIAZÁBAL CHEESE: One of most important cheeses made in the Basque Country, this hard, aged cheese received Spanish Denominación de Origen status in 1987. That means that strict standards govern its production, including that it must be made from the raw milk of Laxta and Carranza sheep, two long-haired breeds that graze in the rolling hills of the Basque Country. Boasting a rich, nutty, flavor, it was traditionally lightly smoked by hanging the wheels to dry near a fireplace. Today, most Idiazábal sold in the Basque Country is unsmoked. In the United States, smoked wheels are common, to distinguish it from Roncal, the Basque Country's other popular U.S. import. I like to steep the smoky Idiazábal rinds in warm milk and then use them in croquettes and in creamed corn or other non-Basque favorites. Idiazábal is used in a variety of traditional dishes in the Basque Country and is also a popular dessert cheese, often paired with quince jam.

that makes it ideal for frying in olive oil and sprinkling with salt, as it's often served in the Basque Country.

CHEYENNE: Compact and medium hot, this bright-orange pepper often shows up in Basque cooking dried and ground into powder. Difficult to track down in the United States, it can be substituted with dried and ground cayenne pepper.

Dairy and eggs

Pasturing animals is a Basque tradition, and in keeping with that heritage, we seek out pastured eggs, dairy products, and meats at Txikito and at home as much as possible. They taste better and are, for lack of a better word, grassier.

RONCAL CHEESE: Like Idiazábal, Roncal is a traditional Basque sheep's milk cheese with D.O. status. Firm and slightly grainy, it is made from the raw milk of the latxa and rasa sheep that graze in Navarra's Roncal Valley. Pressed and aged for six months, it has a robust, herbaceous, sweet-spicy flavor and musty aroma that pair well with a glass of Tempranillo; it's particularly delicious when stuffed into piquillo peppers.

PARMESAN CHEESE: Although it is an Italian cheese and not a typical Basque ingredient, at Txikito we use this hard cow's milk cheese frequently as a seasoning. It creates a nice umami effect in a number of dishes.

GOAT'S MILK: We recommend buying goat's milk, which is sweet and slightly tangy, from a farmers' market vendor because it will more taste like goat, but it's also widely available at grocery and health food stores. We use it in desserts like *cuajada* (page 259), cheesecakes, and ice cream.

HEAVY CREAM: Always buy heavy cream with at least 36 to 40 percent butterfat, as it will have greater flavor and add incomparable richness to any recipe. Whenever possible, avoid ultrapasteurized cream, which carries a slight cooked taste.

CRÈME FRAÎCHE: I like to add crème fraîche to scrambled eggs and sauces to enhance their flavor and texture, and I often whip it for finishing cakes and flans. For the best flavor and texture, purchase a local organic product or Cabot Creamery brand.

EGGS: Buy pastured eggs, which come from hens that are allowed to roam free, eating plants and insects. At the grocery store, they're often labeled "pasture raised." The eggs have rich, yellow yolks, wonderful flavor, and are of generally higher quality than eggs from hens raised on a conventional diet. Look for them at farmers' markets or roadside farm stands. I have also found that Japanese gourmet stores are a good source. The one I go to in the East Village has no fewer than five brands of organic eggs.

Wine and alcohol

We delve deeper into the vinicultural traditions of the Basque Country in chapter 9. What follows here is a short list of the wines and spirits you'll need for cooking.

WHITE COOKING WINE: As the adage goes, if you wouldn't drink it, don't cook with it. Txakoli, an effervescent, extremely dry white, works particularly well with mussels and clams. Viura from Rioja is great for adding freshness to braises and fish stews.

RED COOKING WINE: Reds from Navarra are generally affordable and fruit forward; I would steer clear of wines with strong oaky notes for cooking.

MANZANILLA SHERRY: For more on sherry, see page 271. Because it's fortified (i.e., higher proof), an open bottle of sherry will last longer than other wines: for drinking, it lasts about a week, but for cooking, it's good for about a month. It works well in sauces and for deglazing pans and is wonderful for steaming bivalves and for adding a bit of freshness at the end of cooking. Avoid Chinese and grocery-store brands; this is something that must be from Jerez and that you need to buy in a liquor store.

Fish and seafood

Buying good fish has everything to do with trust and being able to see it with your own eyes. When possible, you will want to see your fish with its head still attached. When it comes to crustaceans and mollusks, look for either living or frozen critters and pass up anything in between. The exception is squid, which, like fish, is usually kept in a slushy ice bed on the way home. Anytime you can clean your own fish and shrimp, you are guaranteed a better product.

SALT COD: Store-bought salt cod—*bakalao* in Basque, *bacalao* in Spanish—is sold in a wide range of varying quality. At Txikito, we always cure our cod (see page 142), but if you want to take an expensive shortcut, plan ahead and keep Giraldo or a similar high-quality brand of salt cod in your refrigerator. Giraldo, which is available online, is a Spanish brand that has been around since the 1970s. The company cures its cod for several months before desalting it naturally, without bleach or preservatives, and then lets it drain thoroughly. The resulting product has a beautiful, flaky texture and is sold in a number of different cuts. Although we don't recommend

it for raw preparations—we prefer the texture of our homemade salt cod—it is a real treat when used for cooked dishes.

SQUID INK: What is marketed as squid ink is more often than not cuttlefish ink, which is similar to squid ink but "inkier." This is what we use at the restaurant and is what we mean when we say "squid ink" throughout the book. Harvesting ink from squid is daunting and can yield an inconsistent product. You can buy the ink from your fishmonger or from Spanish or Italian markets. Sometimes it's frozen, and sometimes it's kept in little soy sauce–like packets that can be stored in the cupboard. If you buy it frozen, keep it frozen until you're ready to use it.

SQUID: Fishmongers will often clean squid for customers, though we recommend you do it yourself (see page 172). Look for squid that hasn't been chemically treated (the precleaned stuff often is); once you clean it, it keeps well in the freezer, where it will even tenderize over time. If you must buy frozen cleaned squid, try to buy it from a boat, so you know it wasn't cleaned in a factory. Cuttlefish is reliably tender and makes a great squid substitute in rice dishes and soups.

OCTOPUS: At Txikito, we buy our octopus frozen, not fresh, and we recommend you do the same. Look for the biggest octopus you can get your hands on; "baby" octopi are actually a different species and not nearly as tasty. Octopus freezes well because the process tenderizes the meat. Try to buy octopus imported from Spain, caught near Cádiz or Morocco, or alternatively imported from Portugal—the species from the south of Spain and along the Atlantic coast are better—and avoid any that has been injected with water (ask your fishmonger), which affects the texture, salt level, and cost (octopus is priced by the pound). You can also buy excellent marinated octopus in delis and Italian specialty stores, which is great for making *pintxos*.

HEAD-ON SHRIMP: Shrimp heads contain a delicious iodine fat, so be sure to buy your shrimp with the head on. If sucking shrimp heads isn't your thing, you can use them to make great stocks. Head or no head, buy the best-quality shrimp you can afford. At Txikito, we use imported Catalan *langostinos* (langoustines); closer to home, some great domestic crustaceans are Carolina brown, Florida royal reds, and Hawaiian shrimp. If you can't find fresh shrimp, it's okay to buy them frozen.

Canned and jarred goods

Canned and *jarred* are not bad words in Spain and in the Basque Country. On the contrary, canned and jarred foods, called *conservas*, are highly regarded and expensive. Seafood like tuna, mackerel, mussels, sardines, and anchovies are caught and preserved in tins with little more than olive oil and salt, and because there are so few ingredients, each one must be perfect. The same goes for vegetables like white asparagus and peppers, which take on a luscious texture when they're preserved. And like wine, many *conservas* improve with age. Because they're so prized, *conservas* are often saved for special occasions and served without much adornment to better showcase their virtues.

WHITE ASPARAGUS: White asparagus is a source of national pride in the Basque Country. The Cojonudos variety from Navarra is insanely huge, with a diameter almost as big as a quarter. We prefer to buy asparagus on the slightly smaller size, though what's most important is the quality. In addition to being delicious eaten straight out of the can, white asparagus makes a tasty partner to mayonnaise and eggs and in *salsa verde* with hake. You can find white asparagus in specialty stores and through online Spanish purveyors, but, like piquillo peppers, they've also started popping up in stores like Whole Foods.

PIQUILLO PEPPERS: Wood-roasted, peeled, and canned, piquillos (*pikillos* in Basque) are a signature Basque product that is gaining traction in the United States largely because they are extremely sweet and deeply flavorful. Peeled by hand, they are packed in their own juices without ever being rinsed in water, which further enhances their flavor. I recommend buying tambourine-size tins: larger-format tins house the best and largest peppers. Look for *piquillos de Lodosa*, a specialty of Navarra, which are available online or in Spanish import stores. If you discover that a local farmer is growing them, you can roast and peel your own.

BLACK TRUFFLE PASTE: Although it lacks the mind-bending potency of a real truffle, the paste is an affordable alternative. Rustichella is my preferred brand.

CANNED TOMATOES: Many excellent brands of canned tomatoes are available and any type will do, though look for those without basil leaves, which alter the pure tomato flavor. I buy canned whole tomatoes for the restaurant, but at home I use Pomì brand, which comes in a Tetra Pak (aseptic packaging). When cooking with tomatoes, the key is to know your acid level and to use or reduce it to your advantage.

PICKLED GREEN GUINDILLA PEPPERS: Guindilla peppers (aka piparras) are almost always sold pickled. Look for the smallest ones you can find: the smaller the pepper, the bigger the flavor and generally the better the texture. They are yellowish green and have a tangy-sweet taste. Matiz brand has particularly nice ones. If you find fresh guindillas, blister them as you would a shishito or pickle them. I do.

BONITO DEL NORTE: Tender, firm, silky, and torpedo-shaped, bonito del norte is a type of albacore tuna that is beloved in Spain. It is eaten fresh but is also a highly regarded canned food that is cooked in salted water before being packaged. The best canned tuna is packed in olive oil, not water, and has ample contact with the oil, which enhances its texture and flavor. I like two brands in particular: Serrats and Ortiz. Serrats is accessible in price and excellent in quality; Ortiz is worth

ARTICHOKE HEARTS: I recommend that you buy fresh artichokes and clean them yourself, but if you opt to buy them already cleaned, look for halved or quartered hearts in jars with a minimum of citric acid and other additives. The María Jesús brand from Navarra puts up some very precious canned ones. Otherwise, I recommend frozen hearts from Peru. You can also look for good-quality frozen artichoke hearts at Whole Foods or other high-end grocers. Do not buy Italian-style hearts in vinegar, as they are too acidic and soft.

CHORICERO PEPPER PASTE: Make your own (page 39) or buy it at a specialty foods store. I like Gutarra brand from Navarra. Mexican guajillo paste is a good substitute.

every penny. You can also make your own variation by buying skipjack or other bluefish when in season.

ANCHOVIES: In the Basque Country, anchovies are an artisanal product that is processed in small factories in fishing villages throughout the region. At the Ortiz factories along the northern coast of Spain, the whole fish are stored in salt-filled wooden barrels until they are ready to be shipped, and then they are cleaned, boned, and packed under oil by women who process them according to methods that go back to Roman times. These women take a huge amount of pride in their work. They also have the world's softest hands, a benefit of being up to their wrists in oil day after day. Once the anchovies are submerged in oil, they begin to break down, much like tuna. Unlike tuna, which is cooked, anchovies are *semi-conserva* (semi-raw) and should be kept refrigerated once you bring them home.

Anchovies are sold two ways: under salt and under oil. I prefer the second kind, and I like those sold by Ortiz and Don Bocarte. Excellent Basque options are Maisor and Nardín. Although smaller, lesser anchovies have their uses—they provide a big umami punch in vinaigrettes and sauces—I recommend investing more money in the larger, meatier loins that are as great in dishes as they are on their own. These anchovies are meant to be eaten straight out of the tin or jar and are so exceptionally delicious that the very best thing you can do to them is nothing at all. They oxidize quickly, however, so cover them in oil after opening—or better still, finish them.

You will also sometimes find anchovies sold as *boquerones*. The term is applied to both fresh and processed anchovies, though it can also mean almost any small fish in the bluefish or whitebait family. For our purposes, a *boquerone* is just a vinegared white anchovy. You can find them at many delicatessens or fine grocery stores, where they are typically sold in transparent packaging that allows you to see the large, white loins. *Boquerones* should be labeled as such; if possible, buy them without the garlic and parsley that often accompanies them. If you can't find excellent Spanish brands, look for Italian *alici marinate*, which receive the same treatment.

Meat

Charcuterie is embedded in Spanish culture, and the Basques have their own traditions and recipes for fully utilizing the pig and all its parts. At a *txariboda*, which is a *matanza*, or pig slaughter, a family or community breaks down the pig and makes the most of it, cooking, salting, casing, and storing it over the course of a day.

JAMÓN SERRANO: A type of dry-cured ham, *jamón serrano* is generally served in thin slices or occasionally diced. Never purchase *jamón serrano* less than 18 months of age, because it will taste insufficiently cured. Buy it sliced as close to the day of consumption as possible, and let it come to room temperature before consuming it. You can also buy a large

rear-leg ham. Because it weighs less, the *paleta* is cheaper, though it is still an excellent product. You can buy the whole *paleta* and shave off as much as you need or buy small pouches of the ham in Cryovac packets that protect the meat from drying out once it is sliced. If you shop at stores carrying imported Spanish foods, end pieces of *jamón*, which are good for cooking, are increasingly available. They are usually on the counter in a basket and sell for much less per pound than the *jamón*, much like the difference between Parmesan cheese and Parmesan rinds.

JAMÓN FAT: Whenever you buy large chunks or a whole *jamón*, don't just trim and toss the fat. Save it for seasoning sauces and rice dishes or for pressing into toasty warm sandwiches called *serranitos* (page 61). Or make friends with your Spanish *jamón* deli counter specialist and have him or her save you the fat. As my mother says, *el que no llora no mama* (the squeaky wheel gets the spoils).

CHORIZO: Chorizo is a paprika-laced dry-cured sausage eaten throughout Spain. In the Basque Country, *chorizo ibérico* can be purchased at charcuterie stores and gourmet markets at virtually every price point. Compared to what can be found here in the United States, Basque chorizo is exceptional: its fat melts on your tongue. For *pintxos* and standard dishes, we use Palacios, Dehesa, and Fermín brands. For fresh chorizo, we recommend you make your own chorizo hash (page 62), which is fresh chorizo minus the casing.

piece or even a whole *jamón* (rear-leg ham) or *paleta* (front-leg ham), which will last you practically forever. I like the Navidul and Redondo Iglesias brands.

JAMÓN IBÉRICO: *Jamón iberico* is considered the crème de la crème of Spanish dry-cured ham; a Denominación de Origen product, it's made from black Iberian pigs and cured for a minimum of 12 months. Its highest grade, *jamón ibérico de bellota*, is made from pigs finished on a strict diet of acorns before they are slaughtered. Because the pig's diet has such a great impact on its flavor, it in turn determines the grade of the ham. When it comes to buying *jamón ibérico*, look for the *paleta* or *paletilla*, which is the front-leg ham, rather than the larger

Miscellaneous pantry items

Most of the ingredients that round out the Basque pantry will no doubt be familiar to many American cooks; all are versatile workhorses that show up frequently in the Basque repertoire. Ingredients like beans and spices shouldn't be kept indefinitely, so buy them in small quantities from sources with a high turnover, which ensures better quality.

BEANS: We like Rancho Gordo's heirloom Rio Zape and Sangre de Toro beans, two dark red dried bean varieties that have thin skins and produce a great liquor when cooked. In the Basque Country, Tolosa is famous for its beans, but I find that if you don't bring them back with you, imported beans sit for so long in warehouses here that you end up paying a premium for what is often an inferior product. At Txikito, we wait until the end of the summer to load up on local fresh beans like *pochas* (white beans), which are grown for us, and lima beans. We also love chickpeas and lentils. Although we prefer dried chickpeas, which can often be found in the grocery store bulk section, the canned versions will also work in these recipes. Lentil-wise, we're partial to the tan Spanish Pardina and slate-green French Le Puy varieties; you can find them in finer grocery stores and also online.

BOMBA RICE: This short-grain white rice, reputed to be the very best in Spain—*arroz bomba de Calasparra* even has a Denominación de Origen to prove it—can absorb three times its volume in liquid without losing its firm texture. It's excellent for making risottos and paella and can be as dry or juicy as you prefer. Just make sure you don't stir it when making Basque-style rice. Bayo and Cebolla brands are a step down from Calasparra but still work well. A good substitute is high-quality sushi rice, though you must rinse it well before using to reduce the starch.

CHOCOLATE: High-quality dark (bittersweet) chocolate, with a 68 to 72 percent cacao content, is used in the recipes in this book. I like Valrhona and sometimes use it in combination with Guittard.

GELATIN: Made from animal collagen, gelatin is used to thicken cold soups and molded desserts. We prefer to buy sheet gelatin because it's easy to use and dissolves well. If using powdered gelatin, 1 tablespoon is equivalent to 4 sheets.

MUSHROOMS: Basques are obsessed with mushrooms, whether they're cultivated or foraged. Especially popular are *bolete* (aka porcini), *zizas* (aka chanterelles or hedgehogs), and *niscalos* (aka milk caps). Look for unblemished mushrooms that are relatively clean. If they come from excessively sandy forest floors, you will get impossibly gritty mushrooms. Cultivated button mushrooms are also a favorite. Make sure they are white and firm.

OLIVES: My favorite olive types are Arbequina (little green and brown olives with a mild, buttery flavor grown all over Catalonia and the south of Spain), Empeltre (soft-fleshed black olives that are the

or *pimentón picante*, is a bold, combustible seasoning that plays well with chorizo and other meat dishes. Similar to smoked paprika, sweet smoked paprika, or *pimentón de la Vera dulce*, has a mellow edge that pairs nicely with milder dishes like garlic soup with salt cod and poached monkfish. And smoked paprika, or *pimentón de la Vera*, has a wonderfully woodsy flavor that works beautifully in meat dishes like pork roast and braised veal shank.

SALT: At the restaurant, we use two kinds of salt. For seasoning, we like Diamond kosher salt. Although all kosher salt may appear to be created equal, that couldn't be further from the truth. It can vary enormously in terms of how it's processed and the size of the grind. Diamond and Morton's, for example, are almost identical in appearance but season food very differently: ¼ cup of Morton's weighs twice as much as ¼ cup of Diamond, so the same volume amount is much saltier. If you're not using Diamond for these recipes, we recommend salting your food to taste. But really, just use Diamond if you can.

For finishing dishes, we often use Maldon salt. When we first began using it two decades ago, it was pretty difficult to find; today, it's readily available online and at many grocery stores and specialty food shops.

Basque version of niçoise or Gaeta olives), and Manzanilla (tangy brine-cured olives from Seville and Andalusia). I recommend that you always buy olives with their pits intact (unless you're using them for the *gilda* on page 51). If you can, shop for olives at a store specializing in imported Spanish foods: you'll be buying from someone who cares about the details when it comes to olive quality.

PAPRIKA: In this book you'll find a few varieties of Spanish paprika, or *pimentón de la Vera*, the red powdered spice made from grinding the dried pods of various chile peppers. Sweet Spanish paprika, or *pimentón dulce*, has a sweet, mild flavor that works well with bean and seafood dishes, as well as *refrito*. Hot Spanish paprika,

SOURCES

Thanks to the Internet, there are a number of places where you can find high-quality Spanish and Basque products, regardless of where you live. These are some of our favorites.

DESPAÑA BRAND FOODS
Our friends and purveyors of many years, this New York–based company has great pantry items, salt cod, *jamónes*, and cheeses, as well as their own private label brands.
despanabrandfoods.com

FAGOR
This Basque appliance manufacturer makes my favorite pressure cookers, which I highly recommend if you want to cook beans, stews, and the like in a fraction of the time. You can buy Fagor-brand pressure cookers in many American stores.
fagoramerica.com

FORMAGGIO KITCHEN
With locations in Boston and New York, Formaggio Kitchen is a great place to buy Spanish and Basque imports, including Txakoli vinegar.
formaggiokitchen.com

SPANISH TABLE
With three storefronts along the West Coast, this company is great for cookware and kitchen tools, like flan molds and tortilla flippers; they also carry a good range of meats and *conservas*.
spanishtable.com

LA TIENDA
Based in Williamsburg, Virginia, La Tienda carries an impressive range of *jamónes*, chorizos, cheeses, and wines. It doesn't have a huge array of Basque items, but it often has good marmalades, beans, and anchovies from Basque companies.
tienda.com

ZINGERMAN'S
Although this Ann Arbor, Michigan, deli is best known for its sandwiches, it also sells an excellent variety of specialty and Spanish foods. You'll find numerous kinds of olive oils, vinegars, cured meats, and tinned fish here.
zingermans.com

ACKNOWLEDGMENTS

To our parents and grandparents for the table, the food-making, and the memory-making. Special thanks to Maria Inés Raij and Bruce Harris: there are no words for our gratitude. Txikito would not be but for the two of you.

Dani Aixela, you are the most positive, food loving, uncynical inspiration to both of us. (And thank you for marrying us!)

To Eder's *kuadrilla*, "La Hambrina," thank you for the eternal friendship and fun. To Ernesto Largo and Naiara Pujana, thank you for opening your home and you hearth for this book.

Gracias to all our staff for their hard work and friendship, and especially to Naño, Mivi, Chile, and Dani for their work on the book. We finally have recipes!

Also to Jason Arias for your wisdom and all-around love for this profession; thank you for being there when we could not be, and for making it possible for us enjoy our children.

Mikel Urmeneta, thank you for bringing Txikito to life with your mural and poetry. When you live with a piece of art in your life, day in and day out, it enriches and informs you. Your generous gesture forever changed the restaurant and even the way we see ourselves. Thank you.

Luis Bollo, thank you for introducing us to one another and to the joys of working together.

Carla Raij, Nora Montero, Urtzi Ruiz de Loizaga, Susan Finesman, Jackie Terrebonne, John Willoughby, Anya Von Bremzen, Maricel Presilla, Elena Marsal, Megan Krigbaum, Concha Vecino, André Tamers, thank you for being early and constant believers and supporters.

Amy Wilson: thank you for getting it; Robin Raisfeld, Rob Patronite, and Peter Meehan: thank you for getting us. David Chang and Anthony Bourdain, thanks for remembering us when there is so much to remember.

Mark Kurlansky and Emily Lobsenz, thank you for your appreciation for all things *euskaldun*, for your films, your books, your creativity. We are still learning from you.

Andoni Luis Aduriz and Aitor Basabe, thank you for teaching us how to eat and cook by feeding our souls, our bellies, and our imagination.

Andrew Knowlton, thank you for noticing in the first place and then sticking with the story.

Xavi Sacristá and Rafael Clarasó: when Catalunya was home to Eder, you taught him how to be and how challenging and satisfying a life in cooking could be. We are still in it because you didn't sugar-coat it.

Ashley Christensen, Mikel Zeberio, Javier Urones, Georgina Aspa, Eduard Llanas, Luis Claramonte, Francis Vega, Fernando Zarauz, Louie Sloves, Juan Ángel Vela Del Campo, and Karlos Arguiñano: thank you for sharing our love of food, and showing it in all you do.

Fany Gerson, thank you for being an amazing friend and the sweetest person in sweets on the planet. *Tu eres* "Sweet Mexico."

Aaron Wehner, thank you for believing in this book and making Ten Speed Press the most extraordinary home for it, even before it was its home.

Rebecca Flint Marx, thank you for helping us put this story on paper in a way that so honestly speaks to our experience, and your remarkable talent.

Penny De Los Santos, thank you for the fearless and beautiful pictures you took for this book, and everywhere you go.

Thank you to Hannah Rahill for fighting for this book and giving us the most vibrant and amazing talent to make it.

To Emily Timberlake, and Betsy Stromberg, Emma Campion, and Sharon Silva: how did we get so lucky? You are the most amazing editors and designers anyone could hope to have. Thank you for keeping the book so honest and making it so striking. And for being so engaged. You kept the love, beauty, and humor in this humongous effort alive to the very end.

Eskerrik asko!

—Alex Raij and Eder Montero

Alex Raij, thank you for letting me be your co-writer and collaborator on what has been an incredible and endlessly thought-provoking journey. And thank you above all for introducing me to the Gilda and forever blowing my mind about the addictive potential of olives, anchovies, and peppers.

Emily Timberlake, our editor extraordinaire: thank you for your patience, thoughtfulness, and impeccable care in turning an ungainly Word document into an honest-to-goodness cookbook; we were so fortunate to be in your capable hands. And a hearty cheers to everyone else at Ten Speed: Hannah Rahill, for believing in the potential of this book; Emma Campion and Betsy Stromberg, for making it such a stone-cold stunner; and Sharon Silva, for your extremely impressive attention to detail.

Penny de los Santos, for bringing the food, people, and landscape of the Basque Country to vibrant and beautiful life.

The family of Eder Montero, for your generous hospitality during our travels.

—Rebecca Flint Marx

INDEX

Copyright © 2016 by Alexandra Raij and Eder Montero
Photographs copyright © 2016 by Penny De Los Santos

Published in the United States by Ten Speed Press, an imprint of the Crown
Publishing Group, a division of Penguin Random House LLC, New York.
www.crownpublishing.com
www.tenspeed.com

Ten Speed Press and the Ten Speed Press colophon are registered
trademarks of Penguin Random House LLC.

Library of Congress Cataloging-in-Publication Data is on file with the
publisher.

Hardcover ISBN: 978-1-60774-761-1
eBook ISBN: 978-1-60774-762-8

Printed in China

Design by Betsy Stromberg

10 9 8 7 6 5 4 3 2 1

First Edition